THE
RIGHT BRAIN
AND
RELIGION

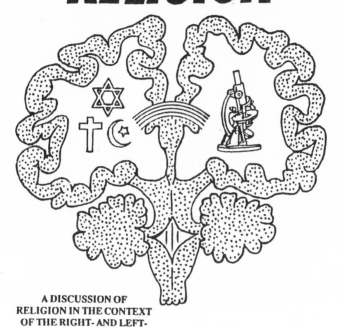

**A DISCUSSION OF
RELIGION IN THE CONTEXT
OF THE RIGHT- AND LEFT-
BRAIN THEORY**

C. W. Dalton!

A BIG BLUE BOOK

Dedicated to all people of goodwill regardless
of their religious or secular orientation

Editorial service and typesetting of text
by L. D. Garland of San Diego, California

Copyright 1990 by C. W. Dalton !
Printed in the United States of America
Library of Congress Catalog Card Number 90-81587
International Standard Book Number 0-916969-02-9

Published by
BIG BLUE BOOKS
Lakeside, California

CONTENTS

PREFACE. The puzzling contradictions of people's beliefs--The a-   1
bility to believe something and not believe it at the same time--The
allowance of contradictions by the bicameral brain--The gingerly
avoidance of religion by neuroscientists--The speculative nature of
the right- and left-brain theory

I. LEFT BRAIN--RIGHT BRAIN. The evolutionary development of   5
intelligence--Physical and functionary characteristics of the bicameral brain--The left brain: province of speech, logic, linear
thinking, technical science, consistency--The right brain: province
of feelings, esthetics, wholistic thinking, intuition, religion--The
cognative dissidence of the hemispheres--Memory, intuition, dreams,
drugs, religion

II. RIGHT BRAIN AND RELIGION. The right-brain province of   15
religion--The value of religion to the individual and society--
Arguments in support of belief in God--Religion's fulfillment of e-
motional, spiritual, esthetic and social needs--Religionists seen as
more free thinkers than atheists--The understanding of religion by
poets--The fulfillment of religions's functions--Marxism, humanism
and Christianity--The risk of faith in pure reason--America as a de
facto Christian nation--The tenacity of religion

III. LEFT BRAIN AND RELIGION. The rationality of the left   23
brain--The indefinability and inconceivability of God--Concept of
soul--The Bible--Conflict between religion and science--Question
of taste versus fact--Religionists' unwavering faith in science--The
impossibility of the supernatural--The disposition to believe versus
the disposition of doubt--The overwhelming popularity of religion

IV. RELIGION AS A CULTURE-TIME-FILLER. Theories of the   49 origin of religion--Needs fulfilled by religion that atheism and humanism are incapable of--A world without religion--Religion as an evolutionary selection--Comparing the good and evil spawned by religion--Religion's obsession with sex--The rationalist assumption of value in truth--Production and consumption as culture fillers

V. THE IDEAL CHRISTIAN AND REALITY. The zealot's rational   69
response to Christian theology--Weak belief as indicated by popular behavior--The form and substance of Christianity--Religion as an addiction--The disturbing doubts of believers--Why religionists hate atheists--The televangelists--The secret contempt for preachers--In defense of proselityzing--Parents with the right religion as more important than the right genes

VI. THE IDEAL ATHEIST AND REALITY. Faith in reason, logic   85
and science--The persecution of atheists despite America's vaunted freedom of religion--The greater factor of temperament over intelligence--Atheists seen as closed-minded--Militant atheists and closet atheists--Tom Paine's miscalculations--Increased literacy and the spread of superstition--Atheists' product nobody wants--Some Biblical atrocities--Wasted time bashing the Bible--The profitable promotion of religion; the expensive promotion of atheism--The cultural compulsive to support religion--Atheists as foredoomed to lose--Religion as a tool for domination--Isaac Asimov on the fight for rationality

VII. THE WILL TO BELIEVE. Creationism versus evolution--The   109
dualism of body and soul--All born atheists--Christian slave morality--The characteristics selected by evolution--The explanation of compassion--Religion as a genetic defect--The unsettled definition of instinct--Religion and Freud's pleasure principle--The reluctance to face death and oblivion--Instinct or early indoctrination? The right-brain need for the absurd and bizarre--The failure of the wonders of science to stir the passions--The ineffectiveness of atheist literature--The exploitation of the will to believe by advertisers--The rejection of science but not its goodies--American atheists and humanists as Don Quixotes--Should the will to believe be encouraged?--The rare victories of truth and justice--The proposition that either truth is impotent or religionists possess the truth--The badly impaired right brain.

CONTENTS

VIII. CULTS AND NEW AGE RELIGIONS. The cult beginning of   135
religions--The charismatic gurus who create and dominate cults--
The strong emotional appeal to the right brain--Some seasoned cults:
Mormons, Jehovah's Witnesses, Christian Scientists, Seventh Day
Adventists--Faith healing amidst doctors and hospitals--The exposure of healing charlatans--The difficulty of defining cults--The
severe control of cult members' lives--Est, a secular cult--Cults or
nascent religions: The Unification Church (Moonies), Hindu Rajneeshees, People's Temple--New Age channelers and UFO buffs--Voo-
doo and Devil worshippers--Deprogramming--The succumbing of
both hemispheres to the will to believe

IX. MORE GOOD THAN HARM? The axiom that religion does   171
more good than harm--Religion as a necessity to civilized society--
The practical benefits of religion--Religion as a cause of war--Re-
ligion as a restraint to the explosive expansion of science--The
selection of religion by evolution--Religion as chief cause of perse-
cution--The Christian Crusades--The reduction of self-responsibility
by religion--The wise and cowardly preaching of morality to others--
Religion as a cruel hoax--Religions's great waste of talent, energy,
wealth--The degradation of women by religion--Crime resulting from
the unnatural, blundering treatment of sex--The Catholic Church's
benefit from clerical sex crimes--Harm from faith healing and serpent handling--The impending disaster from overpopulation--The
overflow of prisons with religionists--Dubious Christian love--The
Protestant Revolt--The replacement of religious faith by economic
enticements

X. TEMPERAMENTAL SIMILARITIES BETWEEN FUNDAMENTALISTS 201
AND ATHEISTS. The sincerity and dedication of both--Intolerance
as a common characteristic of both camps--The inerrant Bible as
basis for perfect left-brain logic of Fundamentalists--The comparison
of right-brain art and music with religion--The hostility, bitterness
and mean-spiritedness of the despised atheists--The sluggish bulk of
the religious center that preserves domestic peace by keeping the
fundamentalists and atheists from each others' throats

XI. THE HOLY SPIRIT AND SECULAR POWER. The desire to serve 211
God and the lust for power--Religion as a tool of rulers--The history

of American fundamentalism--The threat to freedom by mergers of
government and religion--The abandonment of purpose by institu-
ionalized religion--The dependence of religion's success on violation of its own moral codes--Cultural compulsives that blind educators and psychologists to the truth--The need for the crippling effect
of consciences for a durable society--The deep-down suspicion of
the successful that they are frauds--Why my theory of success will
never fly--The greater importance of power compared with salvation,
spirituality or truth--Achievement of power as emulation of God,
the all-powerful

XII. SEARCH FOR THE HOLY GRAIL. Religion as a tolerated ex-   229
crescence rather than an evolutionary selection--Science's facing of
the unknowable--The ebb and flow of religious zeal--The resurrec-
tion of religion in communist countries--Effects of religious liberalism and ecumenism--The end of miracles--The fractionalization of
Christianity--The irrational behavior that can fulfill humankind's
needs while causing most of its problems--The irrelevance of truth--
The shattered hopes of history--The function of conscience--Raised
consciousness--The breakdown of Marxism and its attendant void--
Utopianism--A good society's chance of survival in a predatory
world--The proposition of life that should arouse our indignation and
outrage--The relative unimportance of doomsday--Civilization's
greatest threat: overpopulation

XIII. THROUGH A GLASS DARKLY. Ideologues, realists, skep-   249
tics, cynics--Pragmatists as salt of the earth--The ivory-tower taint
of humanism--Christianity as a pushover--Humanists' need to learn
from religionists--The irrelevance of being right--The collapse of
communism from a malfunctioning reward and punishment system--
Secular education versus religious indoctrination--Two opposite views
of the child--Technical training versus liberal arts--schools as supporters of the status quo--Moral training versus adaptability--When
rulers assume the authority of God--Is religion coasting to its end on
the semantic residue of past ages of belief?--The fading taboo
against discussion of religion--When all realize the emperor wears
no clothes--Two impediments to humanist and atheist hopes: right-
brain preference for superstion and the population explosion--The
left brain as savior of humankind

PREFACE

I had been puzzled most of my life over how most religious people could seemingly hold so many contradictory beliefs.

I had observed that in biology classes most religious young people accepted with little apparent difficulty the theory of evolution, which disputes the Genesis story of creation. The same was true in the study of astronomy — they accepted the inconceivable, infinite size of the universe while believing in their Bible's pea-sized, geocentric universe built by God in six days. In chemistry they accepted the rigid laws governing chemical reactions, along with their belief that Jesus turned water into wine. In their study of physics they could accept the inviolable natural laws governing matter and energy, side by side with the Biblical miracles that violated every natural law in their physics book.

I wondered how they could believe in ghosts, souls, faith healing, salvation and Genesis while at the same time believe in immutable natural laws, medical science, heliocentrism and evolution.

I often entertained the notion that maybe all those people were lying — either about their religious beliefs or their scientific beliefs. But my acquaintance with religious people dispelled this notion; I was convinced of their sincerity.

I was also puzzled by the contradictions between what people profess to believe and what their actions indicate they believe. For example, people believing in punishment for their sins by eternal burning in the fire of Hell, yet living flagrantly sinful lives, and breaking most of the Ten Commandments as a normal pattern of behavior. Or people believing their life on Earth to be a mere few seconds compared with the eternity promised by the Bible for devotion to God, while rarely attending church, seldom praying, never reading the Bible, and expending 99 percent of their time

1

and energy seeking the comparatively infinitesimal rewards and pleasures of their few seconds on Earth.

Or Christians believing that life on Earth is one of trouble and travail — a kind of testing ground to prove one's acceptability to Heaven — yet mourning the death of a relative or friend, when they believe that person was merely delivered from this rotten world into Heaven. Logically, if they believed the theology they professed to believe, they would happily celebrate the release of loved ones from this wretched world, as they would the release of such a person from prison. Funerals would be occasions of joy, not sadness and mourning. So, obviously, most people both believe and disbelieve the theology they profess.

We read about the burning of heretics back in the Middle Ages. The Church authorities ordering the burning presumably believed in their Bible, which promised that such people would be burned in Hell. Obviously, they also didn't believe it, so they made sure the heretics got burned.

How could I account for people's contradictory beliefs as well as for the obvious contradictions between what people say they believe and what their actions and behavior indicate they believe?

It seems that people can believe something and not believe it at the same time, that they can state one belief yet act in a manner based on a contradictory belief. Well, why not? Is it not just an assumption of mine that their beliefs must be consistent and that their actions must be consistent with their beliefs? Why can't normal people be full of contradictions among their stated beliefs as well as between their stated beliefs and their actions-indicated beliefs? I came to the conclusion that there is no mechanism in the human brain that automatically eliminates contradictions. People manage to live almost comfortably harboring cognitive dissonance, glaring contradictions. The problem is confronted only when rare circumstances or reflections happen to bring them to light. It is as if a cat and a mouse lived for years in the same house unaware of each other. The situation could continue indefinitely — until some day the cat and mouse happened to come face to face. (I was getting pretty close to the concept of the right and left brain before I had ever heard of the theory.)

When I came across the theory of the bicameral brain it did not immediately occur to me that here was the answer to my lifelong quandary over the inconsistencies and contradictions of individual's beliefs. The reason it didn't occur to me immediately was that nothing I had read on the subject ever mentioned religion, superstition, supernaturalism or mysticism in relation to the bicameral brain.

One may properly wonder why neuroscientists ignore religion in their speculations about the brain. With religion being one of the most important aspects of human cultures extending back to time immemorial, one of society's most powerful influences, one of the features that distinguish humankind from lower animals and one of the most important philosophical, metaphysical, social and political questions of the day, why would neuroscientists fail to deal with it? I have yet to find a book on the right and left brain that does any more than casually mention religion, supernaturalism or mysticism. Most of the books gingerly avoid those areas.

The gap of omission of religion is so flagrant a person has to wonder why. I suspect that the truth is that our scientists are still too fearful of the church and of the religious sentiments of the populace to dare speculate about religion's province and function in the brain.

Economic, professional and social sanctions against scientists today are not as crude and brutal as those of the Inquisitions, but nevertheless quite effective.

Religion is a tabooed subject for drawing room conversation today just as was also the subject of sex 50 years ago.

As we grow up we are subtly cautioned against discussing religion in our daily secular lives — mostly before we are even old enough to wonder why. We learn that discussing religion is in bad taste. Norman Lear described American culture as "skittish" about the discussion of the sacred.

I suspect that the early conditioning of scientists along with the rest of us has had an inhibiting influence causing them to shy away from religion. In addition, the discussion of religion could evoke heated responses drawing neuroscientists into unwanted religious controversy.

Two fearful Renaissance men would have sympathized with today's neuroscientists. Descartes declared, "On no account will I publish anything that contains a word that might displease the Church," and Bacon, concurring, said, "All knowledge is to be limited by religion." So one of my purposes in writing this book is to fill a flagrant void.

From the knowledge I have gained from reading numerous books and publications on the bicameral brain, I have no doubt that religion, supernaturalism, superstition, mysticism and magic belong in the right hemispheres of the brain along with music, art, theater, folklore, poetry and dancing.

I will endeavor to describe religion and atheism as they relate respectively to the right and left brain. I will avoid as well as I can the fruitless debate over religion versus atheism. I will emphasize the psychological motivations, temperaments and cultural compulsives that determine belief or nonbelief. I will consider what people believe as less important than why they believe it.

I recognize the impossibility of absolute, prejudice-free neutrality in dealing with religion and atheism. For me to claim to be without bias or prejudice would be not only erroneous and dishonest, but arrogant.

I will discuss a smorgasbord of views, insights, opinion, innovative concepts, emotional stances, deep convictions and rigid mindsets. The attempt will be to entertain, stimulate the mind and broaden the mental and spiritual horizons of readers. The reader will be able to discern his or her own preferential brain hemisphere in the course of the book.

A word of caution is in order about neuroscience, the study of the nervous system headquartered in the brain. Neuroscientists recognize that their science is in its infancy and that the right-left -brain theory (upon which my book is based) is highly speculative.

Little is known for sure about how the brain functions. Most theories are tentative and fuzzy. Neuroscience may be ultimately limited by the analogous limitation of the eye seeing itself.

Since neuroscientists seem to be afraid to deal with religion, I have taken a great deal of liberty as a layman in pushing the frontier of speculation a little further—into the realm of religion, superstition, supernaturalism, mysticism and magic.

Chapter I
LEFT BRAIN - RIGHT BRAIN

In the beginning God created man with a right and left brain.

Whether God or evolution is responsible for the asymmetric hemispheres of the human brain, neuroscience is fairly well agreed that the higher functions of the brain are divided, but not rigidly, between its left and right cerebral hemispheres.

Before intelligence could develop, living organisms had to evolve, so let's consider briefly a popular scientific theory on the origin of life on Earth.

Earth was around a long time before it cooled down enough and developed sufficient atmosphere for life to be possible. In the meantime chemical changes were evolving in the primordial ooze. Chemicals were going through an evolution of their own preceding biological evolution. They became more and more complex and began replicating themselves. It would be arbitrary to say just when during a period of perhaps a billion years of evolution, the chemicals reached a stage of development that we might begin to call biological life.

Intelligence developed along with chemical and biological evolution, and was an integral part of it. In fact, intelligence began before life, with the interaction of chemicals leading to the development of chemical compounds.

A primitive form of intelligence can be readily observed today. The one-celled amoeba will move toward a food particle dropped in the water near it. The amoeba will move away from an irritant dropped in the water.

The survival behavior of the amoeba to move toward a source of food and away from a destructive irritant is a characteristic selected by evolution. Obviously, an amoeba acting in a contrary manner would not survive. Thus the development of intelligence fits well into the theory of evolutionary natural selection.

This primitive intelligence is the building block that eventually led to the development of human beings capable of creating nuclear energy, television, computers. Imagining how the simple reactions of one-celled animals eventually reached the development of the human brain requires the same kind of imagination needed to conceive of how the original microscopic one-celled animals developed into ten-ton dinosaurs. It took billions of infinitesimal steps.

The complexity of a brain rather than its size, is the measure of intelligence. The human brain is not the largest brain, weighing only about three pounds, but is the most complex.

The most highly developed part of the human brain is the cerebrum, made up of a right and left hemisphere. This is the part of the brain that makes us Homo sapiens (thinking men). This is the component we will be talking about mostly.

Other parts of the brain include the cerebellum, medulla oblongata, pons, thalamus, hypothalamus, reticular formation, hippocampus, pituitary gland, pineal gland, limbic system, corpus callosum. These various components specialize in different functions although their functions often overlap and intertwine because the brain is highly integrated.

Some of the innumerable functions of these auxiliary parts are: coordinating body movements; filtering and inhibiting neural messages; controlling breathing, heart beat, body temperature, thirst, appetite, sex, sleep; receiving and processing sensory information; registering and controlling emotions; receiving and responding to pain and pleasure; controlling hormone distribution, regulating sleep cycles and storing memory. These functions are in addition to those of the cerebrum, humankind's most highly developed brain component.

The cerebrum, made up of a right and left hemisphere, is the most massive part of the human brain. Its cortex (outer bark) is greatly wrinkled and grooved to produce more surface for its restricted cranial space, the area of surface being of great importance to its functioning capacity.

We are born with all the brain cells (neurons) we will ever have. Mental development from then on depends upon increased interconnections between cells.

Neurons communicate with each other by electro-chemical means from the axon appendages of one neuron to the dendrite appendages of another neuron. There is a gap (synapse) between each axon and dendrite. Self-generating electrical charges pass through a neuron to its axon appendage. A charge, according to its nature and strength, activates chemicals (neurotransmitters) in its axon appendages that fire the nerve message across the gap to adjoining dendrites (adjoining except for the gap) of other neurons. The message is relayed on to the next cell and the next cell until it finally reaches its destination.

When you consider that there are between an estimated ten to one hundred billion neurons making up the brain with their almost infinite number of interconnections, continually firing messages across trillions of synapses, you can appreciate how incomprehensible the brain is. The brain is more like a bucket of microscopic worms than like a clockworks.

The two hemispheres are separated by the corpus callosum, a thick membrane through which pass bundles of nerves that maintain a constant communication between the two hemispheres. These bundles of nerves, called commissures, help integrate the left and right brain, an integration so pervasive that sometimes one hemisphere is able to assume or learn the functions diminished by brain damage on the other side.

We should note that when neurons are destroyed they cannot be repaired or replaced by new ones. That is why other neurons try to take over the function of damaged neurons, even if the damaged ones are in the opposite hemisphere.

The right and left brain, or more properly the right and left hemispheres of the cerebrum, start out with a switcheroo. The nerves connecting the hemispheres with the rest of the body cross over to the opposite side as they enter the brain. This results in the left hemisphere controlling the right side of the body and vice versa. Due to the integration of the two hemispheres via nerve connections through the corpus callosum separating them, such controls are partially shared with the other hemisphere.

Usually one hemisphere is dominant in motor control. If the dominant hemisphere for motor control is the left one, the person will be right-handed — because of the switchover. But this does not mean that the person has a left-brain preference in all other ways. He may or may not. Handedness does not determine personality and talent. A right-handed person may be a gifted artist (right brain) or a statistician (left brain). People have preferences, weak or strong, for one hemisphere or the other.

Because most people are right-handed, the odd left-handers have historically been treated as flawed and inferior. This curious bit of majority conceit has brought us such expressions derogatory to left-handers as left-handed compliment and leftovers, while the right-handers are flattered by such expressions as right, meaning correct, and righteousness.

The most publicized ability of the left brain is language. Language is governed by a specific location in the left cortex called Broca's area. The left brain for whatever reasons, is better suited to process language regardless of the modality by which it is received. Although the sign language of the deaf and mute is received through the eyes while spoken language is received through the ears, both are processed in Broca's area. It is as if the brain has actually been built to reserve an area for language no matter what. So the brains of deaf people are like the brains of hearing people. Speech is located in the Broca area of the left brain for right-handers as well as for almost all left-handers.

THE BICAMERAL BRAIN. The cerebrum, divided into right and left hemispheres, is the part of the brain most responsible for the thoughts, memories and personality traits that make us human. The right hemisphere is the region of what many people refer to as the "heart" (as distinguished from the head). The right is gifted with artistic talent and music ability. It is more in tune with feelings, emotions and compassion. It is more wholistic in its concepts and more spatially oriented. In addition, it seems to be more creative and intuitional. It is spontaneous, childish and subject to emotionalism ranging from hysterical joy to gloomy despair. The right brain is also more autonomous. While one can force oneself to jog, wash the dishes, spade the garden, memorize a poem or read a book, one cannot force oneself to do creative thinking. Creative thinking is in the province of the autonomous right brain.

The right brain understands metaphors, gets the point of jokes and the meaning of fables. It also seems more concerned with pleasure and taste than with logic and facts. The right brain is also the province of religion — superstition, supernaturalism, mysticism, magic.

The right brain doesn't seem to like anything that's dear to the left brain. For example, the right brain with its artistic taste disdains perfect geometric circles, squares, rectangles and even straight lines so favored by the left brain. Similarly, the right brain disdains the truth, honesty and logic of the left brain. The right brain seems to reflect a negative, perverse reaction to whatever the left brain favors. The right brain, being less sensitive to factuality, is easily duped. Most advertising is obviously pitched to the right brain.

The left brain is the thinking or logical brain, the analytical brain. It is better at math, linear thinking, technology. It favors order and does things step by step. With its esteem for logic, the left brain cannot tolerate contradictions, inconsistencies and dishonesty. Left-brained people, although perhaps not any more trustworthy than right-brainers, are more aware of inconsistencies, contradictions and falsities. The left brain can lie, but it needs a good reason for lying. The right brain seems to need no reason at all. In fact, the right brain seems to be a pathological liar. Many left-brainers by contrast make a fetish out of honesty and emphasize it as a personal, virtuous character trait.

A classical example of right-brain performance was former President Ronald Reagan's explanation of his contradictory stories concerning the arms-for-hostages deal with Iran. Said right-brained Reagan: "A few months ago I told the American people I did not trade arms for hostages. My heart and my best intentions still tell me that's true, but the facts and the evidence tell me it is not."

Many people are able to abide gross contradictions in their views and in their behavior. They can go to church on Sunday in all sincerity, and for the other six days of the week act in a manner that repudiates everything they confessed to believe on Sunday. And they may be completely unconscious of their hypocrisy due to poor communication between the two hemispheres.

They allow their right brain to dictate their behavior on Sunday — behavior based on the authoritative tenants of their church. For the other six days their left brain controls their behavior. This does not mean that the right brain is the good brain and the left brain the evil brain. Far from it. Very often such Sunday-only right brainers, who accept religious tenants to guide them on Sunday, have never developed any secular ethics to guide them the other six days and behave like scoundrels.

DREAMS. Offhand, dreams would seem to be a product of the right brain. What could be more creative than dreams with their irrationality, bizarre imagery, grotesqueries, disregard for reality and contempt for truth? All characteristics of the right brain. But on second thought, judging from my own dreams, dreams seem to be of two quite different kinds: the rational dream that is easily recalled and the entirely irrational dream based on such skewed logic, alien values and insane images that about all we can remember is that the dream made no sense whatever. So, maybe both hemispheres indulge in dreaming. In fact, a recent study by the Brain Image Center at the University of California at Irvine found that the right brain was relatively calm during dreams.

My own speculation is that one hemisphere is spinning the yarn while the other is listening. This would explain the listening brain's surprise at what happens. It couldn't be surprised if it were the same brain making up the story.

DRUGS. An interesting question is whether the right brain is the brain of alcohol and drug addiction. It is the brain that rejects reason and common sense; it is the undisciplined brain, the dishonest brain, the brain of denial; it is the brain that says if it feels good, do it.

The psychological profile of the deeply religious person does seem to be similar to the profile of the substance abusing person.

Perhaps alcoholics and drug addicts unconsciously attempt to fill psychological needs religion has failed to fulfill. After all, the atheistic Soviet Union has a greater problem of alcoholism than religious America has.

In the beginning of the drug culture in the 1960s, the effects of drugs were often interpreted as religious or transcendental experiences. Peyote and LSD trips were thought of as mystical. They were mystical, of course, in the secular sense. They enhanced sensory perception, created hallucinations, extinguished time-consciousness, registered music in streaming visual colors, produced out-of-body experiences, etc.

Drugs are still used by many primitive religions to enhance what is believed to be a spiritual, religious experience. So it was only natural for counterculture youth to confuse the effects of drugs with religious supernaturalism. Some of the psychedelic drugs undoubtedly did sometimes stimulate thinking about the expansibility of the mind, the abstruse problems of existence and the wonders of outerspace. But their effects were of the same order as the effects of aspirin in relieving headaches and no more mystical than a dose of castor oil.

The close connection between drug effects and religion does seem to place both in the right hemisphere. A study of the similarity of personality characteristics conducive to drug addiction and religion would make an interesting project for some young social scientists who want to make headlines.

But there is another aspect to drugs that should be mentioned here. One may strongly suspect that there is a significant difference between the abuse of drugs by the hedonistic, mindless herd and the use of drugs by the sophisticated successful.

Celebrities — entertainers, movie stars, athletes — get hooked on drugs or alcohol, go through Betty Ford's glamour mill and come out whistle-clean and more popular than ever. Skeptics become suspicious.

Oh yes, they condemn drugs most passionately. But it is never pointed out that if it weren't for drugs we would never have heard of most of them. Drugs got them up there. But this fact is hushed. I will say no more about it. It's the great American secret!

Let me insert a caution here about the cerebral hemispheres. Some popularizers of right-left-brain theories go overboard in listing the characteristics of each hemisphere. This tendency is called "dichotomania." To help the reader gain a better concept of the hemispheres, I will list a moderate number of such characteristics:

LEFT	RIGHT
Speech	Feeling
Reading	Wholistic
Mathematics	Music
Logic	Art
Analysis	Creativity
Linear thinking	Folklore
Categorizing	Intuition
Technical science	Visual
Legalism	Poetry
Consistency	Religion

I would like to devote special attention to four very important brain functions: intuition, memory, emotions and religion.

INTUITION: Intuition is generally assigned to the right brain. Sometimes I wonder if it really belongs there. Wherever one places it, intuition should be stripped of its popular aura of mysticism.

I will offer three theories explaining intuition. First, intuition is simply rumination and cogitation that go on continually at a subconscious, nonverbal level of the logical left brain. When the process flashes an insight or reaches a solution to a problem, the left brain pulls it up to the conscious level, evaluates it, refines it and then either adopts it or rejects it.

A second theory is that intuition is a process carried on in the right brain, where the ambience is more favorable to free association, flexibility, uninhibited inquiry and creative thinking. The left brain connected through the corpus callosum picks up the output of right-brain ruminations and subjects such output to its rigorous standards and discipline, to either accept or reject.

A third theory sees intuition as non-verbal reasoning that goes on in the old brain, the kind of thinking that preceded the development of language. Its insights are picked up by the left brain and put into verbal form.

MEMORY. Memory is still in its early, nebulous state of speculation. There seems to be no specific area collecting and processing memory, but instead memory involves and pervades the whole brain. There is short-term memory and long-term memory. Whether they are different in kind or degree is not clear.

The latest theories involve complicated electrochemical processes that are too tentative to bother to go into here. We probably can say with some certainty that biochemical changes are produced by the firing of messages across the synapses. The more firing of messages the greater the changes wrought — thus memory. The more you walk on a path through a field, the more trodden the path becomes — neuroscience's word for it is engram, or memory.

We should note that a superb memory is not always good. Some things are better forgotten. The memory of a horrible experience can destroy one's future. In addition, a great memory may keep a person stuck in his ideas, while a poor memory may free him from his mental chains so that he may make new, fresh reappraisals.

EMOTIONS. Emotions range from the subtle emotional promptings essential to all life — promptings to breathe, eat, sleep, quench thirst and avoid pain — to the more dramatic emotions of hate, anger, rage, jealousy, fear, disgust, love, infatuation, compassion and the emotional components of religion.

As with everything else, emotions are a product of evolutionary selection and development, those emotions conducive to the survival of the human species being naturally selected. The existence of our emotions is in itself proof of their benefit to our survival, even though such emotions are responsible for brutality, racial hatred, xenophobia, greed, dishonesty and ruthlessness. Of course, emotions are also responsible for kindness, generosity, loyalty, fidelity, trustworthiness and religion.

Emotion in the form of motivations plays such a vital part in the function of the brain that the brain wouldn't work at all without emotions. No thinking would take place without the desire (motivation) to think, and our idle brains would atrophy. Emotion can't be separated from mental activity.

Considering the pervasive nature of emotions, it becomes obvious that emotions are not confined exclusively to any particular area of the brain, but permeate the entire central and peripheral nervous systems. But the right cerebral hemisphere is believed to be more involved than the left hemisphere in processing emotional information and in producing emotional reactions.

Certain strong emotions, however, seem to be centered in the primitive brain stem and the hypothalamus. But much is yet to be learned about emotions and their functions in the brain.

ASCENSION OF ELIJAH.

RELIGION. I have yet to see religion listed anywhere in a dichotomy of brain functions. Surely, religion with its associated components of supernaturalism, superstition, mysticism and magic is too important in human behavior to totally ignore.

I have little doubt that religion is almost an exclusive product of the right brain — almost exclusive because the two hemispheres are connected by trunks of nerve fibers carrying a high traffic of communication between them.

The right brain is pleasure-loving, more influenced by taste than by truth, and easily satisfied with rationalization (an undisciplined form of logic). The left brain is involved in ascertaining truth, while the right grasps that which is still elusive or uncertain.

Both hemispheres receive the same information input. The difference is in what input they accept and their interpretation of it. The left brain has a strict, rational criterion for what is acceptable; the right brain seems to accept anything that pleases its fancy and isn't too disturbing to any of its present beliefs.

A right-brainer, with little concern for honesty and factuality, might defend religion by comparing religion with art, suggesting that we do not criticize abstract impressionism or cubism because they aren't truthful representation. Religion is truly more of an art than a science.

Right-brainers are essentially hedonists. They have little use for reason or logic. Their rubric seems to be: if it feels good, believe it.

What lies ahead for the evolution of the human brain? Can we rationally project ahead from the course of the past?

The cerebral hemispheres of non-human mammals are symmetrical and perform the same functions. But the functions of the asymmetrical human brain differ considerably between the right and left hemispheres.

It is believed that previous to the development of language, the right hemisphere was dominant. This was the period of evolution during which superstition, supernaturalism, mysticism, myth, magic and low-grade logic developed. It was the period in which the emotions—love, hate, fear, jealousy, vengeance and wishfulness motivated and dominated the cerebral processes.

In time the left brain developed logic and reason along with language. From there on the left brain has striven to reign in the irresponsible, erroneous right brain by subjecting its products to rational scrutiny.

Since the left brain is the truly human brain and appears to be on an evolutionary roll, it seems logical to believe that it will continue to move toward dominance of the cerebrum. But the right hemisphere, like a venerable dynasty, is deeply entrenched, popularly supported, and tough with age. It is not a pushover.

Chapter II
THE RIGHT BRAIN AND RELIGION

Religion is ensconced in the right hemisphere, the hemisphere of art, music, poetry, fantasy, folklore, creativity, imagination.

Religion gains its strength not so much from its theology and the promise of salvation as from the emotional impact of its pageantry and rituals; its organ and choir music, its sacred paintings, sculptures and stained-glass windows; its humbling ambience created by cathedrals, tabernacles and mosques; its aura of mystery. Religion's orderly creeds, as has been said, are not meant to be signed but sung.

Columnist Joe Sobran expressed it clearly: "What really converts men, though, is not argument but beauty and poetry. . . . A faith has to have a radiance that men can love. I've always pitied those who can't respond to the sheer glory of the Catholic faith."

Even the skeptic H. L. Mencken admired the Catholic Church for its insight into the phenomenon of religion: "I find myself constantly admiring the Catholic Church, in spite of its astounding imbecilities. It has always perceived that religion is not a syllogism but a poem. . . . In the face of overwhelming beauty, it isn't necessary to belabor people with logic."

One might add that there is something about the beauty of religion — especially the Catholic religion with its art, music, liturgy and mysticism that permeates its congregants. By contrast, the spiritual bareness of atheism seems to produce the same kind of bareness in its advocates.

Religionists, governed by flexible, imaginative right brains, can range boundlessly over the rich pastures of creeds, phantasies, mysteries and magic, while left-brained atheists are tethered on the short chain of factuality.

Religionists believe as they do because they want to. Atheists believe

15

as they do because reason demands it. In that sense atheists are less free thinkers than religionists.

The right brain is independent and fancy-free while the left brain is a slave to logic and factuality. Any fool can believe in what reason tells him is certain, so it has been said, while faith is the quality of believing beyond reason.

"If a man without a sense of smell declared that this yellow rose I hold had no scent," said Sir Ralph Richardson, "we should know that he was wrong. The defect is in him, not in the flower. It is the same with a man who says there is no God. It merely means that he is without the capacity to discern his presence."

In satirical form, Jim bishop exemplifies a popular mode of Christian logic: "There is no God. All of the wonders around us are accidental. No almighty hand made a thousand-billion stars. They made themselves. No power keeps them on their steady course. The earth spins itself to keep the oceans from falling off toward the sun. Infants teach themselves to cry when they are hungry or hurt. A small flower invented itself so that we could extract digitalis for sick hearts."

Poets understand religious faith:

> Why ask for proof when need of none is shown?
>   Or limit truth by logic's stumbling art?
> Love is real to all who love have known;
>   Faith is no riddle to the trusting heart!
>   — Arthur Wallace Peach

> The world stands out on either side, no wider than the heart is wide.
> Above the world is stretched the sky, no higher than the soul is high.
> East and West will pinch the heart that cannot keep them pushed
>   apart.
> He whose soul is flat the sky will cave in on him, by and by.
>   — Edna St. Vincent Millay

The right brain sees proof of God in the beauty and design of nature. "The heavens declare the glory of God," said the Psalmist. They are a magnificent display of His handiwork.

Mighty oceans, towering mountains, green meadows, spectacular canyons, rushing rivers, mighty Sequoia forests, fields of blooming daisies, wind, rain and sunshine all speak of God.

That inorganic matter produced all of this without the aid of a Divine Intelligence religionists find inconceivable. They ask who gave the peacock, the blue bird and the cardinal their flaming colors? Who taught bees to make honey, spiders to weave webs and beavers to build dams? Who taught the caterpillar to turn into a butterfly, if there is no God?

Many religionists do not consider the foundation upon which their religion is built as a leap into the dark, but as a faith supported by the strongest evidence — the beauty and design of nature. The world is a beautifully synchronized machine. We even set our clocks by the position of the stars and can predict appearances of comets for scores of years in advance.

> There is no unbelief:
> Whoever plants a seed beneath the sod,
> And waits to see it push away the clod.
> He trusts in God.
> There is no unbelief:
> Whoever sees, 'neath fields of winter snow,
> The silent harvest of the future grow.
> God's power must know.
> There is no unbelief:
> Whoever says, when clouds are in the sky,
> "Be patient, heart; light breaketh by and by,"
> Trusts the Most High.
> There is no unbelief:
> Whoever lies down on his couch to sleep.
> Content to lock each sense in slumber deep,
> Knows God will keep.
> — Anonymous

There is a popular cliche around that God is Love. Perhaps love is divine because love is different from all other motives, being the only one that doesn't impel us to act in our own selfish interest. Love is irrational enough to fit comfortably in the right brain. B. Z. Goldberg, author of *The Sacred Fire*, writes: "To the refined, delicate, sensitive soul of modern times, love in its religious aspect offers greater spiritual depth and wider aesthetic experience than the other elements in religion. . . . They who know religion know that no greater love exists and that there is nothing more all-inclusive in life than the love of God."

We might speculate that the logical left brain of primitive man saw the need for justice, a concept that helped greatly to distinguish humans from lower animals, since lower animals show no sign of a sense of justice. Robert Ingersoll suggested as much: "In nature there are neither rewards nor punishment—there are only consequences."

Then the right hemisphere picked up the idea of justice and employed it in its theology in the form of an afterworld of reward and punishment in which all accounts would be evened. The inventive right brain excels at such creations.

Quite extraordinary mutations must have taken place to leap from lower animals to human beings, there being such a great gap between the intelligence of the two.

Some liberals, probably because of their compulsion to put man down, maintain that the tremendously superior intelligence of human beings is not one of kind but merely of degree.

Although I see a great gap between the intelligence of an Australian aborigine and a nuclear scientist, I accept it as a gap due primarily to the difference in cultural advantage. But the gap between the aborigine and a chimpanzee is a difference of kind, not to be overcome by a few generations of cultural uplifting. The gap seems to support the claim of religionists that humankind are uniquely different from lower animals. Perhaps because humans possess souls?

> Under this sod, beneath these trees
> Lie the remains of Soloman Peas.
> Peas isn't here, only his pod,
> He's shelled out and gone to God.

Whether it is instinctual or culturally induced, a strong need to believe is a human characteristic. Columnist Patrick Buchanan expressed it this way: "The necessity to believe is part of human nature; it is written upon the soul; it cannot be erased."

If Buchanan is right, incising religion from the brain may be as difficult as incising art and music from it.

Pragmatically, what may be most important is the fulfillment of the functions of religion, without regard for its truth or falsity.

Emotional fulfillment is one of the primary needs of humans, and religion supplies it. Believers get an emotional lift or high from praying, singing, testifying, partaking of the Eucharist and from sheer commitment to belief.

The church provides people with soul-stirring music and art, elegant homilies on Sundays, spiritual solace at troubled times, consolation for the lonely, and anchorage to the community.

> Now, God be praised, that to
>   believing souls
> Gives light in darkness, comfort
>   in despair.
>   —Shakespeare

The church meets emotional and social needs for acceptance, entertainment, excitement, fellowship, intimacy, pomp and ceremony, recreation and participation in compassionate and charitable activities. It gives the faithful peace, happiness, harmony and a sense of purpose. In addition, faith brings great joy to many religionists through a personal God, particularly the Lord Jesus, who alleviates their fears and their loneliness by watching over them and loving them.

People like the authority figures and moral absolutes of religion to guide them so they can know the right path to trod in a very confusing world. They like to feel that they are walking on the solid rock of infallible religion rather than on the shifting sands of tentative science and moral relativity. People also like the warm, loving acceptance by religious groups, an emotional fulfillment that gives them a closer feeling to God and their church. And mysticism just by itself seems to fulfill a deep, primitive emotional need for most humans.

A sensible purpose of life is filling in the time between birth and death as pleasantly as possible. Religion seems to have been chosen by most of humankind to help fulfill such a purpose. Fantasy, folklore, fables and fairy tales fall far short of religion in filling such need.

The emotional appeal of religion, of course, far outweighs its intellectual appeal. That's why religion belongs to the right brain. Religionists may have good left hemispheres, but have been conditioned to turn them off when it comes to religion.

Another benefit of religion is the raising of one's self-esteem — the feeling that one is superior to soulless lower animals as well as superior to nonbelievers because one is saved and chosen for eternity.

Finally, if a person's emotional, spiritual and psychological health has been sustained all of his life by belief in a guardian angel and in rewards of an afterworld, what difference does it make if there are no guardian angels and no afterworld? The function of his religious beliefs has already been fulfilled. By contrast, the atheist gains nothing by believing nothing.

Religionists maintain that it is religion that has furnished humankind with the inspiration to transcend its savage animal state, develop morality, foster compassion and create justice. They say that anything can bring out the worst in a person. Religion brings out the best.

They say that people need a responsibility to something higher. They say a belief in God buoys up humanity and nurtures the growth of idealism and love, the foundation of civilized behavior.

Many Christians argue that it is the vestige of the Christian heritage in today's secular world that holds it together — not the new humanist ethical concepts, and without regeneration of morality by religion, humankind is headed back to savagery. That is, for only a while can the momentum of Christian love and morality sustain civilization, once Christianity is abandoned.

Any attempt to rob religion of its personal and emotional content and reduce it to intellectualism whether theologic dogma or ethical precepts, is an attempt to destroy the basis for religion and take away the reasons for its existence.

Christianity is transcendental, aimed at lifting humankind to higher moral grounds, to greater nobility, to a more nearly perfect civilization. This is the basis for Christianity's ideological appeal that inspires its followers to commit themselves to it and sacrifice for it. The poet Robert Browning expressed it: "Ah, but a man's reach should exceed his grasp, or what's heaven for?"

Marxist communism also made an ideological appeal. It proclaimed its new order would eliminate corrupt government and end exploitation of labor. Many idealists dedicated their lives to its success and fulfillment. But in the course of human affairs reason was seized upon by the rulers of the new order to be used as a tool, as religion had often been used in the past, for amassing power and enslaving the people.

In a short time in historical measure, we are now witnessing the general failure of Marxist nations and the relative success of Christian nations. There can be little question that God is winning in the balance.

The failure of communism, socialism and fascism have added another layer of disappointment and disillusionment on top of the failure of democracy and Christianity to bring peace and happiness to the world.

There is no evidence that if societies were not based on religion but on scientific truth, they would fare any better. If the ruthless leaders down through the ages have used religion and superstition and lies and myths to dominate, would they not use truth in the same manner? Being ruthless, they will use whatever leads to success, whether it be mythology or science.

They are as receptive to truth as they are to falsehood — as long as it is not applied to them.

Moreover, placing faith in pure reason is risky. Anatole France said: "In ethics all possible views have been maintained. . . . Pure reason, if they had hearkened only to her, would have led them by divers roads to the most monstrous conclusions."

In addition, "pure reason" often leads to monstrous conclusions because it is not pure reason, but a rationalization of prejudices, tastes and economic interests.

The Nazis followed the pure reason of eugenics. The Communists follow the pure reason of dialectic materialism. Pure reason today could easily lead to preemptive nuclear war. Get the other guy before he gets you.

Pure reason is as much the problem as it is the solution; it is no virtue per se.

The idea that truth furnishes a more durable foundation for society than does religion may be just another instance of faith. Maletus made a good point when he said at the trial of Socrates that you cannot look at the roots without killing the tree. Did the Greeks finally kill the tree, bringing their golden age to a premature end?

Why should people have faith in the systems advanced by the intellects of the ages? Their systems have one after the other been discarded by later intellectual insight. They have proved no more infallible than the religions. Confidence would seem to be misplaced in any of the various philosophies, pop psychologies, economic schools and socio-political theories that appear regularly with claims of being the answer to the human predicament. They all end in the dustbin of history.

If all knowledge is tentative, and there are no absolute truths according to modern scientific thinking, can such serve as a basis for human behavior? Is such not too unstable to serve as the roots of a society?

Finally, we have lost faith in education from the discovery that an educated person is not necessarily a good person.

There is overwhelming proof of the success of religion today over rationalism. In the Marxist countries around the world Marxism is losing its support and religion is in a renaissance. Nor is religion yet a basket case in America, where according to recent polls, believers in the supernatural outnumber nonbelievers 95 to 5.

There are 120 religious television stations and 1,700 religious radio stations in America to none for rationalists, atheists, humanists, free thinkers.

Only in our larger cities are there at best a few rationalist organizations as opposed to hundreds of religious organizations. The rationalists likely meet in dingy rented rooms in a run-down neighborhood while the religionists meet in their own buildings ranging from small, frame, neighborhood churches to multi-million-dollar stone cathedrals.

Despite the safeguards in the Bill of Rights to protect our country from theocratic control, America is and has been from the beginning a God-fearing, God-worshiping nation. George Washington clearly expressed his belief in God in his proclamation for a Thanksgiving Day:

"Whereas it is the duty of all nations to acknowledge the providence of Almighty God, to obey His will, to be grateful for His benefits, and humbly to implore His protection and favor, . . . Now, therefore, I do recommend and assign Thursday, the 26th day of November next, to be devoted by the people of these states to the service of that great and glorious Being Who is the beneficent Author of all the good that was, that is, and that will be — that we may then all unite in rendering unto Him our sincere and humble thanks — for the great degree of tranquility, union, and plenty, which we have since enjoyed. . . ."

All must agree that the United States has done very well as a religious nation — primarily a Christian nation. So it is a little puzzling to religionists that anyone would want to destroy the foundation that has served the country so well.

Charles Darwin, an agnostic, wrote: "Nor must we overlook the probability of the constant inculcation in a belief in God on the minds of children producing so strong and perhaps an inherited effect on their brains not yet fully developed, that it would be as difficult for them to throw off their belief in God, as for a monkey to throw off its instinctive fear and hatred of a snake."

If religion is so thoroughly established in our culture, and so deeply engrained in our hereditary nerve patterns as to be called instinctive, anyone assaying to eradicate it would seem to religionists to be both vain and foolish.

The fact is that religion has been selected over rationalism in the course of human history. Its very evolutionary selection and predominance is proof enough of its superiority over rationalism. The right brain has spoken.

Chapter III
THE LEFT BRAIN AND RELIGION

The chief characteristics of the left brain—logic and reason—mix poorly with religion. Religion thrives in the right brain, which is characterized by fantasy, emotion, imagination and aesthetic pleasure. In the left brain religion is overwhelmed and routed by reason, logic and scientific discipline.

Religion is more a question of taste; some people savor the absurd, the ridiculous, the mystical. As the third century church leader, Tertullian, expressed it: "I reverence it [Christianity] because it is contemptible; I adore it because it is absurd; I believe it because it is impossible."

Religionists ignore logic and reason and follow their feelings. They believe whatever they wish to believe and then rationalize it. However, there is a kind of weak, undisciplined reasoning underlying most religion. But one hesitates to dignify it as reason.

A primitive culture might sacrifice three lambs at seeding time to gain the favor of the gods to grant them a good harvest. If a drought destroys their crop they don't conclude that the sacrifice was in vain. They suspect that a witch among them cast a spell on their crop so they burn an old woman. The next year they again sacrifice three lambs. A plague of locusts devours their crop. They burn two old women.

We often read in the newspaper of the few survivors of a tragedy thanking God for bringing them through alive. If God was good enough to save them, atheists wonder, why wasn't He good enough to save all the others who were burned alive in fire or crushed to death in a tornado or drowned in a shark-infested ocean?

In fact, atheists would ask why did this benevolent God allow the tragedy to happen in the first place? (A question that persistently troubles many religionists.)

When the Catholic Church canceled St. Christopher's saintly credentials two decades ago, protests were heard from far and wide. Catholics who had dangled little figurines of St. Christopher from the dashboard of the family car became fearful of even driving to work. The Church had robbed the Saint of his power to protect them from accidents.

Said a Miami woman: "It's like taking a crutch away from a cripple. My father was the worst driver in the world and he lived 10 years past his time because of his St. Christopher medal."

Accident statistics would undoubtedly show the same percentage of accidents involving cars with St. Christopher as those without. But the right brain has little interest in statistics.

Reason is obliterated by religion. Religion relishes bizarre explanations, miracles, faith, authority and God's mysterious ways. Religionists live in a world of verbiage and symbolism. Their world exists only in their heads, divorced from the objective, extentional world of reality with which science deals.

Some New Age cultists, mystics and parapsychologists think they have transcended reason. Rationalists think nobody has ever transcended reason. Our power to reason is what distinguishes us from lower animals. If we possess any divine attribute, that is it.

Joseph Bronowski put it well: "Rationalism is the exploration of the world as human adventure, and it is not less human because it is an intellectual adventure—it is more human. Why do those who belittle science always behave as if the mind were the least human of our gifts? The inquiring mind is the godhead of man."

The left brain accepts as true that there is a logical explanation, a cause for everything. The right brain is not so demanding. The beliefs of right-brainers are guided more by their wishes. As Francis Bacon suggested, "People prefer to believe what they prefer to be true." People don't like to believe in their returning to nothing at death so they believe in an afterlife. They yearn for justice so they believe in Heaven and Hell. People feel alone on Earth at the mercy of an uncaring nature so they believe in guardian angels.

Science is appealing because it gives clean-cut answers and can prove them. It is eschewed because its answers are limited and often unpleasant. Religion is appealing because its answers are unlimited and pleasing to right-brainers. It is eschewed by rationalists because it insults the intelligence.

Science is probably the single area of human involvement where honesty predominates. This is so because in the realm of science dishonesty doesn't work. You can't fool nature or violate her laws and get away with it.

Rationalists maintain that honesty in science is the reason science has brought us the only measurable advancements in human history.

Science deals with the natural world, while religion deals with the purported supernatural world. The problem is that there really isn't such a thing and cannot be such a thing as the supernatural. If something exists, it is natural. If it doesn't exist, it isn't anything. So, there can be no supernatural.

But even many rationalists, atheists and humanists use the term "supernatural," not even realizing that they are talking nonsense. It is stupid to dignify such a nonsense word by seriously using it.

In actual practice what we generally mean by the supernatural is the unknown. Once we did not know that bacteria cause disease, we did not know that fly eggs cause maggots, we did not know the cause of pregnancy. Now, does that mean that bacteria, maggots and pregnancy were supernatural? Apparently they were at one time thought to be.

Of course, the ne plus ultra in the category of the supernatural is God. But there are a lot of problems with God.

A popular argument in favor of God is based on logic and runs like this: You have a watch. Someone had to make it. A watchmaker made it. Now we have the watchmaker. Somebody had to make the watchmaker. God made him. The sequence blows up into absurdity when it is explained who made God. God made Himself.

Bertrand Russell wrote that "if there can be anything without a cause (or maker) it may just as well be the world as God."

There is an argument for God based on design. Everything fits together so well, the stars are so orderly, nature is so beautiful, everything must have been made or designed by a benevolent Creator.

Well, life on Earth is really not so idyllic and orderly; life is a bloody struggle for survival. The carnage that goes on day and night causes Earth to resemble a giant slaughterhouse.

Besides, the apparent fitting together has come about by the components of nature evolving around, adjusting to and coordinating with one another.

A cat probably thinks God put mice on Earth for cats to eat. (One wonders if mice believe God put them on Earth so cats could eat them.)

Lake trout probably think God put lakes on Earth for them to swim around in. (If there were no lakes, lake trout would still be living in the ocean as saltwater fish.)

Squirrels probably think God put trees on Earth for them to climb around in. (Were there no trees, the squirrels would be living on the ground with most of the other mammals.)

Also, one might ask: if the world has been so well-planned and designed, why has the history of humankind been filled with endless disasters of floods, fires, cyclones, earthquakes, locust plagues and disease epidemics?

Religionists argue that it is incomprehensible how matter could have produced all the living things on Earth by mere chance without the aid of a god. Of course, atheists would respond that it is even more incomprehensible how a god could have produced all of this — a god who created himself out of nothing before he existed.

But before we explore the question of the existence of God, we must first define God so we know what we are talking about. Here we face a formidable task. (Actually, the term "God" is just a later nom de plume in religious history for Jupiter, Zeus, Jehovah, Yahweh, Baal and others.)

We find that God is not only indefinable and indescribable but inconceivable. Meaningless cliches don't help any: God is Love, God is Nature, God is the Great Spirit, God is Ultimate Reality, God is Spiritual Essence, God is First Cause.

The problem is the unknowable, inconceivable nature of an omnipotent, omniscient God. Atheists argue that since God is infinite power and wisdom, one must be able to conceive of infinites before one can conceive of God. For example, one would have to be able to conceive of a straight string without ends, or an endless number, or a boundless universe. Yet there are people who claim they can conceive of the Creator of these infinites!

If God is inconceivable and unknowable, "God" becomes a meaningless word. Herbert Spencer maintained that God is unknowable and that those who claim knowledge of Him are deluded victims of wishful thinking.

Theists grant that God is unknowable, then proceed to describe Him. Since God is definable, indescribable and inconceivable, it is impossible for atheists to even know what it is they don't believe in.

God sometimes ends up in semantics. John Stuart Mill wrote: "The tendency has always been strong to believe that whatever received a name must be an entity or being, having an independent existence of its own. And if no real entity answering to the name could be found, men did not for that reason suppose that none existed, but imagined that it was something peculiarly abstruse and mysterious."

God is such a reification, an abstract word that has taken on the characteristics of something real. God personifies the unknown, and retreats daily as the known encroaches on His territory. God, being accredited as responsible for everything we cannot explain otherwise, becomes the symbol of our ignorance.

"Religion is the daughter of hope and fear, explaining to the ignorant the unknowable," said Ambrose Bierce.

Some nonreligionists call themselves agnostics. If they mean the belief that God is unknown and unknowable, most atheists would agree. But the strict constructionists go a little further. While atheists say there is no God, puristic agnostics say they don't know, there might be. On the surface such a stand sounds reasonable and unassailable. But a little further study shows the agnostic position to be ridiculous, if not dishonest.

Moslems believe an animal named Alborak had a human face, two wings and a peacock tail and carried Mohammed to Heaven. Agnostics would have to say it could be true, since they don't know that it isn't. But would they be speaking truthfully about what they really think? Could they really believe such a fantastic story possible? Consider how much less credible is God's creating the universe in six days—a proposition such agnostics claim to neither believe or disbelieve.

Certainly atheists are correct in arguing that the God of the Christian Bible could not possibly have created the infinite universe because He is obviously a finite God possessing the personal characteristics of the ancient Jews who created Him.

This parochial God, accredited with creating the universe, selected a small desert tribe on the spec-of-dust Earth as his chosen people to whom to reveal Himself.

One wonders why since then this coy, enigmatic God has been incommunicado. (Yes, He did send his son Jesus down 2000 years ago.)

One finds it inexplicable that an all-powerful God would try to make his will known to the world by revealing himself to such few people. It was revelation only to those few; to the rest of the world and future generations it was hearsay—passed by word of mouth for many generations. Yet such hearsay is the very foundation of Judeo-Christianity.

Probably not one person in ten thousand around the world was ever made aware of the revelation of the Judeo-Christian God at the time of such revelation.

One wonders why God would choose a Bible to reveal himself thousands of years before the invention of the printing press and at a time when few people could read.

John Baillie, in his book on Revelation, complains: "Hearken we ever so diligently, we are rewarded only with a stony silence. After all, has not mankind listened attentively enough these thousands of years? How men have searched for God! How that old firmament above us has been scanned on starry nights with all the agony of prayer! How the paths of logic have been scoured and scoured again, if haply they might reveal some sign or hint of the divine reality! And what, we may ask, has been the result but a tense and oppressive silence? That Sphinx in the Egyptian desert is the true representation of Deity. Upon our stormy questionings it turns an inscrutable, expressionless face, but no one has ever heard it speak."

The fact is, in the two thousand years since Jesus was here, God has not revealed himself again in a verifiable manner. Yet, according to the Bible, He demands that we believe in Him, threatening us with Hell if we don't.

Atheists wonder what is this God doing, playing a hide-and-seek game with us? If he is so desirous for our believing in Him, He could ensure such belief by simply, openly and honestly revealing Himself. But, instead, He insists that we violate the reason He endowed us with by believing in Him without one shred of verifiable evidence.

Religionists expect us to eschew the rules of evidence required by our courts and the critical proofs, cross-checks and corroborations required by science, and accept the dubious hearsay and sloppy translations found in the ancient Bible as proof of God's existence.

Oh, we have heard of many reports of people talking with God, but none have been verified. Wouldn't it be nice to talk with God?

We could learn if there is intelligent life on other planets, if there is a Hell of fiery brimstone, or how He managed to create Himself and the universe out of nothing. Things that scientists devote their entire lives to learn, God could tell us in a minute.

He could even tell us who killed Jack Kennedy, whether Marilyn Monroe really committed suicide, what happened to Jimmy Hoffa and whether Elvis Presley is still alive. Since God knows the answers to all these questions but won't tell us, He must be a mean-spirited god.

Those people who define God in abstract terms such as Ultimate Reality have fled so far from the God of Moses that they should hang their heads in shame at their equivocation. Can you imagine Ultimate Reality handing Moses on Mount Sinai the Ten Commandments etched on stone? Or Ultimate Reality sneaking into Joseph's bedroom and impregnating his wife? It's difficult enough to imagine a ghost doing it.

Our next problem to deal with is the soul. Upon death our souls putatively leave our bodies and go to the next world.

For Heaven to be meaningful the soul would have to possess the memory of how grievous life was on Earth in order to appreciate the blissfulness of Heaven. So the soul would have to retain its memory, its sensitivity to its heavenly reward, and its sensory and emotional capacity. That is, the soul after leaving the body of its host at death would have to go on as a conscious, perceiving, cogitating, emotion-registering entity — a human personality. Atheists wonder what need there was for a brain if the soul can perform all these functions. Wasn't the brain redundant?

Spirit is in the same religious category as soul and presents the same problem of concept. Spirit has been variously described as something without form or dimensions, without material content, intangible and invisible. Is there a better definition of nothing?

When we come to the question of justice, the abstract concept is as simplistic as the execution is difficult.

George Eliot observed that "Justice is like the kingdom of God — it is not without us as a fact, it is within us as a great yearning." Justice is the yearning for order in a disorderly world.

Man's left brain couldn't accept amoral nature so it invented justice, a logical and orderly system of reward and punishment.

But failing to achieve justice on Earth, man went a step further in his quest for justice. Here his right brain took over and created an afterworld where all accounts would be squared — the good rewarded, the evil punished. One does not need to think long about the mechanics of Heaven to realize that such an idea came from the right brain.

The question of how Heaven and Hell are supposed to operate was addressed by George Bernard Shaw in his introduction to *Androcles and the Lion*. Shaw wondered just what possible reward a good person can expect in Heaven. He has earned his passage to Heaven by foregoing sinful behavior on Earth. Obviously he preferred the sinful behavior, otherwise he gave up nothing to earn a reward. Is his reward to be divine indulgence to sin all he pleases in the next world? Certainly, reasoned Shaw, the opportunity to be good in the next world is no reward.

Islamic Heaven makes much more sense than Christian Heaven. As described in the Koran, Islamic Heaven is a paradise abounding with beautiful, willing, perpetual virgins. There is an incentive (at least for men) to be good Moslems so they can go to Heaven. No wonder the jihad is so successful in recruiting soldiers for suicide missions.

All concepts of Heaven are absurd in view of people's varying tastes, desires and value systems. Thomas Moore expressed it:

> Vain things! — as lust or vanity inspires,
> The heaven of each is but what each desires.

Of course, Heaven is an impossibility. Heaven is supposed to engender only bliss, but bliss is meaningless without misery to contradistinguish it. What value could kindness have in Heaven where there is no unkindness? What value could beauty have in Heaven where there is no ugliness? What value could love have in Heaven where there is no such thing as hate?

Success would have no meaning were there no such thing as failure. Sporting games would be meaningless where both sides always win. What value would a heavenly Olympic gold have when everybody wins a gold? Heaven would be insufferably boring.

Well, perhaps not so boring. Hell seems to have been designed as much to please the righteous as to punish sinners. Gregory the Great opined: "The bliss of the elect in heaven would not be perfect unless they were able to look across the abyss and enjoy the agonies of their brethren in eternal fire."

Nevertheless, an afterlife was devised by religionists to help satisfy the human yearning for justice. It is sometimes difficult, though, to reconcile the love for justice with the Judeo-Christian Bible that reeks so of flagrant injustice as to shock the sensibilities. Relatively few Americans have ever read the entire Bible and would undoubtedly be appalled if they ever did.

In the course of the Bible, God violates most of His Ten Commandments. A few of His crimes: He damned the whole human race because of the sins of Adam and Eve; He killed Egyptian babies during the Passover; He ordered the Israelites to "utterly destroy all in the city, both men and women, young and old, oxen, sheep, asses, with the edge of the sword." He sent a pestilence that killed seventy thousand people; He sent two bears to kill forty-two children for making fun of Elisha's bald head; He punished children unto the third and fourth generation for sins of their forebears; He killed everybody in Sodom and Gomorrah for sexual deviance. He sanctioned slavery, religious persecution and the degradation of women. And finally, He drowned almost everybody in the world with a flood.

The enormity of God's punishments is appalling. He required the death penalty for such crimes as working on the Sabbath, reviling one's parents, irreverence toward Him, homosexuality, witchcraft, adultery and heresy.

Let's not forget that God punished the whole human race for Eve's peccadillo. Well, one small-town preacher didn't think it was a mere peccadillo: "Listen, friends, so great was that sin in the sight of God, that He not only cursed man from the Garden of Eden, imposed the penalty of death upon him and upon his offspring, but God even cursed the entire creation, the earth, the birds, the animals, and every creature."

How the enormity of God's punishments are reconciled with a merciful God is for the right brain to explain. The really incredible part of Christian theology is God's demanding after perpetrating His brutal crimes and injustices on humankind and ordering His own son murdered — demanding that humankind honor Him, worship Him, kneel down to Him, and sing His praises day night forever.

While God routinely punishes the innocent, He perversely rewards the guilty. According to one Christian scheme of salvation the worst sinners, no matter how much raping, robbing, swindling, murdering and mutilating they have done in their rotten lifetime, can get into Heaven by merely acknowledging God's son Jesus as their Savior; they can enjoy eternal bliss right along with good people who have earned it.

The Bible says that "there shall be joy in Heaven over one sinner that repenteth, more than ninety and nine righteous persons who need no repentance." This outrage prompted Ibsen to exclaim: "Your God is an old man whom you cheat."

Since God has complete foreknowledge (being omniscient) of each person's fate, many people are born for no other purpose, according to this theology, than to fill a quota for the lower region.

And of course God has His *Catch 22.* He commanded His children to go forth and populate the earth; then He made sex a sin — "Behold I was shapen in iniquity and in sin did my mother conceive me." (Psalm 51-5) This mischievous Father must chuckle as He watches His children struggle with the moral bind He put them into.

The most grotesque and heinous act of injustice was God's having His own son murdered to expiate the sins committed by other people. Here was innocent Jesus dying nailed to a cross as punishment for sins committed by people Jesus didn't even know. And the whole enormous injustice designed by Jesus's own Father. Verily, the right brain has a peculiar sense of justice.

While some of the deeply religious were apologizing for the Bible, others equally religious became biblical scholars. The unintended net effect of the latters' investigations has been to pretty well destroy the authenticity and inerrancy of the Bible. One can only marvel how the Christian religion with its biblical foundation virtually destroyed retains its vitality.

Religion, along with many of its other right-brain compeers — art, poetry, folklore and literary fiction — shows a light regard for truth. Lacking logic, the right brain doesn't recognize falsehood when it sees it. Of course, religionists along with artists, poets and writers claim to reach higher truths. But rationalists believe that true, like unique, correct and absolute is not subject to degree. There is no higher truth than truth. The concept of higher truth boils down to taste, not truth, and belongs in the right brain along with gormetism. I fail to see any relation between beauty and truth. Beauty is a subjective emotional reaction. How can an emotional titillation be called truth? Besides, sometimes truth is very ugly.

The mystic considers truth to be wisdom either internally generated or coming to him through his spiritual contact with "Reality." Doubters call his truths fantasies hardened by conviction. Some religionists claim that they get truth from their intuitions. But they never explain where their intuitions got it. But one must admit that these methods of obtaining truth beat many years of study and tedious laboratory research.

The atheist makes little distinction among superstition, supernaturalism, mysticism and religion. They all fit into his category of bunkum. Similarly, the atheist makes little distinction among reason, rationality, scientific principles and common sense (which is not so common as it sounds). They all fit into his category of logical thinking.

Atheists have observed that over the years as one religious belief after another has been discredited as a result of scientific and intellectual enlightenment, the discards have passed into the categories of superstition and myth. The religion of the Greeks and the Romans we today call Greek and Roman mythology.

Even many of the beliefs of religious conservatives today are viewed as superstitions by religious liberals.

Egyptian mythology yielded to Greek mythology, Greek to Roman mythology and Roman to Judeo-Christianity. Today nobody worships the Greek or Roman gods. Religions are called mythologies after people cease to believe in them. Someday Christianity will be called Judeo-Christian mythology.

In view of the thousands of discredited and abandoned religions of the past, it is logical to believe that someday all current religions will be discredited and abandoned, and replaced by new ones.

Every god is sooner or later repudiated. Most Gods seem to have been cruel hoaxes invented by the evil conniving minds of ancient priests to victimize humankind. Even a religion like Christianity purportedly created to champion the poor and downtrodden was later taken over by the rich and powerful for their own benefit. People were told to be good, obey the authorities, humble themselves before the Church, and they would be greatly rewarded in an afterworld. In the meantime the priests and their princely cohorts enjoyed most of the goodies of Earth. (There is something suspiciously similar between those ancient priests and modern swindling con men. Both appeal to greed in seducing their victims with promises of fabulous rewards: the con man's 200 percent profit on a 3-month investment, and the priest's eternal life in return for a petty tithe. Such fabulous promises alone should arouse the suspicions of a prudent man.)

But, think of the magnitude of such a criminal hoax on simple, devout parishioners — provided, of course, that there is no such afterworld.

There are three popular bases for truth: verifiability, authority and faith. The rational man quickly discards authority and faith as having nothing whatever to do with truth.

The Christian, dominated by his right brain, believes he has attained truth through the authority of the Bible. If the Bible is true, he possesses the truth. But he never subjects the Bible to critical study. He devotes his time and energy to defending his religious views, little to questioning them.

It seems to me that the Bible writers (with the possible exception of the author of Revelations) showed a lack of imagination.

People are still looking for fire coming from a bush — when we have nuclear flashes that strike one blind a hundred miles from the source. The explosion of one of our nuclear bombs exceeds the power of all the bombs, shells, mortars, bazookas, land mines, cannons, torpedoes and missiles exploded in all the wars in history. (Even so, a bush catching on fire without a cause would be a far greater happening.)

Religionists exclaim over the wondrous miracles of those glorious biblical days. They even get excited over purported miracles today, like a weeping Madonna in a grotto (later proved to be a total fraud — as always).

Jehovah scratched some messages on a stone, while today we send color photographs to Earth from Neptune, 2.3 billion miles away.

Religionists become ecstatic over some backwoods faith healer's claim to have cured a sinner of gonorrhea by laying a sanctimonious hand on the fellow's penis, while medical science has wiped out polio, scarlet fever, diphtheria, bubonic plague and typhoid fever. (However if it came to pass that even a mouse was cured of mange by divine intervention through the agency of a faith healer, all the great wonders of science would be as nothing.)

Religionists are surrounded by the invisible world they have been talking about for centuries — omnipresent voices — both radio and television; invisible, ghost-like images passing through the air. The Bible writers could not imagine such miracles and such spiritual omnipresence as are commonplace in our daily lives.

The spirits, ghosts and angels flitting about in biblical days were nothing compared with the omnipresent radio and television signals we are totally emersed in 24 hours a day. Television programs — news, stock market, weather and sports reports as well as movies and soap operas — permeate even our bodies.

There are greater wonders today inside our gallbladders than all the miracles of the church that have allegedly occurred in five thousand years. We can pick up People's Court or Wheel of Fortune or even a pornographic movie by inserting a tiny antenna even into our gallbladders. A hundred radio and television programs are available in there. But few religionists are awed. They are watching for a flaming bush or the faint likeness of the Madonna on a watertower.

No wonder rationalists and atheists have difficulty understanding the religious mind. With a cavalier contempt for logic, Christians believe in the Trinity, where three equals one — the Father, Son and Holy Ghost all being the same person. This leads to the absurdity of Jesus on the cross asking God: "Why doest Thou forsake me?" This is Jesus (God) talking to Himself asking why He is forsaking Himself. (The Trinity has placed an incomprehensible riddle at the heart of Christianity and made the greatest virtue that of believing the absurd.)

One, of course, finds it difficult to grasp the logic and justice in punishing one person for the sins of others. And one finds it hard to visualize the God of the universe leaving his other millions of worlds to come to Earth to be crucified by proxy because Adam and Eve ate an apple.

The easy access to Heaven by merely acknowledging Christ seems to be catering to something-for-nothing greed. And one doubts (to say the least) that the wine and crackers dispensed every Sunday to church congregations turn, with a little priestly incantation, into the real blood and flesh of Christ.

One wonders how Christians can still believe in Jesus after He told His disciples He would come back to Earth in their lifetime. That was 2000 years ago and He hasn't showed up yet.

One wonders also why Jesus was never mentioned by contemporary writers and historians. It is just incredible that God had come to Earth in the form of Jesus and performed astonishing miracles and finally been publicly crucified, buried and three days later, arisen and ascended to Heaven without contemporary writers and historians even mentioning it. Also not mentioned were the dead people arising from their graves and marching into town during the crucifixion of Jesus, as Matthew reports in the Gospel. We might mention that even more incredible was Mark, Luke and John describing the same episode and not even mentioning the marching dead people. Did these other Gospel writers fail to see those dead people or did they think it not worth reporting?

Although atheists find such things impossible to believe, religionists seem to have little difficulty believing them. There are 880,500,000 Moslems who believe that the Koran was brought by an angel from heaven; 663,500,000 Hindus who believe their god, Shiva, has four arms, 311,800,000 Buddhists who believe they will be reincarnated; 1,669,500,000 Christians who believe that God created the world in six days.

If human beings are smart enough to go to the moon, build nuclear bombs, make microprocessing chips, invent television, build supersonic airplanes and develop genetic engineering, one wonders how they can still believe in ghosts, miracles, afterworlds and the Bible. Answer: The right brain.

Atheists find it futile to argue with religionists because religionists base their arguments on their feelings which they verbalize with semantic gobbledegook. They say they know in their hearts that there is a God, while atheists base their beliefs on evidence. Religionists accord no validity to atheists' evidence just as atheists accord no validity to religionists' feelings, faith or authorities.

Arguments between them are as futile as arguments between a Frenchman who speaks no English and an Englishman who speaks no French.

The right brain can believe anything it wishes to believe, however fantastic. No proof required. The only criterion is whether the belief feels good. If proof is insisted upon, rationalization and flimsy logic are readily offered. As long as the right brain dominates, contradictions, inconsistencies and irrationalities are easily swept aside. Each hemisphere of the bicameral brain has its own method of arriving at truth. After all, it's a free country.

One should not be surprised that because of the contrary characteristics of the right and the left brain, conflict takes place between them, conflict that transfers on a world scale into the conflict between religion and science.

But when viewed in the perspective of the worldwide and historic savage conflicts among religions, the religion-science conflict pales by comparison.

Since the foremost religion in America is Christianity, its foundation, the Bible, is vitally important. Atheists, of course, see the Bible as a disorderly compilation of anecdotes, pornography, cruelty, injustice, contradictions and absurdities, while Christians see the Bible as the sacred word of God and as a valid guide for moral behavior and the uplifting of humankind. Some less pious people consider the Bible just a great piece of folk literature and a valuable historical document.

The Bible is a veritable hodgepodge of books attributed to various authors, who scholars agree are often not the ones who wrote them. Various Christian sects differ on which books are authentic and which are fraudulent (apocryphal).

The Jews and the Christians, being stuck with the Bible, devote much time and effort softening its crude impact by new translations, reinterpretations, substitution of euphemisms, deletions of the apocryphal, and explaining vile stories as allegorical. These religionists apologize that although the Bible was inspired by God, it was, unfortunately, written by ancient, ignorant, half-civilized people.

The apologists give new meanings to old texts; they allay disturbing doubt by explaining that what the Bible says had a different meaning in biblical days and that the Bible does not always mean what it says or say what it means. Nevertheless, with all their doctoring up, the Bible still demonstrates a twisted and inverted sense of justice and a strong propensity to fabricate and exaggerate.

At any rate, the Bible writers lived in a time when Earth was thought to be flat with four corners and that if you walked far enough you would fall off. They believed that Earth was bigger than the sun and was the center of the universe. They thought that the blind and mentally ill were possessed of demons which could be driven out of them with whips, that there were witches and they should be killed, that diseases and earthquakes were divine visitations which could be forfended by burning goats, sheep and even each other.

Atheists see biblical truth as made up of horror stories, parables with usually no rhyme nor reason, phony miracles, worthless promises, cryptic doctrines and dubious prophesies—all passed down from questionable witnesses through generations by word of mouth until recorded and then translated into modern languages; finally a council of prelates deciding by majority vote which parts of the Bible were true and which false. The resultant inerrant Bible was then promulgated by preachers and priests whose status and income depended on it.

Unfortunately, since the Bible is the foundation of Christianity it is incumbent on Christians to believe in it. Blackstone asked: "If you do not accept the testimony of the Bible as conclusive, what proof have you that God exists and that man is immortal?"

More specifically, Christians are obligated by calling themselves Christians to believe that Christ was the Son of God. It is not enough to say, as many religious liberals say, that Jesus, though not divine, was a great moral and ethical teacher. That won't wash. Jesus spoke of God as his father.

So, accepting the Bible's depiction of Jesus, if Jesus was not divine, He was either a charlatan or suffering from delusions of grandeur. Christians have to take their pick. Accepting the divinity of Christ is what qualifies a person as a Christian. All others claiming to be Christians would seem to be hypocrites.

The fragile evidence of the appearance of Jesus on Earth has to be accepted with the help of considerable faith. It is true there are some reputable scholars who believe that the Bible is historically true. Would anyone have ever heard of Jesus if He hadn't been promoted by the Bible? Most scholars find no record of Jesus in any historical documents of His day. In other words, we know of Him only through the Bible. No Bible, no Jesus.

Many Christians believe there is only one valid way by which to arrive at knowledge: by faith. According to Martin Luther, "Faith must trample under foot all reason, sense, and understanding and whatever it sees it must put out of sight, and wish to know nothing but the word of God." (Here was Martin Luther prescribing for the followers of his new religion the very rules he himself violated in breaking away from the Catholic Church.)

Christian leaders have always realized that Christianity could not hold up against reason so they substituted faith for reason and made doubt a major sin. Their fears have been justified: whenever reason has been applied to Christianity, belief has crumbled.

From the earliest Christian times, the Church has defended itself against exposure of its fraudulent nature by persecuting scientists, torturing dissidents, censoring literature, burning blasphemers, brainstuffing the laity—in every way possible keeping the populace steeped in ignorance, terrorized by fear and subjugated to the Church. At the same time the Church hierarchy had to fight off heretics bent not on exposing its fraudulence but upon gaining power to propagate their own fraud.

Pious fraud aimed at the spiritual and mental subjection of the people was viewed by the Church as praiseworthy. Any end in the name of Jesus Christ justified the means. Of course, the real end was the greater power and glory of the Church.

The early Christian Church was a rich soil for the nourishment of the right brain. We are still overwhelmed by our legacy of pious fraud, hypocrisy, dishonesty, holy pretensions, irrationality, superstition and ignorance.

It logically follows that if Christianity is true, then reason is false. If human reason is false, how does one account for the great marvels created by science based on human reason?

We must understand the difference between questions of taste and questions of fact. Taste is governed by what feels good. Religion feels good. Arguments over questions of taste are senseless. If you say you like pumpkin pie better than apple pie, it would be silly for me to dispute you.

Fact or truth as related to scientific verification admits of no exercise of taste. In building a new library the board of trustees have a choice between classic and modern design. This is a matter of artistic taste. But the builder has no choice between scientific and unscientific engineering principles in its construction.

Although most religionists reject scientific principles applied to their religion, fearing their religion would collapse under the impact, they accept with unquestioning faith all the modern inventions produced by the application of scientific principles. They have little doubt that when they snap on their television, a picture will appear. If it should not appear, they call a technician, not a faith healer.

During a drought religionists will assemble at the church to pray for rain—with the sprinklers turned on full in the church lawn and not an umbrella in the whole congregation. They give lip service to their right-brain religious faith. Whether religionists are engaged in exorcism or passing out *Watchtowers*, their faith is really in science.

They don't have enough faith in God to move a bottle cork, but they do not doubt that with sufficient mechanical equipment (or a medium-sized nuclear bomb), engineers, wishing a mountain moved, will move it.

Science gains the respect of the public, but very little love. People are surrounded by the stark evidence of the success of science—television, microwave ovens, digital watches, pocket calculators and jet planes as well as fiber optics, laser beams, nuclear generators and genetic engineering. They all work. Yet the public's real love seems to center on supernaturalism, superstition, astrology, faith healing, palmistry, crystal worship, exorcism and medical quackery despite the absence of evidence that any of them work.

The most outspoken religionists have unwavering faith in science, while widely denouncing science. Televangelists have the insolence to berate science from their television pulpits while shamelessly raking in hundreds of millions of dollars from the gullible made possible by science's greatest creation for folk enjoyment.

Much of humankind's intellectual and emotional struggle has been not for truth, but against truth. The advance of science has been sporadically fought against for thousands of years. Man fancies himself in his little world of make-believe at the center of the universe, as a creation in the image of God. From Earth, unlike all the mortal animals with whom he shares Earth, he goes to another life provided for him by God.

But such vanity sets him up to be pummeled and humiliated by every advancement in science and learning. So he spends much of his psychic energy defending his precious ego against the truth.

The heliocentric theory of Copernicus rudely removed man from the center of the universe and placed him on a speck of dust orbiting around an obscure star which, in the course of cosmological discovery, turned out to be only one of billions of stars in its galaxy, which is only one galaxy in billions. The magnitude of the reduction of man's importance in the universe by the discoveries of astronomy is inconceivable. From a god-like hero in the center of the universe, he has been reduced to almost nothing. How much more humiliation was in store for him? Much more.

Darwin determined that man was not made in the image of God, but had evolved from the lower animals among whom he lived; that he, although incomparably smarter, was very much like those animals.

Karl Marx came along and told man he wasn't a creature of free choice who molded his own world, but was a product of the economic system under which he lived.

Sigmund Freud heaped more indignity on man by suggesting that man did not act from the noble motives that he pretended, but from ulterior motives that he was too ashamed of to even admit he had. So he kept them buried deep in his unconscious.

Then B. F. Skinner, the behavioral psychologist, compounded the indignity of Marxism by asserting that the character and personality of a person are determined by the conditioning factors in his environment, not by his own will. So the early demigod man was reduced to a puppet on a string.

But the advances of science have not been accepted gracefully. They have been denounced by the church and resisted by the populace. The leaders of scientific discovery have been vilified, harassed, persecuted, tortured, imprisoned, executed. But the weight of evidence and practical results piled up by science is invincible — something that many of today's fundamentalists still haven't learned.

The Western world was under the rule of the Church, whose power derived from the Bible, a product of the right brain. Science was in its infancy, but with almost every step it took it collided with religion.

Science is an aberration in a human history of ignorance, superstition, dishonesty and depravity tolerated because it produces irresistible, seductive material goodies for a society of consumer addicts, and furnishes superior armaments upon which ruling establishments are absolutely dependent.

For hundreds of years the clergy has been dividing its energy between fighting against science on the one hand and proclaiming on the other hand that there is no conflict between science and religion.

But despite the apologetics, we have a glaring conflict between science and religion. Side by side we have two irreconcilable allegiances, one supported by demonstrable, corroborated proof, the other by faith and authority. Or, another way of viewing it, the clash between science and religion is a clash between cerebral hemispheres.

Nobody doubts that telephones, radios, digital watches and televisions work; that Polaroids take instant pictures, airplanes fly, submarines navigate under the seas, space ships zoom to the moon. But atheists wonder how many Americans really hold no doubt that faith healing works, that guardian angels protect them, that their prayers are answered, that they are immortal. Surveys aren't very helpful. Surveys often tell us only what the right brain believes, not what a person's behavior indicates the left brain believes.

Science, with its irrefutable proofs, should be easy to believe, but most people, with their right-brain preference, seem to find religion, despite its fuzzy foundation, easier to believe.

Science does not question the existence of God — it totally ignores such a possibility. Nowhere in the fields of astronomy, physics, psychiatry, medicine, nuclear science, neuroscience or genetic engineering is there any consideration given to the possibility of a soul or God.

Scientists predict eclipses of the sun and the moon with minute precision convinced that God has nothing to do with it.

When a matriculating freshman enters the portals of a secular college he must leave God outside the door as his grandfather left his dog outside the door of the little red school house. Psychology professors don't bother to argue away God and soul, but just ignore the possibility of a spiritual world, allowing students to draw their own conclusions.

The physical and biological sciences are even less concerned about a God governing all natural phenomena.

Of course, religious schools are a horse of another color. The Rev. Jerry Falwell, speaking of Liberty University that he founded, wrote: "Every teacher at Liberty must sign our doctrinal statement, which clearly espouses a belief in the literal and direct Creation of the universe by God. There are no exceptions — including the professors in the biology department. We are so committed to the doctrine of special Creation that we require every student to study Creation."

If supernatural forces were really at work, one could not trust his rear-view mirror in driving, nor his brakes, nor his steering wheel. One could not trust the trajectory of a rifle bullet aimed at a deer. It might circle around and strike the hunter in the head.

There could be no radio or television. Programs would be constantly interfered with by supernatural forces. We could not risk building and operating nuclear energy plants if supernatural forces were abroad that might cause meltdowns at the whim of some evil spirits.

While religionists insist upon the existence of supernatural forces, our whole modern world is built and operated on the assumption that there are no such things. As a matter of logic, as argued earlier, there can be no such thing as the supernatural.

Educators, doctors, entertainers, writers and scientists must all show a certain obeisance to religion whether they believe in it or not. Their professional success, their social status and in rare cases even their lives depend on their patronizing the prevailing mythology. So their fear of religion and their occasional pusillanimous behavior is easily understood.

A classic case of pusillanimity was that of Galileo in bowing before the Church's Tribunal and declaring that he didn't believe the Earth revolved around the sun (when, of course, he did) in order to save his neck.

Galileo remembered what they had done to Bruno for Bruno's scientific expositions — they had burned him at the stake. Who can blame Gali leo?

Galileo was worth more to the world as a live scientist than as a dead scientist. A curious lack of concern over science martyrs gives them little value while religious martyrs are often worth more dead than alive. Christ, for example. If He had not been crucified He probably would have sooner or later been exposed as a fraud and forgotten.

ADAM AND EVE DRIVEN FROM EDEN.

There is little fear in debunking astrology, palmistry, spiritualism, crystal worship, reincarnation and telepathy because most Christians view these to be superstitions, even if atheists don't recognize any significant differences between such beliefs and Christian beliefs.

While superstitions are safe to attack, religions are no-nos. God, who atheists believe to be the biggest hoax of all, is sacrosanct.

It is a sad situation when intelligent persons fear to stand above the superstitious herd. In fear of economic sanctions and social ostracism — in short, the wrath of the mob — they must timidly deny disbelief in gods, ghosts, angels and devils as if they were ashamed of their higher ability to reason. For today's mob and its leaders still have effective ways of dealing with heretics without resort to the use of the physical torture of the past when the churches were at their zenith of power.

Establishmentarian scientists frequently indulge in equivocations to protect their jobs and reputations. They affirm their belief in God, but their

God is an abstract concept that bears little resemblance to the personal God of the people. Nevertheless, the defensive preachers are so hungry for any little crumb the eminent scientists may toss them that they greedily pounce on it without inspecting its purity.

Even liberal preachers indulge in such deceitful equivocations rather than come out honestly and confess their disbelief in the God inside the heads of most of their parishioners. After years of seminary study and years of establishing themselves as the spiritual leader in their community, they can hardly be blamed for not wanting to destroy themselves.

University professors and scientists, living opulent lives and enjoying revered status, face every morning a day of compromising their integrity in order to preserve their soft berths. So their throwing a sop to the mob about God every time they write or speak is easily understood.

There is scant evidence of humankind's ability to adapt to the secular world, the real world. Over 95 percent of human beings still cling to the ancient myths. For the sake of the goodies that science produces, they bend, but they do not adapt. This forced bending is the cause of much of the tension from which modern people suffer.

While scientists have led us into the miraculous twentieth century, our holy men have performed the incredible feat of preserving the public's child-like behavior and adherence to the beliefs of Year One. And few educators have opposed them. Educators and scientists seem to care little about the failure of the mental advancement of the masses as long as they themselves are rich and comfortable. They have remained indifferent to the inevitable disaster that atheists see as the result of humankind's failure to adapt — to overrule its right brain.

In fact, many modern liberals give up the infallibility of the Bible in matters of physics, but try to keep it in matters of faith and morals — a bit of intricate intellectual hocus-pocus. The prestigious University of California at Berkeley has even shamed itself by bowing to the demands of the superstitious in offering doctorates in parapsychology.

Generally the least literate societies are the most strongly religious, and historically, the periods of greatest ignorance have been the periods of greatest religious fervor.

In addition, atheists point out that most of the greatest people in almost all professions have been nonbelievers in religion — lawyers, writers, scientists, artists, philosophers, statesmen, educators, psychiatrists, mathematicians. Such illustrious persons include: William Shakespeare, Mark Twain, George Eliot, Sinclair Lewis, Henry L. Mencken, George Bernard Shaw, W. Somerset Maugham, Sir Thomas Moore, Buckminster Fuller, S.

I. Hayakawa, Alfred Korzybski, Charles Darwin, Thomas Paine, Thomas Jefferson, James Madison, Thomas Huxley, Herbert Spencer, Bertrand Russell, H. G. Wells, Voltaire, Spinoza, John Stewart Mill, Sigmund Freud, John Dewey, Clarence Darrow, Margaret Sanger, Michelangelo, Beethoven and Alice in Wonderland.

Why religionists believe what they believe is often more irrational than what they believe. When you consider that religious beliefs result from the mere happenstance of birth and that hundreds of millions of Christians, Jews, Moslems and Hindus are willing to die for their religious beliefs, the whole religious world takes on the aspect of insanity.

Here are a million Moslems ready and willing to slay Hindus. But if they had happened to be born in Hindustan, they would instead be Hindus ready and willing to slay Moslems.

Worldwide, probably less than one percent of religionists choose their religion. It was instead imposed on them by heredity; they were indoctrinated with it in their vulnerable childhood.

Arthur Koestler explained it clearly: "How many men *choose* the belief system for which they are prepared to die? Your credo is just as much a matter of the hazards of birth as your citizenship. If you were born in Jordan, you'd be a good Moslem. Once the credo is imprinted, man's schizoid brain permits his faith to coexist with his reason, even when they contradict on every point."

It is obvious that relatively few people are ever faced with making a religious choice, the choice having already been made by forbears. It is not by choice or by coincidence that a Catholic's parents, grandparents, uncles, aunts, brothers and sisters are also Catholic.

So, can we rightly say that the religious opinions of such people — the vast majority of people — are worthless because those people had nothing to do with forming those opinions, but were merely indoctrinated with them — brain-stuffed victims of a system that promotes mindlessness? H. L. Mencken opined: "The most curious social convention of the great age in which we live is the one to the effect that religious opinions should be respected."

The religionist believes that his religion is based on truth while other people's religions are based on false doctrines, myths and superstitions. Surely, if religionists ever did any serious thinking on the mater, they would see the absurdity of the 5,000 religions in the world each with a different belief and each convinced its view is right, and the other 4,999 wrong.

Each of the 5,000 religions describes God in a different way. Can you imagine them describing a horse in 5,000 different ways? Will Durant suggests: "Where there are a thousand faiths, we are apt to become skeptical of all of them."

Even where choice of a belief is rendered, it is probably less the result of cognition than of temperament. Then the chooser spends the rest of his life rationalizing his temperament.

There are, of course, a few crossovers among sectarian lines and among the many Protestant and Jewish denominations, as well as movements from traditional Western sects to Eastern religions and to cults. Such shifts of faith take place even though they imply that the subject had been wrong all his or her previous life.

The reasons for these shifts of faith are many and varied — convenience, economic advantage, friendly persuasion, disillusionment, chronic discontent, searching, brain-washing, seduction, marriage, proselytizing, spiritual awakening.

Conversion to atheism is a major shift of preference from the right brain to the left brain. It is almost always irreversible. After a person discovers the clay feet of the idol he can never be easily persuaded to believe again that the feet are of flesh and blood.

The main reason Christianity grew to such world stature was that it came along on the heels of the crumbling Roman Empire making it easy to displace Roman mythology. In time Christopher (the Christ-Bearer) Columbus had the serendipitous luck to discover America from which followed the Christianization of the New World. Riding the industrial development and growing military might of Europe and America, Christianity in time became the dominant world religion. Of course, there were many competing cults around in the early days of Christianity. Christians ask why among them all it was the Christian cult that succeeded. They attribute Christianity's success to its inherent truth.

So far as the teachings of Jesus are concerned, they had to be rejected almost totally for the Western world to rise to dominance. To begin with, Jesus taught communism and slave morality. The West was not won by rich men giving everything they owned to the poor, nor by turning the other cheek to predatory nations, nor by opening one's safe to thieves (give him also your cloak), nor by lending freely to borrowers, nor by not judging lest ye be judged.

Just as extrinsic factors determined the global spread of Christianity, the success of the Islamic religion today — the second largest and fastest growing religion in the world — got its big boost from oil, not Allah.

The sex repression inspired by the Bible (for which Saint Paul is probably more to blame than Jesus) laid the basis for unhealthy sexual cultural development, leaving its miserable trail of sexual neurosis, perversion, rape, child abuse, sadism, withered celibate lives, sex antagonism, venereal disease and pornography.

In view of Christianity's bankrupt doctrines and morality, atheists are puzzled at its tenacity and success. About the only explanation they can come up with is the sine qua non of any religion's success—the need and will to believe. Man is surely a gluttonous, coprophagous animal.

Truth and reason seem to have little impact on society. People's passions are aroused by supernaturalism and mysticism, not by science and reason. Man seems to prefer falsehood to truth, hypocrisy to honesty, chicanery to integrity.

As one after another of his myths are destroyed, he creates new ones to take their places. He has replaced his shattered belief in gods, angels and devils with belief in flying saucers, paranormal powers, quartz crystals, magical organic foods, nostrums and rejuvenators.

The disposition to believe or not believe is the determining factor and the right brain has a disposition to believe. Atheism is not so much a sign of intelligence as it is a sign of the disposition to doubt—to look for fallacies, contradictions, absurdities.

The schizoid nature of the brain with its right and left hemispheres makes possible for scientists whose professional thinking is dominated by their left brain to indulge also in the low-level thinking of their right brain in matters of religion.

A few decades ago some Filipino psychic surgeons made quite a splash in the tabloids by claiming to remove tumors from internal organs by reaching their bare hands into the side of their patient's body and plucking out the tumor without leaving any sign of an entry lesion.

The sad part of this story is that four doctors traveled to the Philippines to observe these surgeons, and came away convinced that they had observed miracles.

The doctors actually believed that those Filipino surgeons had supernatural powers. First of all, the doctors had to be stupid and superstitious enough to believe such a miracle possible or they wouldn't have traveled all the way to the Philippine Islands to observe. That marked them as kind of dumb doctors to start with.

So, even scientifically trained people can succumb to the prompting of their right brain—the hemisphere with the will to believe.

One is rightly puzzled over why religious supernaturalism and superstition have prevailed throughout history in evolutionary selection over reason and rationality. That they have is evident by the overwhelming plurality of religionists over rationalists in the world. One would have expected reason and rationality to have overwhelmed ignorance and superstition long ago. But the latter have inexplicable tenacity.

Atheists have to live with the fact that religion has succeeded over atheism by most standards of measurement. Even in this 20th century with its explosion of science and rationality, religion is still vastly more popular than atheism. The atheists can only console themselves with the conviction that popularity proves nothing. In Salem, Massachusetts it was very popular in 1692 to hang witches.

In addition, although convinced that they are on the side of truth, atheists are nevertheless vilified and maligned their entire lives by the vast majority of the population, a majority atheists see as on the side of darkness and error. The good guys lose; the bad guys win.

Of course, there are religious minorities — Mormons, Jehovah's Witnesses, Moonies, Christian Scientists, Hare Krishnas — who are similarly vilified and maligned. Each group probably agrees that the good guys lose and the bad guys win — with some difference in opinion about who the good guys are. But religionists are all under the umbrella of believers. Atheists are on the outside.

In view of the inconsequential number of atheists, an atheist must surely feel a little arrogant who says that religion is bunk, God is a myth, Abraham was a fictitious character, Moses was a ruthless dictator, Jesus Christ was a fraud, the Twelve Disciples were dupes, the Catholic Church is the biggest parasite on Earth, Martin Luther and John Calvin wasted their lives supplanting one brand of rubbish with another; and that all the priests, preachers, monks, nuns, rabbis, bishops, deacons, popes, shamans, ayatollahs and other assorted holy men throughout history wasted their lives propagating falsehoods!

But, of course, preachers, priests and popes are hardly paragons of humility themselves, pretending to have been especially selected (having gotten the call) by God Himself to be His earthly representatives.

A big question in the controversy between atheists and religionists is who's to decide what criteria are to be used.

The left-brainers, of course, accept only the criterion of logic. By their criterion they win hands down. But religionists have their own criteria.

After one has given all the logical arguments for atheism, one has to face the fact that religion doesn't deal with logic. Religion has its own paths to truth. Religion is concerned with spirituality, with logic can't touch.

In addition, there are frequently overlooked arguments favoring religion: Religion has persisted since time immemorial and has successfully resisted every attempt to destroy it. Religion has apparently been chosen by evolution as an indispensable guide for human society. All over the world for thousands of years — in Hindu lands, in Moslem countries, in Christendom — the greatest art, architecture and music have been inspired by and dedicated to religion. There is nothing comparable inspired by atheism.

Probably the best argument for religion is that religion works while atheism doesn't. It is somewhat similar to capitalism. Capitalism works, while socialism, despite its foundation in humanitarian aims and the impeccable logic of Marxism, doesn't work.

It may all come down to the old proverb that the proof of the pudding is in the eating — performance is the true test, not appearances and promises. Humankind have apparently found religion more palatable than atheism. The atheist response is predictable: What has that got to do with truth? The religionist answer: Everything.

Chapter IV
RELIGION AS A
CULTURE-TIME-FILLER

If we accept evolution, there can be little doubt that if we go back far enough we reach a state of pre-religion in humankind's history. Or, if you scratch a priest deep enough you find an atheist.

This is not to deny the existence of God, but to point out that according to the Bible, God didn't reveal Himself until four or five thousand years ago. Primitive man couldn't have known anything about God a million years before God revealed Himself.

Nevertheless, primitive people were prone to superstition, supernaturalism and magic as far back as anthropologists and archeologists have been able to dig. Since there is no sign of religion in the other primates from whom humans developed, somewhere along the evolutionary path between men-like apes and ape-like men, religion entered the human psyche. Even our closest cousins, the chimpanzees, show no signs of religion.

It most probably entered after the development of the bicameral brain because other primates have such a brain, but don't have religion. So, somewhere this virus or neurotic obsession, as Freud called it, entered into the right brain.

Many theories explaining the origin of religion have ben suggested. No single theory may be the exclusive cause, a combination being more likely. Moreover, religions in different societies may have had different origins.

Let's consider very briefly eight theories.

(1)   Primitive man confused his shadow or shade with a spirit that

followed him around. We have in our dictionary today such definitions of shadow and shade as "phantom, ghost."

(2)   The origin of the concept of spirit or soul may have arisen from primitives' dreams convincing them that their spirit left their bodies every night and cavorted about the village.

(3)   Early man did not know about hormones, endocrines, neurotransmitters, endorphins, glands, messenger chemicals, pain receptors and other biochemical factors governing emotions and moods. When a person became angry it was believed that a demon had entered the body. (Possibly a good early defense in murder cases.)

(4)   Religion among some primitives may have arisen from the worship of ancestors. A son's father dies and the son is unable to sever his father's image from his memory. If the father was dictatorial the son's memory of his father continues to guide him and rule him. He continues to feel the fear of his parent that he felt when the parent was alive.

There naturally develops from this fear of and reverence for ancestors a hierarchy of spirits corresponding to the family and tribal hierarchies on Earth. One would expect the greatest of the spirits to be a male, since males generally enjoyed the top status on Earth. So God became a monarch governing his earthly subjects and they acknowledged his benevolence and supplicated his favors.

(5)   In this precarious life there is a natural desire for a faithful, trustworthy friend who will help one in time of need. Loyal friends, wives, husbands, partners and servants are always in short supply. So the right brain created protective gods, guardian angels and saviors to reduce fear and anxiety. These protective divinities never forsook or betrayed a troubled person but stood by him even when all his earthly friends deserted him.

(6)   Primitive people sought to understand nature and to devise means for controlling nature. But they had yet only a poorly developed cerebral cortex and their pitiful attempts to use reason and logic led them astray. Their efforts were counterproductive, leading them into a morass of total misconceptions, misunderstandings and failures—in short into religion. Religion arose from man's mistaken interpretations of natural phenomena.

(7)   Early people, deploring the total lack of justice in nature, attempted to set themselves above amoral nature by establishing a system of justice to live under. But injustice among human beings continued rampant, and the yearning for justice was inextinguishable. In time the right brain dreamed up an afterworld in which all accounts would be squared.

(8)   The overwhelming reluctance of man to accept the finality of death, a reluctance that prompted him to invent two basic elements of religion — a soul and an afterlife.

(9)   Man's bewilderment over the metaphysics of his own existence in response to which his right brain devised answers called religion.

(10)   Finally there is the theory that the right brain, prone to create, imagine and hallucinate, overcame man's primitive, poorly developed, reasoning left brain by playing God and issuing orders through the cerebral commissure to the auditory and speech centers of the left brain. Such right brain dominance of human behavior persists today in spite of the left brain's explosive advancements.

Whatever the origins of religion, the fact that religion has persisted down through history in defiance of logic, reason and scientific refutation is powerful proof that it fulfills many basic human needs.

More important than what people believe is the reason they believe it, and generally the reason is that such beliefs fulfill their needs. So let us consider the needs religion and the church fulfill.

Religion and the church fulfill the needs for ego enhancement, social contact, economic advantage, prestige, belonging, feelings of righteousness, getting something for nothing, esthetic pleasure, emotional experience, drama, transcendental euphoria, spiritual solace. In addition, humans do not like to feel alone in this big impersonal indifferent universe. A personal God is a great comfort.

The emotional element stands out in the more primitive religions. Today's more sophisticated Christian denominations have eschewed the emotional element as beneath their intellectual level. As a result their memberships have fallen off drastically. The charismatic movement and cults have stepped in to fulfill this neglected emotional need and have enjoyed spectacular success.

Emotionalism in Christianity has a long history, being brought to America by settlers from Europe. Sects in Europe and England were given to emotional extravagance at their meetings. When smitten by the Holy Spirit, followers had convulsions and trances and visions; they babbled in tongues, swooned and made violent cluckings. They danced, jumped for joy, moaned, wept and fainted in religious ecstasy. They jerked, rolled, barked and gobbled.

Such heritage was imported to America undiluted. An observer described early American Methodist and Presbyterian evangelical meetings: "The people remained on the grounds day and night, listening to the most exciting sermons, and engaging in a mode of worship which consisted of alternate crying, laughing, singing and shouting . . . trembling, weeping, and swooning away, until every appearance of life was gone and the extremities of the body assumed the coldness of a corpse. At one meeting no less than a thousand persons fell to the ground."

The theatrics and audience participation of the early revival camp meetings helped fulfill the emotional needs of early Americans. Without the time- and culture-fillers of radio, television, movies, rock concerts, professional sports, shopping malls, vacation travel, easy transportation and general reading literacy, religion had little competition for the public's patronage and devotion. It often became the all-absorbing entertainment and passion of small town and rural America.

One famous camp meeting at Cane Ridge, Kentucky in 1801 was attended by 25,000. In view of the small population at that time and transportation by foot or horse, such a gathering can be seen as spectacular. Participants said that Cane Ridge was beyond description. Emotionalism and unrestrained spontaneity governed; primness and prudery were discarded. Was Woodstock of 1969 essentially a counterculture Cane Ridge without the Holy Spirit!

True or false, religion fulfills needs. Whether God really exists or not makes little practical difference. Religious people love Him and praise Him; ministers devote their lives teaching about Him. People follow His alleged precepts whether He is imaginary or not.

Religious people are like crows that shun a field wherein is staked a scarecrow. The birds shun the field just as they would if a real live man were stationed in it. Their imaginations conceive a real man where, in fact, there is none. The effect on the birds is the same.

Most atheists regard the vicars of Christ, the holy men, the prophets, the ayatollahs, the redeemers and he Bible writers as mostly romantic liars. Whether they are called Buddha, Shiva, Krishnamurti, Christ, Mohammed, Mrs. Eddy, Joe Smith or Sun Myung Moon. But it doesn't really make a great deal of difference — the need for infantile diversions of an immature species is fulfilled.

Most primitive peoples did not need the full 24 hours of a day for sleeping, eating, food-gathering, hunting, shelter-building and home-making. Most of them lived in mild climates where food was abundant. They had to do something to fill the remainder of their day. Religion was one of those things — ceremonies, rites, prayers, magic, feasts, initiations, weddings, funerals. Their religion was integrated with their cultural arts that developed with it — dancing, painting, sculpturing, carving, costume designing, music, drama and story telling. Unlike modern people, they did not escalate their wants to keep right on the heels of their capacity to produce. They enjoyed leisure time. Other time-fillers such as education and the development of science were to come later.

This leisure time, this discretionary time, was the time out of which human culture has been developed. What humans have done with their spare time has determined the course of history.

Hundreds of diverse religions and gods have been created to fill human beings' discretionary time. So, lumping all religions into one category is playing it loosely. Some religions, like the Judeo-Christian religion, believe in an active, personal God, an anthropomorphic God. Others, including some Eastern and Oriental religions believe God to be Spiritual Essence (whatever that is). One suspects that religions which define God as Spiritual Essence, Cosmic Consciousness, Divine Principle, Ultimate Purpose, etc. are masquerading reality with semantic gobbledegook. In our society today one frequently hears God defined as Love. The problem here is that love is about as difficult to define as God.

Even the personal Christian God is interpreted quite differently among different sects in arriving at their own values. The more fundamentalist sects value humility, piety, poverty and faith, while some modern sects see God as a heavenly agent to seek help from in attaining success and wealth.

Polytheistic religions were more popular in the past. Gods were assigned separate functions covering the various aspects of nature and human life. Some ancient religions believed that Earth was already here before their gods ever showed up. Their gods were finite.

The Christian God is a kind of hybrid, being both a monotheistic God and a trinity of Gods. Some Christians, as in Mexico, even use the plural for God — Dios.

Yoga, an offshoot of ancient Hindu Vedanta philosophy, has in recent years become popular among religious dilettantes in America. The aerobic calisthenics aspect of Yoga has had the greatest appeal. Yoga is presented over American television as a program of reducing exercises.

The theology of Yoga involves a complicated system of reincarnations, several layers of gods, spiritual cycles and wheels, personal gods (Atman), thought waves, and a tripartite brain (located in the anus, the chest and top of the head).

Upon completing the seven stages to gain perfect knowledge of your Atman, you achieve pure undifferentiated consciousness and oneness with your Atman. But you are not through yet. You must reach the final step of union with Brahman.

In ancient India discretionary time for religion must have been plentiful, since there was little to do beside herding sheep and tilling the soil.

Animals have often been invested with religious properties. The totem animal of ancient tribal life was worshiped as the protector of the tribe. The cow in India even today is treated as sacrosanct.

In Egypt many thousand years ago house cats were treated as sacrosanct. Cats were worshiped in temples and in homes. The cat was the first to be rescued from a burning house, and the death of a cat was cause for deep mourning. Killing a sacred cat was a capital offense. But there was a dark side to it from the standpoint of cats. In keeping with religious contradictions and inconsistencies, cats were also strangled and offered as sacrifices to the ancient cat goddess, Bastet. Cats were regularly mummified before burial. In the 1800s, around 300,000 cat mummies were shipped from Egypt to England where they were ground up as fertilizer for English gardens.

One can hardly trust his intuitions and feelings in matters of religion. Fundamentalists' early-imbued religious feelings dominate their thinking process, but as Charles Darwin suggested, a sense of sublimity is no argument for God. The Christian walks and talks with his God and feels His presence, the Shintoist feels the same thing when he kneels in worship of his ancestors. The Hindu mother of olden times felt the presence of her God when she sacrificed her infant child; the sun worshiper when he tore the flesh from his body, the druid when he performed his mystic harvest rites, the Aztec priest when he plunged the knife into the heart of his human victim on the sacrificial altar. John Calvin felt he was striking a match for Jesus when he burned Servitas at the stake.

Only our secular civil government, not our religious feelings, protects us from the potential savagery of religion. The policy of our government as declared in the Constitution is to allow its citizens to sink to whatever depth of ignorance and superstition they wish as long as they don't hurt anybody—at least not in explicit, obvious ways.

A Reuter's dispatch from Jakarta, Indonesia, illustrates how government must sometimes protect people from religious madness. Indonesia, although proud of its religious tolerance, has had to launch a campaign leading to bloody fighting against the wild followers of some of 150 to 200 strange new sects now spreading in the island republic.

In Tjirojom, West Java, a man named Nawawi formed a sect which he called "Hakeko" (derived from the Arabic word for truth). He told his followers he had permission from God to marry three virgins. Believers were instructed to divorce their partners, then dance together stark naked at night in the local mosque. Male members of the sect were given permission to rape the wives of disbelievers whom they dubbed "heathens."

A village leader reported the orgies to a nearby army post, which sent a sergeant and two village guards to investigate. As they approached the mosque where dancing was going on, Nawawi and his naked followers burst out and attacked them with bamboo spears and machetes, screaming "Allah Akbar [God the great]. Who does not follow us is a pig." The sergeant and one village guard escaped, the third man was killed.

The next morning the army post commander went to the mosque. He was attacked and chopped to pieces. Later, troops moved into the mosque, firing over the heads of Nawawi's men. The belief of the sect was that its members were bulletproof, and as the devotees screaming war cries and insults attacked the approaching soldiers, the troops fired into them, killing 22 and wounding dozens.

Another culture-filler involves saints and miracles of the Catholic Church. Saints are people who have led exemplary religious lives, suffered from persecution and martyrdom or performed miracles. The Catholic Church has a roster of over 2,500 saints. The plethora of saints had become confusing and their feastdays were crowding the liturgical calendar. Room had to be made for new saints. So about two decades ago the Church defrocked 200 of its saints, including 46 that the Church admitted had never even existed. Celebrations and feasts honoring 2,500 saints can soak up a lot of discretionary time.

One of the demoted saints, San Gennaro, of Naples, continued to work his annual miracle despite the loss of Vatican sponsorship. Neapolitans crowded into the Church of San Gennaro as usual to wait suspensefully for the miracle — the liquefaction of his blood in a glass reliquary. After appropriate supplication and exhortation the miracle happened — right on schedule accompanied by whoops of triumphant joy.

Miracles, too, add much to enrich the lives of believers. Miracles add mystery, drama, hope and outings to holy shrines. Miracles are happenings that defy natural law. The Catholic Church has a long list of authenticated miracles. Of course, atheists believe every one of them is a hoax. The Vatican itself disavows most purported miracles.

We often read about weeping Marys appearing in grottos or in the morning mist of distant hills, and Christian crosses miraculously etched on window panes. The Vatican is much too savvy to give recognition to these hoaxes, but believers flock to see them, often to the enrichment of the perpetrators.

The most popular dispenser of miraculous cures is the Lourdes grotto in France, site of the famous Catholic shrine where many people believe the Virgin Mary appeared in 1858. Over five million pilgrims go to Lourdes every year. They dip their sick and crippled into a spring pool of near ice water to cure them.

A *60 Minutes* feature on Lourdes showed a woman who had taken her husband there five times. He appeared to be a little balmy. The wife admitted Lourdes had not cured him of anything. For her the pilgrimage was primarily a time-filling outing.

But Lourdes claims over 200 miracle cures. With five million pilgrims going there every year, one would expect after a number of years at least 200 of them by chance to get well about the time they were journeying home from Lourdes, whether they were dipped in the ice water or not. The Catholic Church admits that the water at Lourdes is no different from any other kind of water (except perhaps a little colder). Maybe that is why, when the Pope gets sick, he doesn't fly to Lourdes, but seeks the best doctors in Europe and America.

At Lourdes they say that "for those who believe no explanation is necessary; for those who don't believe no explanation is possible." But Lourdes fills a need—a time-consuming, cultural emotional experience, a religious outing.

Nature keeps people pretty busy just struggling to survive. If it weren't for the struggle against the onslaughts of nature humankind would no doubt get into more mischief than it does.

Flies and mosquitos torment us, disease germs mortify us, insects destroy our agriculture, natural disasters wreak havoc on us. Mark Twain lamented the fact that the Creator "devised a special affliction agent for each and every detail in man's structure."

Would the world be a paradise if we didn't have to struggle against diseases (thus slashing the cost of doctors and hospitals), if the production of food required only half as much work in the absence of insects, if we didn't have to expend so much time and resources on replacing the damage of earthquakes, tornadoes, hurricanes, volcanic eruptions, floods, tidal waves and droughts? Not likely.

Such a relief from the struggle to survive would only enable nations to build twice bigger military forces. And they would because the size of nations' military forces are the maximum their economies can afford.

Disease, insects and natural disasters may be blessings in disguise, keeping humankind too busy contending with the hostile forces of nature to get into idle-time mischief. A flood half the size of Noah's would keep nations so busy in reconstruction that they wouldn't have the time nor the money for warring. Peace would reign for a hundred years.

Primitives spent much of their time attempting to manipulate nature to act in their favor by ritually supplicating the gods they believed controlled the weather, the harvests, the locusts, the supply of fish and game.

Even in our modern day, there are religious people in various countries who believe that gods control the weather. In 1987, Prime Minister Rajiv Gandhi of India appeared at a nine-day ritualistic festival to implore the Hindu god of fire, Agna, to end the drought that was devastating large parts of monsoon-dependent rural India.

Four hundred loincloth-clad priests chanted around 20 fire pits in which coconut husks, clarified butter, sacrifices of grain and sweetmeats lay smoldering.

The purpose of religious festivals and pilgrimages isn't always to seek miracle cures or to supplicate deities to restrain nature's uncaring ways. Sometimes the motives seem to be more concerned with pleasure-seeking and time-filling as described in an AP report about a Taiwanese pilgrimage that stole its motifs from carnivals, rock concerts, birthday parties, the Rose Bowl parade and the Fourth of July:

> Peikang, Taiwan. Folk religion is flourishing on this island as caravans of pilgrims make their way by foot, covered wagon, motorcycle and bus to worship a sea goddess sacred to both sides of the Taiwan Straits. "I've been to the Ma Tzu festival at Peikang," say sassy red and yellow pennants carried by jaunty pilgrims, snapping from motorcycles and festooning tour buses.
>
> For two weeks every year hundreds of thousands of Buddhists stream across Taiwan to this small town on the east central coast to say "happy birthday" to the goddess Ma Tzu.
>
> Firecrackers, dragon dancers, neon-lighted floats, even self-flagellation, are part of the contemporary ritual.
>
> Taiwan itself currently is experiencing a religious revival and a surge in new temple construction. Authorities here have been trying to discourage costly religious celebrations and remind citizens they ought to put money in the bank.
>
> Despite such urging, the Ma Tzu celebrations in Peikang are said to generate nearly $300,000 annually in purchases of offerings.
>
> The experience of Ma Tzu is one of molten piety in the temple and ferocious gaiety in the streets. The air is acrid and sweet from firecrackers and incense.
>
> Mechanized floats with neon lights, steam-snorting dragons, Chinese rock 'n' roll bands and beauty queens careen among worshipers and hawkers. Dragon dancers coil through alleys.

Pilgrims take offerings of roast duck and mangoes and leave them on sagging banquet tables. Shopkeepers selling television sets and designer scarves leave sacrificial meals for Ma Tzu in their stalls.

Peasants doubled over with age and svelte women in spike-heeled shoes devoutly burn incense and throw down wooden blocks to learn their fortune.

On a corner stands a lone figure, a Christian missionary, holding a yellow banner. "Learn from the Bible," it says. "Please repent and believe in Jesus."

Restless, unfulfilled right-brainers seize every opportunity to enrich their culture with superstition and supernaturalism, to indulge their coprophagous proclivities.

In 1987 New Age religion exponents made pilgrimages to various sacred scenic spots. One such was Mount Shasta in California, where thousands of worshipers attended a two-day planetary purification rite to celebrate harmonic convergence of the planets, an alignment that purportedly hadn't happened in 23,412 years. The alignment was to produce a cleansing energy focus on humanity.

The prediction and the computations were by the courtesy of Jose Arguelles, a writer and art historian who interprets the ancient Mayan and Aztec calendars.

Entrepreneurs showed up to hawk New Age T-shirts, crystals, beads and Buddhist drums. "Nobody knows what's going to happen," said a spokesman at Harmonic Convergence Headquarters.

James Cornell of the Harvard-Smithsonian Center of Astrophysics, described the event as "a mass-media madness having to do with harmless, but totally worthless delusions. This is simply a coming-out party for all the befuddled minds — for people who believe in astrology, UFOs and the Loch Ness monster."

Well, nothing happened — except a weekend of culture-filling nonsense.

Some religious sects and cults have become obsessed with their religion. Instead of being the masters of their religion, they have become the slaves and victims of it. Instead of using religion to fill their discretionary time, they have surrendered their entire lives to religion. Religion doesn't enrich their culture, it steals their culture from them.

A good example is the ultraorthodox Hasidic Jews of which there are about 200,000 in the United States alone. They follow the Jewish Torah and the Talmud to the letter. Even other Orthodox Jews consider them extremists.

The Hasidim live in small isolated groups separated from society at large, with their own synagogues and schools and generally work for one another.

Unshaven, they sport earlocks, wear skull caps and eat only kosher. From the moment he awakes early in the morning until he goes to sleep at night, the Hasidic Jew follows strict rituals. He wears his skull cap all night and when he awakens in the morning he reaches over to wash his hands in a small bowl on the floor. He prays and then spills water over each hand three times, because the Law says that when he awakens, the evil spirit leaves from his body except from his fingers. So he has to wash it out of his fingers.

I think no more needs to be said about religions that consume lives rather than enrich them.

There are, of course, many other culture-fillers besides religion. Let us look into the area of fantasy, folklore, fables and fairy tales involving Santa Claus, the Easter bunny, Halloween witches, the animal characters in Aesop's fables and in Harris's "Uncle Remus" stories.

What can we say about Santa Claus and God, both embedded in the right brain? Are they comparable? There are many similarities. When we grow up and cease to believe in Santa Claus, we go right on celebrating Christmas with plastic Santas, candied Santas, Christmas card Santas and live department store Santas as if nothing had happened since our innocent childhood.

I suspect that many Christians who lose their belief in Christian theology go right on acting and talking as if nothing had happened. One might say that in relation to Santa Claus, all adults are atheists, but since no stigma is attached, adults don't hide in the closet.

One need not puzzle over how children can believe in the Easter bunny, a rabbit that lays eggs, paints them and hides them in the woods for children to find on Easter morning, or in Santa Claus, who lives at the North Pole and makes toys to deliver on Christmas Eve in his sleigh pulled across the sky by galloping reindeer. Even such fairy tales as these are easier to believe than many of the religious stories that are believed by adult minds, such as the story of Joshua commanding the sun and the moon to stand still, Noah packing pairs of all the creatures of Earth into his little ark, and God creating the universe in six days.

Perhaps the fairy tales we impose on our children are harmless enough, but one cannot say that about the myths of religion. The perpetration of frauds on adults is in a different category. Children do not try to kill each other over the mythical legends adults impose on them, but millions of

FALLING OF THE WALLS OF JERICHO.

adults have been slain over differences in their mythical beliefs — and the slaying is still going on today.

Even the myth of Heaven is responsible for many heinous crimes. One such crime was the 1983 suicide attacks on American and French peacekeeping forces in Beirut, Lebanon killing 225 American marines and 56 French soldiers — attacks carried out by religious fanatics expecting a glorious reception in Islamic Heaven by luscious damsels with open arms, as promised in their bible, the Koran.

Aldous Huxley said: "If we must play the theological game, let us never forget that it is a game. Religion, it seems to me, can survive only as a consciously accepted system of make believe." That is how Santa Claus has survived.

Some atheists (e.g., Sigmund Freud) see religion as a sickness. Perhaps religion should better be viewed as merely a product of the right brain along with other products such as dance, poetry, music, art. We wouldn't call them sicknesses.

But not calling religion a sickness is not saying that religion is true. And one must not be awed by the overwhelming beauty of religion, especially the Catholic religion. That overwhelming beauty is often paid for with tithes extracted by such overwhelming beauty from parishioners who can't afford tithing.

Believing has its rewards. Credulous people enjoy the wonders of a circus sideshow. They are not fools for believing everything they see. The fools are the skeptics who pay good money to get in and are too skeptical to enjoy the wonders of it. They cheat themselves.

Pragmatists are correct in observing that people fare better in any society by accepting the society's religion, mores, values; by conforming rather than by dissenting. People living in a religious community find that they fit in better, adjust more easily, prosper better, feel more secure and are happier if they accept the prevailing religion.

A person living in a society of flat-earthers would fare better if he believed that the earth is flat. If he lived in a society in which the majority were atheists, he would find social adjustment easier by becoming an atheist.

Blaise Pascal suggested that a person should voluntarily believe in God. At no cost to the person, asserted Pascal, believing gives him the possibility of Heaven if the theology proves correct. If the theology proves wrong, the person has lost nothing by believing in it.

But Pascal neglected telling us how a person can voluntarily believe in a theology. Obviously, the person previously found the theology too irrational to believe.

There are many other rewards for believing. Believers often develop a sense of mysticism that elevates their self-esteem to pleasing heights. Albert Schweitzer pontificated: "For those who through the Spirit have attained fullness of knowledge, the whole panorama to its fullest ranges lies in clear daylight; . . . for those who are wise 'with the wisdom of this world' all is still veiled in cloud."

Many Christians involve themselves with seeking solutions to human problems, an activity that gives substance and direction to their religion and their lives. It is as good a time-filler as any, and along the way they may dispense a lot of Christian charity even if they solve nothing.

Although the right brain has been the chief source of the benign religious art, music, pageantry, mysticism, rituals and drama that have filled and enriched cultural life since time immemorial, we must not forget that the right brain has also been involved in much more than artistic activity, hymn singing and praying. It has also been the chief source of religious atrocities, injustice, enslavement and war.

We need only to reflect on the Thirty Years War, the Inquisition, the autos-de-fe, the Saint Bartholomew's Day massacre, the bloody Crusades, Moslem conquests in the name of Mohammed, the Salem witch trials, today's jihad terrorists, the interminable inter-religious slaughter going on in Lebanon. All religious culture-fillers, however bloody. Some benign culture-fillers of religion help compensate for the evils of religion: activities such as sermons, Sunday schools, recreational activities, seminaries, catechism recitation, confessions, hymn singing, chanting, praying (Moslems pray five times a day), camp meetings, church socials, national conventions and bingo. All catalyzed by religious art, music and mystery.

I suspect that when the Catholic Church changed its liturgies from Latin to English it gained nothing. The appeal was never an intellectual appeal but an emotional appeal. The Church probably lost by eliminating the mystical effect of an exotic language.

Anyhow, chants, creeds and prayers soon lose their meaning by repetition. Repeating them is like dancing in a circle. You're not getting anywhere, but you're dancing just the same. You're filling time in a manner you enjoy.

The scriptures, prayers and hymns of the Ethiopian Christian Church are written in the ancient Ge'ez language which nobody speaks today. The priests all memorize the Ge'ez scriptures and teach them by rote in church schools. It is rare to find a priest who knows the meaning of the mysterious words he chants. Does it really make any difference?

There may be a definite advantage to congregants in such use of unintelligible language. Their rational left brains aren't exposed daily to irrational theologies. There may even be some benefit to preachers. Every intelligible word a preacher utters testifies to the doubt in his left brain. He overcomes these disturbing doubts by constant repetition of his creedal beliefs — more to keep himself convinced, I suspect, than to convince his congregants. The repetition drives absurd beliefs past the critical defenses of the left brain deep into the credulous right brain.

The efforts of the church to suppress sex have also occupied much of the time and attention of the churches. Without denying that some sex repression has developed as a means of controlling the birthrate and of promoting family life, most repression is historically based in religion. The unfortunate Christian obsession with suppressing sexuality in devising our moral code grew out of the necessity for early Hebrews, in order to promote their new religion, to denounce and vilify the prevailing, competing religions built around the worship of the gods and goddesses of generation—that is, around phallus worship. The Hebrews did the obvious, effective thing: they turned their people against the phallic worshipers by declaring sex to be a sin. The Judeo-Christian religions have been stuck with sex repression ever since.

Such obsession has caused a relatively weak emphasis on much more important sins such as murder, robbery, mutilation, slander, blackmail, arson. In fact, there is serious doubt that sexual behavior even belongs in the category of sin and immorality. Sexual behavior may more properly be a problem of health and economic prudence.

The normal healthful activities of sexual procreation are wholly incongruous with crimes of violence, as well as with white-collar crimes that rob the public of billions of dollars annually. Only rape and other sexual abuses should be treated as crimes. (We do not treat all commerce as criminal and immoral because commercial swindling is criminal and immoral, so why treat all sexual activity as criminal and immoral?) But our Judeo-Christian background (with its conceived-in-sin doctrine) has left us with a general conscientious disapproval of sex.

Had all the efforts of police, preachers, teachers, moralists and misled parents that have been aimed at the suppression of sex been directed rather at the suppression of real crimes, we would have a much better society today. Instead, we have created a society mired in sex-sin pathology. Only our natural skeptical and outer-directed children escape pernicious psychological damage from our sex-repressive morality.

What could be more negative thinking than belief that sex and procreation, without which there could be no life on Earth, are dirty and sinful! Our obsession with sex morality has produced a sexually sick, sadistic, perverted, frustrated, aggressive, violence-prone society.

Some primitive societies enforced (a few backward societies still do) their rules governing sexual behavior by direct and brutally crude means. They sewed or clamped the end of boys' foreskins; they incised girls' clitorises and sewed shut their labia until marriage. A boy with a hog ring clamped through his foreskin was not likely to masturbate or seduce his cousin, nor was his sister likely to get pregnant with her organ of sensual pleasure cut out and her labia sewed shut. In our own advanced society we still practice one of the vestiges of such brutal mutilations—circumcision. Ghastly culture-fillers.

It may be argued that atheism is incapable of supplying cultural needs

THE WISE MEN AND THE INFANT CHRIST.

and filling discretionary time, that only religion can perform such functions. The quality of a society is then chiefly determined by its religious customs, tenets, compassion and tolerance.

The Greek philosopher Protagoras declared: "Man is the measure of all things, determining what does and what does not exist." Near the end of his life, Protagoras wrote a book that began with these words: "As for the gods, I do not know whether they exist or not."

The Greek establishment, accepting Protagoras's dictum that man is the measure of all things, believed that the gods did exist. They measured Protagoras and found him wanting; they banished him from Athens and burned his books.

Alexander Pope over two thousand years later wrote: "Know then thyself, Presume not God to scan; the proper study of mankind is man."

This early expression of humanism did not go down well with religion, either.

Religions like to speculate concerning matters which, by their very nature, lie beyond the reach of man's comprehension. But if that is what fulfills people's needs, why should anyone wish to deprive them of it?

Religion reaches into society offering hope, dreams, excitement, spiritual awakening, mystical experience, redemption, emotional fulfillment. At a recent faith healing meeting, 6,000 people showed up at our local sports arena, including the sick, lame and blind (50 people in wheelchairs). The nature of the session was a kind of do-it-yourself arrangement in which 1,000 believers who had been through a recent training program took part in the healing procedure.

A small musical combo and six singers entertained the crowd with hymns and disco tunes with religious lyrics.

Two thousand worshipers streamed down for a mass baptism. All over the arena people were swaying side to side with their eyes closed, both arms waving in the air, alternately praising Jesus and speaking in tongues by mumbling unintelligible gibberish.

Could an atheist or humanist organization have offered the public a comparable evening?

Suppose we could perfect man according to the criteria of rationalists, atheists and humanists. We would purge man of his superstition, supernaturalism, mythology and ignorance. We would eliminate his undesirable character traits of selfishness, ruthlessness, arrogance, hatred, bigotry, cruelty, greed, vanity, conceit, pomposity, self-righteousness, infidelity and murderous proclivity.

Then there would be no more theft, robbery, embezzlement, political corruption, poverty, divorce, rape, murder, terrorism or war.

Society stripped of its dishonesty and vanity, its crime and sin; relieved of its burden of primitive ritual, baseless pageantry, religious fiction and man-made purposes; disencumbered of its political chicanery, economic barbarism, international strife, and power politics; disenslaved by its propaganda, false advertising, dollar worship and consumer addiction; disburdened of its empty status-seeking, frustrating struggle for success, and vain display of wealth; discouraged by its ethnocentric evaluations, illusions of absolutes and shattered hopes; enlightened to the relativity of morality, anthropomorphism and the doctrine of determinism; relieved of its illusion of progress and faith in man's divine fatherhood, there would be little left of human society.

There also would be no more church services, televangelism, choirs, cathedrals, synagogues, mosques, Easters, Christmases. No more Protestants, Catholics, Jehovah's Witnesses, Mormons, Christian Scientists, Moonies, Children of God. No more Billy Graham crusades, revivals, faith healings, Christmas caroling. No more need for police, lawyers, courts, army, navy, air force, marines or defense industry. And no more political wrangling in Washington.

Wouldn't life be great? It might be more like nihilism than paradise.

> Little by little we subtract
> Faith and Fallacy from Fact,
> The Illusory from the True,
> And starve upon the residue.
> —Samuel Hoffenstein

Does it really matter that man slithers from the womb, lives in a make-believe world of his own illusions, sees himself as noble, courageous, master of nature, and child of God when really he is a sniveling, cowardly, pretentious, superstitious, brutal, self-glorifying, thieving, lying little varmint?

> But, man, proud man,
> Drest in a little brief authority,
> Most ignorant of what he's
>   most assured,
> His glassy essence, like an angry ape,
>   Plays such fantastic tricks before
>   high heaven
> As makes the angels weep.
> —Shakespeare

What a dull world, indeed, stripped of the right brain! I sometimes wonder if a world strip of illusion, religion and deception would be possible. Maybe that is part of man's predicament — that a rational world would offer insufficient incentive for living.

In the last analysis, life is what humans make it. We individually choose our own purposes for living. Billy Graham's choice: "The purpose of life is not simply to feel happy or at peace. The purpose of life is to live for God and let Him use us for His glory."

But suppose there is no God. Then Graham is living a life of total illusion. What difference would it make? He is filling his time and that of his followers with religious culture, and when they die they will never find out it was all lies and illusions, for they will be as dead as the rest of us.

Religion has played another interesting role in the history (and fate) of humankind. One wonders, had humankind devoted to education and science as much time in the past as it devoted to religion, would we have developed the nuclear bomb several thousand years sooner and blown ourselves to bits long before Christ was born!

We understand little about the world in which we live. We don't know where we are, how we got here or where we're going. We don't know how the universe was created, nor when it was created nor how big it is. We can't conceive of the beginning of the universe nor can we conceive of the universe not having had a beginning. We live out our lives in the darkness of dazed incomprehension.

With science unable to give us the answers, religion steps in and fills the gap of our ignorance with nonsense, fantasies and pretentious lies. Prophets and priests rush in where scientists fear to tread.

Atheists, calling themselves truth-seekers, have deep faith in truth. However, as mentioned earlier, there are reasons to question the social value of truth. The ruling element of any society is interested only in using what is available for its purpose. Whether a culture is based on religion and mysticism or on science and rationality is not of vital concern to rulers. They will put to their use whatever is. For this reason the common people might be no better off in a society based on truth than in one based on lies and superstitions.

Of course, we have a problem when we discuss truth in relation to religion and science. Religionists claim that their truth is absolute and rock solid, while scientists concede that their truth is tentative and relative.

The problem is not solved by atheists, who consider that the truth of religion, based as it is on faith, feelings and forged documents, is of a lower order and not comparable with the truth of science based on confirmable evidence. The problem is not solved by religionists, who consider that the truth of science is of a low mental order and not comparable with the high spiritual truth derived from holy men and inerrant scriptures.

It is true that the shifting sands of science result in every new century rejecting much of the scientific truth of the previous century. The early evolutionary theory based on acquired characteristics has been replaced by a new theory based on mutations; eugenics has been renounced; Euclidian geometry has been superseded; scientific Marxism is being dismantled. Dugdale's widely accepted 19th century study of the Jukes family proving hereditary criminality is now refuted.

By extension we can only assume that many of today's scientific truths will be discarded tomorrow. People of the future will be amused by our ideas just as we are amused by the ancient Greek concept of the stars glued to transparent concentric spheres of varying distances from Earth, or by the Medieval physiological concept of the four body-regulating humors — yellow bile, black bile, blood and phlegm.

The job of a school teacher is to educate and indoctrinate a child with the current ideas and beliefs — right or wrong (future research and discovery will prove most of them wrong). Fortunately for the child, after graduation it will be competing with others indoctrinated with the same mistaken ideas.

One may wonder how teachers can teach with any enthusiasm and confidence when most of what they teach will eventually be proven wrong. Perhaps few teachers are reflective enough to realize it.

One may even conclude that scientific truth is as erroneous as religious truth, that science is just another culture-filler like religion.

The Hobson's choice seems to be between living by faith in religious falsehood or spending life searching for unattainable truth.

Nevertheless, the religious herd is not dismayed by the conflict between science and religion. Eager shoppers crowd the shopping malls to buy the latest byproducts of scientific research and discovery — synthetic clothing, quartz watches, pocket calculators, radio-controlled racing cars, electronic games, television sets, compact discs, VCRs, computers. The science-demeaning populace wallows with joy amidst science's consumer goods. Production and consumption take their place alongside religion as culture fillers.

Chapter V
THE IDEAL CHRISTIAN AND REALITY

Ideal Christians are respectable, law-abiding citizens, community-minded, church-supporting and devout. They are active in their church's social and recreational activities, in its charitable endeavors and are a moral influence on the community.

Ideal Christians make good neighbors and are tolerant of the beliefs and creeds of other sects and other religions. They support the constitutional principle of separation of church and state.

They are monogamous and faithful in their marital relations, and understand the need for laws and moral rules. They discipline themselves, however frustrating such self-restraint may be. They are good parents — non-abusive, non-authoritarian, giving their children the freedom to grow.

They are trustworthy in their business dealings, their word being as good as their bond.

Ideal Christians live soberly, are compassionate toward the unfortunate, stand up for justice and practice the principles of the Sermon on the Mount as closely as is practicable.

Their guiding role model is Jesus Christ of the Bible liberally modified by their own lights. They are saddened by the behavior of such televangelists as Jim Bakker and Jimmie Swaggart for the shame they have brought on Christianity.

Ideal Christians accept the Bible as the inspired word of God and excuse the injustices and atrocities of ancient Jewish and Christian leaders detailed in the Bible as inevitable reflections of the primitive stage of moral development in biblical times. They winnow the good from the bad of the Bible.

Ideal Christians regret the barbarous atrocities committed during later periods of Christian development—the Inquisition, the Crusades, the savage intolerance of early American Christians, etc. They see the wrongs as object lessons to help guide contemporary Christianity along better paths.

Ideal Christians are people who even atheists would welcome as next door neighbors.

These ideal Christians—law-abiding, well-groomed, clean-shaven, neatly-dressed, gainfully-employed, family-oriented establishmentarians are, of course, a far cry from Jesus of Nazareth—an unshaven, dissident, itinerant, revolution-preaching vagabond. But history shows that the creators of revolutionary change and reform are a different cut from their followers. Their followers are faced with carrying on the movement, and the disparity between them and their founder is no ill-reflection on the followers. Rooting a new religion into society requires quite different kinds of talents from those of the creators.

(The contrast, nevertheless, certainly is striking—Christ, a long-haired hippy-type in sandals riding astride a donkey compared with today's evangelists and popes riding in their private jet planes, Cadillacs and limousines.)

The kind of persons atheists would not want next door are the true believers—the fundamentalists who believe the Bible to be inerrant, take its teachings literally and devote their lives to zealously carrying out the Bible's commands.

Although the Bible is the basis for Christianity, few Christians seem to really believe what the Bible says. But the fundamentalists take the logical position that if the Bible is the word of God, you have to believe it and live by it. Based on such belief, logic dictates that they devote themselves totally to gaining the incomparable reward of Heaven for such devotion.

What we call fanaticism, true believers see as the only rational response they can have to Christianity. Although they are popularly seen as a little crazy, Christian zealots are the ones, in the light of Christian theology, it can be argued, who are behaving rationally, logically, sanely.

Believing in eternal Heaven promised by the Bible, the true believer sees his life on Earth as but a passing moment of trial and tribulation. All one can do in this brief span is to prepare as well as possible for the great life to come. Death is not the end of life, but the true beginning. Beyond it lies the great hereafter unspoiled by suffering and remorse, unbounded in its divine pleasures and heavenly bliss. Common sense tells the true believer that he should show more concern for the billion dollars' worth of life in the hereafter than for the penny's worth on Earth.

Given that the Bible is true, the fanatical behavior of many fundamentalists is easily understood. Deuteronomy XXVIII tells the fundamentalist what will happen to him should he not hearkeneth to the Lord and keep His commandments and laws. Deuteronomy warns him that he shall be cursed unremittingly; he shall be cursed coming and going; the pestilence shall cleave to him; the Lord shall smite him in the knees and in the legs; the Lord shall smite him with hemorrhoids, scabs and the itch; the Lord shall smite him with madness, blindness and heart disease; he shalt betroth a wife and another man shall lie with her; all the grain of his fields the locusts shall consume; worms shall eat all the grapes of his vineyard; his enemies shall eat the fruit of his cattle and his land; his enemies will besiege him and he shall in his desperation eat the flesh of his children; the Lord shall pursue him and overtake him with these curses until he perishes; his carcass shall then be meat unto the fowls of the air and the beasts of Earth.

Christian theology is such that if anyone doesn't get fanatic about it, he or she just isn't a sincere believer.

But the consensus seems to be that true believer—the fanatic fundamentalists and the zealous cultists—are not ideal Christians. The fanatic's left brain fails to reject superstitious religion, but responds to its theology in a totally rational manner. The ideal Christian also accepts religious superstition but his response to it is more pragmatic than rational. The response of the ideal Christian is socially acceptable; the response of the zealot is socially insufferable.

The fundamentalist also sees the promise of eternal life in exchange for a little tithing and good works on Earth as an irresistible bargain.

In addition, fundamentalists see the Bible as an easy, ready and cheap access to knowledge. Nobody wants to think of himself as ignorant. How much easier it is to become knowledgeable by tuning in your radio or television a few hours a day to hear electronic preachers explain the Bible, or even to leisurely read the Bible yourself than to grind away for six or eight years in grueling study at a university. After all, our own former President Reagan said of the Bible: "Inside its pages are all the answers to all the problems man has ever known."

But following the Bible literally often has unfortunate side effects. Sometimes its true believers end up in jail, the loony bin or even the morgue.

There seems to be a steady flow in the news of disasters caused by religious people trying to follow the Bible too literally or misreading it.

A Christian Science couple in California were cleared of a charge of involuntary manslaughter but convicted of child endangerment for relying on Christian Science faith healers instead of medical treatment for their infant daughter dying from meningitis.

In Yakima, Washington four members of a Christian religious cult were charged with beating to death a 3-year-old boy in exorcist rites because they believed he was possessed by the devil. They cited biblical guidance for their act.

In 1989 a former Seventh-day Adventist preacher and his wife and their two children in Carverton, Pennsylvania went 42 days without food after the father lost his truck-driving job. They had $3,775 in the bank but wouldn't draw it out to buy food because the father said it was a tithe belonging to God. He said God would take care of them.

Their 14-year-old son died of starvation. The couple and their 12-year-old daughter were sent to the hospital.

Michael Ryan, the leader of a Christian cult in Nebraska and his 16-year-old son in 1986 were convicted of the torture slaying of a cult member. They whipped him, shot him in the fingers, sexually abused him and skinned him alive. The elder Ryan, who called himself Yahweh, also faces trial for the torture murder of a five-year-old cult member. The child was forced to wear the devil's number 666 and then tortured, sexually abused and murdered.

Michael Ryan was a true believer in Armageddon, stockpiling weapons for the final fight between the forces of good and evil.

Christians have no monopoly on fanaticism. In Nabativeh, Lebanon the Shiite Moslems celebrate the day of the slaying of the Shiite martyr, Imam Hossein 14 centuries ago by beating their heads and chests, and bloodying themselves with swords amid shrieks of joy and pain. Ambulances rush the bleeding zealots to hospitals after they render themselves unconscious. (Only the right brain could believe that such self-flagellation pleases a merciful God or proves his existence.)

No doubt fanatics are true believers, but one doubts that even they ever consider the full extent of the implications of religious belief. Why should Christians fear nuclear annihilation? If you are a good Christian nuclear Armageddon just means you will get to Heaven a little sooner. (Even if you are a Buddhist, it just means that you will get to your next reincarnation a little sooner.) So what's all the fretting about? Do most people think they're going to Hell?

It is certainly significant that while Christian Americans accept the assurance of Psalm XXIII of the Bible that the Lord is their shepherd and that "though I walk through the valley of the shadow of death, I will fear no evil for thou art with me," insurance is the biggest business in America.

Why did the Christians of the Middle Ages and Reformation burn heretics at the stake, knowing according to their own theology that the heretics were going to suffer eternal burning after death anyhow? Obviously, the church authorities didn't really believe what they preached, so they made damn sure the heretics got burned.

If zealots and fanatics themselves don't really believe in the Bible and Christian theology, one should not expect to find much sincerity among average nominal Christians.

Run-of-the-mill Christians show little evidence in their behavior of any consciousness of Christian theology. Even church-goers, who purportedly believe that life on Earth is but a few miserable seconds compared with eternal life after death, devote only an hour or so a weak serving God — presumably the means of earning their passport to Heaven — while devoting the bulk of their time seeking the trivial pleasures and transitory possessions of Earth.

How do we explain the vast differences between what people profess to believe and what their actions indicate they believe? How can a whole nation profess to believe one thing while acting as if it believed something else? The answer is the amazing bicameral brain. No computer is likely to ever be programmed to simulate it.

I think many, if not most, Christians are highly dubious about the Bible while clinging to an unfaltering belief in Jesus Christ. But Christianity is founded on the Bible, and since the only evidence for Christ is in the Bible, one wonders how it is possible to doubt the Bible without doubting Christ.

Christianity's incredible theology along with its unreasonable demands for behavior assure its generally half-hearted acceptance and feeble compliance. The desire for respectability and the urge to conform produce a society of nominal Christians. We are primarily a nation of hypocrites and our trumpeted belief in the Bible is a dishonest pretension.

Personal dishonesty seems to be a necessary basis for religion. That is understandable. Children are indoctrinated with a code of behavior that is instinctually impossible to follow. So they regularly violate the code and to avoid punishment cover up the violations by lying. For them, lying becomes part of their religion.

Nowhere is Vance Packard's description of middle-class Americans as pretentious, hypocritical and dishonest better illustrated than in their wholehearted support of institutional religion.

Among Christian liberals are physicists who make no allowance for the effects of supernatural forces in their calculations; astronomers who don't search stellar space for Heaven; anatomists who identify no organ as housing the soul. (Yet these people call themselves Christians.)

Observing that humankind are so incorrigibly dishonest and hypocritical, one wonders if an honest society is even feasible. In any case, dishonesty and hypocrisy survive well under the rubric of pragmatism.

Most people are practical, adjustable, flexible — pragmatic. If honesty is demanded, they will be honest; if corruption is the prevailing mode they will be corrupt.

You can never change things to suit you, so you might as well adjust to things as they are. Conformity is the easiest road. Adopt the prevailing religion, morality, values — whether laudable or lamentable.

It is true, most people take their religion triflingly. It makes no real difference in their lives. They take religious obligations lightly — go to church or not, read the Bible or not, pray or not according to their whim or fancy. They accept religion as far as it doesn't interfere with their livelihood or their love and sex lives.

The average person in fulfilling his need to believe, in yielding to the urge of his herd instinct and in reaping the many advantages religion offers is following the path of the least resistance and greatest reward.

After all, this is the way recommended by modern psychology. Psychiatrists help people adjust to the imperfect real world, while preachers want people to adjust to a world reflecting the kingdom of God.

Despite their professed religious belief, most Christians seek salvation through themselves — through self-improvement, education, vocational training.

Aldous Huxley believed that Christianity has been transformed "from a religion into a system for the justification of wealth and the preachment of industrious respectability . . . one that exalts the Pharisees above every other human type."

The Church of Religious Science is a good example of a modern Pharisee church. The essential teaching is that God wants us to be healthy and wealthy. Money is good; the more you can make, the better. The popularity of such a theology to guilt-ridden affluent congregations is understandable.

But the Church's critics maintain that the Religious Science ministers use the Bible and Jesus' name just to lend credibility and respectability to their church. One acerbic critic had no doubt that Religious Science is a great motivator, but wondered if it was religion.

But such churches can find support in the Gospel parable in Matthew of the lord who gave talents (money) to his three servants. The first servant to whom the lord gave talents doubled his talents by loaning them at interest. The second servant likewise invested them and doubled them. The lord said to those two servants: "Well done, thou good and faithful servant: thou hast been faithful over a few things. I will make thee ruler over many things."

But the third servant had buried his money. The lord told him he should have loaned his money at usury. "Take therefore the money from him and give it unto [the others]," said the lord. "And cast ye the unprofitable servant into outer darkness: there shall be weeping and gnashing of teeth."

The most pragmatic people are the orientals who, unsure which religion among those the missionaries are pushing is the true one, join them all; nor do they give up their native religions.

The ancient Greeks took a somewhat similar pragmatic view in building altars inscribed to "Unknown God." These "to whom it may concern" altars were erected during plagues, since the Athenians did not know what god was offended and needed propitiation.

Most run-of-the-mill Christians have a very hazy concept of their theology. Few have ever read the Bible, the foundation of Christianity, so they really don't know what it is they believe in. A Gallup Poll showed that 38 percent of Americans believe the Bible to be the actual word of God. How many in that 38 percent have ever read the Bible. Two percent? Three percent?

For the general run of nominal Christians, the Christian terminology of faith, grace, unction, justification, propitiation, anointment, sanctification, immanence, atonement and salvation has an emotional impact on them but little intellectual meaning. They believe chiefly because they were taught to believe when children, and doubting either never occurred to them or was suppressed.

Liberals who have actually read the Bible rationalize their adherence to Christianity by saying that the Bible doesn't really mean what it says. In calling themselves Christians, they are appropriating a hallowed name and applying it to a made-up religion of their own.

Most Christians enjoy the forms of Christianity if not its substance. They like the art, music and mysticism of the church. They like the rituals, the pageantry, the socialization, the brotherliness; they like the feeling good about themselves that church membership imparts.

Nevertheless, most Christians feel the need to defend their faith, despite their fuzzy notion of what it is they are defending. Over the years their religion has become bonded to their egos. They may be willing to fight to the death to defend their beliefs while hardly knowing what they are.

Immature and defenseless children are early indoctrinated with religious ideas by their parents, grandparents, Sunday school teachers, etc. By adulthood they become convinced that they possess the truth, and spend the rest of their lives elaborating and defending their religion.

So thoroughly do their beliefs become bound to their egos that to reject their beliefs would be to reject all their past behavior based on those beliefs, to cancel out half their childhood. And such rejection would alienate them from their family and friends and cost them their niche in the social, political and vocational world.

Such perils bear constantly on religionists' unconscious minds, ever hardening the shell around their cluster of beliefs. Apostasy becomes unthinkable.

Clergymen are often caught in a particularly vicious trap. They start out attending a seminary whose purpose is to thoroughly indoctrinate the novitiates with its doctrines and creeds. Finally, promises of faith, obedience and service are required for ordination. Such commitments make it difficult for clergymen to abandon their calling, for they have already invested so much in it.

The more years they preach, the deeper they become a prisoner of their theology. When some new clergymen begin their ministry they soon find themselves saying things in public they don't believe. Being public figures, clergymen are trapped by a world that holds them to their creed.

Religion as a product of the right brain thrives on the esthetic taste and mysticism that predominate in the right brain. The Catholic Church has long perceived this and emphasizes emotion as against reason, art and ceremony as against discussion and debate. Too often Protestant churches consent to reason, only to see religious beliefs fade away.

Religion possesses many of the characteristics of an addiction. Believers get an emotional lift or high from their religion. They are driven by their addiction to go to church every Sunday for their fix, in some cases even after they have ceased to believe in its theology. But if one sees religion as a good thing, addiction to it cannot be considered evil.

Religious addicts are similar to drug addicts in that they want to pull others into their addiction—either because there is comfort in numbers or because of a benevolent desire to share their euphoria with others.

Religion is about the only addiction that is popularly encouraged. If society encouraged and pressured everybody to drink alcohol or shoot heroin, we'd surely all be alcoholics or heroin addicts.

A hundred years ago Karl Marx observed that religion is the opiate of the people. Thousands of seedy evangelists, greedy electronic preachers and others take advantage of this characteristic of religion by addicting the vulnerable in order to exploit their piety, faith, hope and trust. The awesome power addictive religion places in the hands of these ofttimes shady characters is glaringly apparent all around us.

Non-professional Christians are also promoters and proselytizers of religion, following Christ's instruction to "Go ye therefore, and teach all nations, baptising them in the name of the Father, and the Son, and the Holy Ghost." But there are also more subtle reasons for proselytizing. Many religionists live in a state of constant doubt about their beliefs. Surely, their left brains find it difficult to accept faith as a valid source of knowledge and truth. So they seek new recruits to allay their disturbing doubts and reinforce their convictions.

Religious faith itself is founded on doubt, it implies doubt. If something is obviously and unquestionably true, such as rain coming from the clouds, it requires no faith to believe it. Faith is accepting belief without proof. As Archie Bunker put it, if a bit hyperbolically: "Faith is believing something that nobody in his right mind would believe."

The common behavior of believers in proclaiming their beliefs repetitiously and with emotional intensity is in itself evidence of doubt. They wish to overwhelm their doubts with decibels and iteration.

So we have to conclude that religionists feel less secure in their certainties than they would have us believe. Surely, if they enjoyed steadfast certainty of their religious convictions, they would feel little concern for what anybody else believed. If they really believed with unquavering conviction in God and the Bible and Heaven, they would be smugly indifferent, knowing that they themselves were on the right path.

But religionists live in a state of continuous internal struggle to quell their misgivings. They resent any questioning of their beliefs that aggravate their internal torment.

The fact that atheism and apostasy can have no possible bearing on the truth of their religious beliefs doesn't seem to alleviate their dismay. One suspects that many religionists live in fear of the discovery of the clay feet of their idols. They live the precarious lives of embezzlers, forever fearful that their fraud will be exposed.

If they did not have disturbing doubts about their theology, they would not fight so unremittingly the attempts to examine it.

Through their influence, critical discussions of religion are taboo in the daily press, in schools and colleges, over radio and television, in drawing rooms and in family circles.

If people really believed that God is the controlling force of their lives, if people really believed that they live and die by the grace of God, people's attentions would not be almost totally absorbed by sports, politics, employment, entertainment, celebrity-worship, production and consumption.

One does not need to puzzle long over why religionists hate atheists so venomously. Atheists stir up the suppressed doubts of believers to the point of producing anguish. This is the anguish that incited believers to burn heretics and atheists at the stake in olden times to remove the source of the unsettling, disturbing doubts that plagued the believers.

But because of their various sects, religionists also disturb one another by their conflicting doctrines.

The mere existence of atheists constitutes a statement to believers that believers have wasted their lives worshiping a God that doesn't exist, that their beliefs — the very foundation of their personhoods — are false and ridiculous, that believers are dupes and fools.

Atheists by contrast enjoy a kind of ultimate metaphysical security. There are no props to be knocked out from under them. And they live in no fear that God will be discovered and refute them and send them to Hell. (There are many other things, however, that do disturb atheists as we shall see in the next chapter.)

Religionists, whose faith is continually assaulted and shaken, seek to reinforce their faith by proselytizing — driven by the feeling, however irrational, that the more people who accept their belief, the truer it will be, and less the disturbing doubts.

Truth by majority vote! Well, that was the method used by the Council of Nicaea in 325.

It logically follows that the small sects, which feel the most alone and least supported in their views, work the hardest for new converts to dispel their nagging doubts.

So the public is pursued on the street, in the parks and to the privacy of their homes by unhappy little people seeking supporters to allay their doubts; little solicitors, as George Orwell speaks less charitably of them, for "all the smelly little orthodoxies which are now contending for our souls."

Other than removing the source of disturbing doubts, atheists wonder why religionists should care that atheists don't accept God. The religionists know that they themselves are going to Heaven and the atheists to Hell. They may say that it is due to Christian love. The slaying of hundreds of thousands of atheists and heretics by Christians down through history were not acts of love. The clergy was only following God's instructions on dealing with atheists and heretics in Deuteronomy XIII: "Thou shalt surely kill him;

. . . And thou shalt stone him with stones, that he die; because he hath sought to thrust thee away from the Lord thy God."

Atheists suspect, anyway, that Christian love is more self-love. Christians want to be among the precious souls to enjoy eternal life even if they have to stoop to converting slimy atheists to earn their Brownie points.

Among the less ideal Christians, most people would agree, are the televangelists recently exposed for their sexual immorality, obscene indulgence in high living, hypocrisy to the Nth degree and cynical exploitation of people's faith and trust to amass fabulous personal fortunes.

It is little wonder that these generally ignorant, seedy, morally shoddy types achieve amazing success. They are treated as sacrosanct by a government fearful of offending religion. Not held financially accountable as are other businessmen, and enjoying religious exemptions from various taxes and from numerous government regulations, they easily amass millions of dollars from a gullible public.

Although atheists see most televangelists, tent revivalists and faith healers as unscrupulous, greedy buffoons, one has to admit that they follow the entrepreneurial prescription for success: Find a need and fill it.

They do fill the need for reassurance of faith, emotional gratification, participation in religious drama and restoration of hope. While atheists search in vain for needs they can fill.

Preachers offer their congregants and couch potatoes (who don't even have to get up from their TV chairs) a pretty good deal—everlasting life for a 10 percent, tax-deductible tithe from their earnings in this short earthly life. That's an infinitely better deal than even IRA accounts. However, as the saying goes: If it sounds too good to be true, it probably isn't true. But people take the bait anyhow because people are always looking for something for nothing. The irony is that after the victims of the swindle die, they are much too dead to ever find out they've been had. Preachers operate a pretty safe con game.

Religion can promise people Heaven. All that atheists can promise is a life on Earth of low compatibility with superstitious neighbors.

Underneath America's great respect for religion lies a festering doubt and a secret contempt for preachers. To a certain degree the term "preacher" has become one of contempt. There are myriad ribald jokes about preachers, jokes inspired by hostility, pointing out the weakness of the flesh of preachers and their hypocrisy. Perhaps some of the besmirching of preachers is the result of the human urge to pull anybody down who assumes a moral superior stance to his neighbors.

But most of the followers of preachers worship them. Surely, some of the millions of dollars showered on evangelists, cult leaders et al. are expressions of love — not all of their offerings are bribes for God's providence.

The followers of the religious cults — Hare Krishna, Divine Light Mission, Unification church, Bhagwan Shree Rajneesh, Children of God — adore their leaders. Rennie Davis, a former sixties activist, said of Guru Maharaj Ji: "I would cross the planet on my hands and knees to touch his toes." Disciples dedicate their lives to cult leaders, many spending their full working day begging in the streets for money to purchase their guru another Cadillac or Mercedes.

Ideal Christians live fulfilling and rewarding lives and feel that even if there is no such thing as Heaven they will be out nothing for living a good life. A good life has its own rewards.

The less than ideal Christians aren't too happy about their lives. They see themselves as sacrificing many of the pleasures of life and suffering through this vale of tears for a questionable heavenly reward. They would liken the absence of a heavenly reward to working all summer on the promise of a handsome pay check at the end, but instead being fired at the end of the summer and paid nothing.

Religion thrives on its appeal to human selfishness. Even Jesus made his pitch to human selfishness. In His Sermon on the Mount, Jesus said: "But love your enemies, and do good, and lend, expecting nothing in return, and *your reward will be great* . . ." (Italics mine.)

Selfishness is an evolutionary selection. It is the first law of nature. The question of selfishness re Christianity has much to do with the depth of one's belief. Logically, people who believe sincerely that they will be rewarded manyfold in an afterlife for serving God, spreading the Word, proselytizing, obeying the Bible and doing good works during their life on Earth are likely to do so, while people who have considerable doubts about Christian theology are not as likely to make sacrifices for questionable rewards.

When I look about me in this nominally Christian society I can only conclude that belief in heavenly rewards is not overwhelming; even so, one must conclude that such belief that does exist should have a good effect on society. The trouble with such a conclusion, though, is that it would logically lead to the adverse conclusion that rationalists, atheists, humanists et al., who don't believe in an afterworld, should have an evil effect on society. But statistics on crime and on prison populations indicate the very opposite: that precentagewise, nonbelievers have a better record for good behavior than believers in all measurable ways.

NOAH BUILDING THE ARK.

When atheists see the hordes of churchgoers pouring out of the churches on Sunday they think to themselves, "Do these greedy little simpletons really believe they are going to be rewarded with everlasting life for sitting through a boring sermon every Sunday and dropping a few inflated dollars into the collection tray!"

To be realistic, though, probably only a small percentage of them are so motivated. There are a dozen other motives — less pejorative — for attending church.

Probably the foregoing assessment applies more accurately to the Jehovah's Witness proselytizers who, like the U.S. mailmen are stayed by "neither snow nor rain nor heat nor gloom of night . . ."

At one time I somewhat admired the Jehovah's Witnesses who rapped on my door. I thought, now here are true believers willing to give up their whole weekend to work for the Lord. Where will you find a bunch of orthodox church people willing to do that?

These Witnesses tramp from house to house distributing their Watchtowers and their pitch for Jesus. They get doors slammed in their faces, are sworn at and vilified and sometimes even assaulted — usually by other followers of Christ.

So I was inclined to admire them and to feel some sympathy for the mistreatment they suffered. Until one day I took the time to read one of their Watchtowers. I learned that they believe that at the time of Armageddon 144,000 select Jehovah's Witnesses will be immediately transported to Heaven. The remaining Witnesses will all survive Armageddon and live eternally and blissfully on Earth. The rest of us will be horribly burned to death in the fiery struggle of Armageddon between the forces of Jehovah and the forces of Satan.

Then I realized that these courageous Witnesses aren't working for the Lord, aren't suffering blistered feet, personal abuse and battery to save the souls of others. They are working for themselves. They are selfish egoists who want their precious little souls to be among the saved while the rest of us end up in a horrible holocaust.

They want to be among the 144,000 selected to be saved and flown to Heaven. You get selected by tramping from house to house passing out Watchtowers. A wholly left-brain response to evidence the left brain should have rejected at the start.

Foreign missionaries are the quintessential proselytizers. One wonders how much of their zeal comes from the desire to spread the word of God and how much from the competitive desire to spread their particular sect's interpretation of that word.

Aside from their generously financed function of teaching natives to wear clothes — particularly work clothes — and breaking them of the nasty habit of cannibalism, the missionaries in their fierce competition with one another have trampled and laid waste most of the indigenous religions of the regions their military supporters open to them. Of course, missionaries would argue that they are replacing cultist savagery with Christian love. Be that as it may.

Ideal Christians should, of course, follow the biblical command to spread the word. A friend of mine offered her explanation of religious proselytizing, a kinder and gentler explanation than mine, involving motives suitable for ideal Christians. She said that if you genuinely believe that a neighbor's soul is doomed to perdition because of atheism, homosexuality, support of abortion or belief in evolution, and you think his soul will go to Hell if you don't do something, you would be an unfeeling bastard not to try to save him.

At any rate, my hat is off to American missionaries. I can understand their zeal in spreading the only true religion of the thousands of religions of Earth. How fortunate that our nation is blessed with the world's only true religion and that we also have the material wealth and military power to share it with Earth's benighted and beggarly.

Lucky is the native who by chance is reached first by a missionary of the one and only true religion. Come to think of it, though, his or her fate is no more of a crapshoot than that of the average sectarian — who had no choice of parents.

But the number one proselytizing target of Christian fundamentalists are the Jews. Recently (1989), 15 evangelical scholars issued a declaration that was later endorsed by the World Evangelical Fellowship, a declaration to reaffirm the historic Christian position that the gospel is preached to the Jew first. The declaration asserts that Jews can be saved only by accepting Christ, and describes "evangelizing of Jewish people as a priority." A spokesman for the World Evangelical Fellowship explained: "We had no alternative other than to affirm Jesus Christ as the promised messiah and acceptance of him as the only basis for salvation." One may find it curious that almost everybody accepts the divinity of the Jewish Jesus but the Jews.

One can easily imagine how grateful the Jews must feel toward the fundamentalists for their compassionate concern for Jewish souls — that only the fundamentalists can save from perdition.

Since most religionists do not select their religions, but are imbued and indoctrinated with the religion of their parents, they can only hope that the religion of their parents is the true one. It would seem that more important than having parents with the right genes is having parents with the right religion.

In addition to the many different world religions, Christianity is itself highly fragmented. One reason for so many Christian sects is that the Bible on which they are based is such an ambiguous, theologically complex, cryptic, contradictory book that a thousand interpretations can be made of it. As a result, as Shakespeare wrote, even "the devil can cite Scripture for his purpose."

Christians have always picked out of the Bible their justifications for slavery, degradation of women, crusades of conquest, Jewish pogroms, holy wars, and the persecution and murder of heretics, scientists and witches.

Each world religion — Jewish, Christian, Islamic, Hindu, Buddhist, Shinto — looks down on all the others as false, erroneous, mistaken. Even among Christians, each of their many sects believes that its interpretation of the Bible is correct and the others are wrong.

The sectarian looks down his nose at all the other sectarians and muses: "Those foolish, misled people think they have the truth. We know they don't have the truth because we have it."

And, of course, the atheist looks down upon all of them. He knows none of them has the truth because he has it.

1. ATHOR.   2. PTAH.   3. ISIS.   4. OSIRIS.   5. NEITH.   6. BUBASTIS.   7. APIS (THE BULL).   8. HORUS (THE HAWK). 9. IBIS (THE CRANE).   10. SHAU (THE CAT).   11. SCARABÆUS (BEETLE).

The idols of Egypt

Chapter VI
THE IDEAL ATHEIST AND REALITY

The problem with describing the ideal atheist stems from the popular belief that anyone who doesn't believe in God is an awful person. This notion is harbored even by those whose religion is thin as paper and totally irrelevant to their behavior. So the task becomes one of describing the ideal awful person — a kind of oxymoron. But I will try.

Ideal atheists are people of high principles and unassailable integrity. They cannot abide deception, dishonesty, injustice or superstition. They refuse to compromise their principles by overlooking the ignorance, injustice, lies and moral depravity they see fostered by religion, even if they would be more comfortable and popular by doing so.

They do not excuse the atrocities religion has left in its historic wake. They are incensed by hypocrites who use religion for self-aggrandizement and enrichment.

Placing their faith in reason, logic and the scientific route to knowledge and truth, atheists deplore the propagation of superstitions and supernaturalism — especially when such propagation is aimed at the minds of children, inflicting them with what atheists see as mental impairment while children are still vulnerable and defenseless.

Ideal atheists may be militant or passive according to their various temperaments. But the outspoken atheists are few and far between for the simple reason that, despite our vaunted freedom of religion, atheists in America are probably as much stigmatized as are religionists in atheistic communist countries. Since Thomas Paine wrote *The Age of Reason*, three publishers have been imprisoned for publishing it. One publisher was sentenced to a year in prison, another to 18 months plus standing in the pillory, and another to three years plus a heavy fine.

DESTRUCTION OF SODOM.

The road of the atheist in America is such a rough and lonely one that most atheists are less than ideal. They compromise their principles, adjust to a religious society, remain in the closet or follow a line of employment in which their atheism would not handicap them.

Many atheists refrain from direct attacks on religion and on the church. They find it much safer to attack superstitions such as astrology, parapsychology, faith healing and folk superstitions (Abominable Snowman, Big Foot, Loch Ness monster, flying saucers, crystal power, etc.) than to attack the established religions—even though they don't recognize a hair's difference between the two categories. For example, 186 noted scientists including 18 Nobel Prize winners endorsed a statement challenging "the pretentious claims of astrological charlatans."

The statement further lamented, "We are especially disturbed by the continued uncritical dissemination of astrological charts, forecasts and horoscopes by the media and by otherwise reputable newspapers, magazines and book publishers."

The American Humanist Association sponsors an ongoing committee called the "Committee for the Scientific Investigation of Claims of the Paranormal" dedicated to exposing the chicanery of mystics and charlatans who exploit the stupidity, ignorance and gullibility of the public. The CSICOP has 300 members, including such people as astronomer Carl Sagan, psychologist professor B. F. Skinner of Harvard University and paleontologist Stephen Jay Gould.

Worldwide, the CSICOP and other groups and individuals dangle several hundred thousand dollars for anyone who can perform a paranormal claim under scientific conditions. Not a penny has had to be paid out yet. In simple terms, the debunkers demand the same standards of proof from psychics as required for scientific discovery. They have investigated faith healers, poltergeists, telepaths, astrologers, mystics, UFOs, Bigfoot and other alleged supernatural happenings.

"We're disturbed about the growth of irrationality and pseudoscience. Paranormal is the new folk religion," lamented humanist leader Paul Kurtz.

The CSKOP sent letters to 1800 newspapers asking them to print disclaimers with astrology columns. Only five agreed to.

These scientists, predominantly atheists, are unafraid to expose and castigate a motley bunch of second-rate charlatans. Would they criticize Billy Graham or Pope John II in a similar fashion? They wouldn't dare. And who could blame them for not wanting to destroy themselves! The atheist cause is served better by scientists, writers and university professors using their influential positions prudently than by disemployed persons, regardless of their unassailable intellectual integrity.

Many atheists harbor deep resentment against religion as a result of the trauma caused by their disillusionment with the religion they were inculcated with in childhood. They feel they were deceived, imposed upon, lied to. They are the earnest type who respected the authority of elders. The deeper they were committed to religion, the more militant is their atheism once they are disillusioned.

It is to be noted that the children of such earnest atheists, having not suffered from the trauma of disillusionment, generally take a more benign view of religion. In addition, we have the nominal believers, whose religious convictions were shallow and half-hearted to begin with. Should they cease entirely to believe, they experience little traumatic effect. They seldom become militant atheists. Add to these the vast bulk of the population that believe in one hemisphere and disbelieve in the other with little discomfort.

People are probably believers or nonbelievers according to their hemispheric preference, a preference guided by their temperaments as much as by any innate superiority in either hemisphere (the left brain being the hemisphere of logic and reason while the right brain is the hemisphere of fantasy and esthetic taste).

An adherence to atheism is not necessarily an indication of superior intelligence; often it merely indicates that a person is by nature a nonconforming rebel or bohemian type predisposed by temperament to reject anything that is popular.

Conversely, an adherence to religion is no indication by itself of an inferior intelligence. Surely, no one would describe Reinhold Niebuhr as a stupid person. He is a crippled intellectual giant, who, atheists would say, had been crippled by inerasable early religious indoctrination.

Such religious indoctrination may be seen as right-brain pollution which, nevertheless, does not necessarily impair the reasoning power of the left brain — but people with right-brain preference eschew their left brain.

Religious polemicists often argue that atheists are as closed-minded as religionists. If they mean (which they don't) that atheists are closed to the promptings of their mystical superstitious right hemisphere, atheists would readily agree.

The ideal, science-respecting, left-brained atheist has an open mind to religion, as he has to everything else. Open-mindedness is the very heart of science.

Closet atheists are nonbelievers who hide their atheism in order to avoid the social stigma, political handicaps or economic penalties which the religious majority commonly inflicts on atheists. They may be compared with closet homosexuals, who likewise live double lives to avoid popular abuse.

In addition, atheism has been associated in the public mind with communism, another reason for atheists to conceal their belief.

The closetry of atheism, of course, increases the loneliness of atheists, each feeling he or she is the only one in the neighborhood.

The inclination of atheists to conceal their atheism (including concealment from pollsters) casts considerable doubt on religious statistics. One may reasonably guess that the number of atheists in this country far exceeds survey indications.

I would not find it difficult to believe that Johnny Carson, Phil Donahue and William Buckley Jr. are atheists. In fact, I find it harder to believe that anyone of their intellectual caliber isn't. How can we know? What would happen to their careers if they confessed being atheists? Why should anyone suppose they are suicidal?

I might find it a little harder to believe that Pope John Paul II is an atheist. But, again, would he dare admit it if he were?

Many closet atheists avoid acrimony and harassment by joining less-declaimed groups such as general semanticists, rationalists, truth-seekers, freethinkers, separationists and humanists. All are predominately atheistic but they avoid the awful A word. Atheists find compatibility in such groups while avoiding harassment and ostracism for their anti-religious views. Even most Unitarian-Universalist churches are friendly havens for timid infidels.

Among various kinds of atheists are the militant atheists. They do not shy away from the prejudicial term, but consider "atheist" a term denoting superior intelligence.

They are outspoken against religion, zealous proselytizers for atheism and aggressive in the use of the courts to stop religious practices that violate the First Amendment to the Constitution — prayer in public schools, crosses and creches on public property, subsidization of religious schools, teaching Creationism in public schools, etc.

Militant atheists see themselves as the vanguard against the creeping tendency of religion to chip away at the First Amendment. They see peril to our democracy from the religious right that would turn our country into a theocracy.

But there is reason to wonder if such militancy doesn't do more harm than good by uniting the religionists and provoking them to work ever harder to achieve their aims. Has the effect of atheist attacks on religion been to weaken religion by chipping away at it, or to strengthen religion by the solidifying effects of such attacks? Have atheists unwittingly furnished religionists with a handy devil image to fan congregational fervor?

Atheists are so numerically and politically weak that they are bound to lose ultimately in direct confrontation with religionists. The fact is atheism has little to offer compared with what religion has to offer — in this world as well as in the next.

I suspect that most effective proselytizing by atheists has been of an unintentional nature, an undesigned boring from within. Atheists, active in liberal, open-minded organizations, inevitably chip away at their associates' religious views. Any slipping is almost certain to be from religion to atheism.

One can only discover that the feet of the idols are not flesh, but clay. Never the reverse.

So, when passive atheists and humanists work with Christian liberals the most likely outcome is the weakening of the faith of the liberals. Militant atheists tend to strengthen and solidify Christian opposition, while passive atheists and humanists tend to crumble it.

Although I have to admire honest, courageous, militant atheists, I sometimes feel more pity for them than admiration—the pity I feel for anyone who spends his lifetime in a losing battle. Most atheists do waste their lives battling against the unconquerable monster of religion—a monster impervious to the spears of reason, impenetrable by the bullets of logic, and insensible to even the thrusts of common sense.

In relation to the bicameral brain, atheist attacks on religion are the left cerebral hemisphere attempting to destroy a major component of the right hemisphere. An exercise in futility.

At the close of his *The Age of Reason*, Thomas Paine wrote: "I have shown in all the foregoing parts of this work that the Bible and Testament are impositions and forgeries; and I leave the evidence I have produced in proof of it to be refuted, if anyone can do it; and I leave the ideas that are suggested in the conclusion of the work to rest on the mind of the reader; certain, as I am, that when opinions are free, either in matter of government or religion, truth will finally and powerfully prevail."

But Paine was wrong. We just recently voted a Bible-believer to two terms of office as president of our country.

"Soon after I had published the pamphlet, *Common Sense*," Paine wrote about 200 years ago in *The Age of Reason*, "I saw the exceeding probability that a Revolution in the System of Government would be followed by a revolution in the system of religion. The adulterous connection of church and state, wherever it had taken place—whether Jewish, Christian, or Turkish—had so effectually prohibited, by pains and penalties, every discussion upon established creeds and upon first principles of religion, that until the system of government should be changed those subjects could not be brought fairly and openly before the world, but that whenever this should be done, a revolution in the system of religion would follow."

Paine believed that the advent of democratic governments would encourage open inspection of religions. He believed that religions such as the Christian religion would collapse with the freedom of press, speech and inquiry ushered in by democracy. Paine overlooked the fact that increased literacy in democratic societies increases the accessibility of the masses to religious propaganda and religious shysters.

Paine was expecting our country's policy of freedom of religion to open up critical discussion of religion. (Previously, one risked being clamped in the stocks for questioning the Bible.) But no great surge of critical discussion ensued. Paine expected that increasing literacy would increase the knowledge of the populace and raise their intellectual level. But it seems to have only made religious tracts and indoctrinating literature more accessible to more people. Paine believed the increasing literacy would result in more people reading the Bible and discovering what a horrible, obscene, fraudulent book it is. No doubt more people did read the Bible, but they liked it. The ability to read is itself a very low order of intelligence.

Paine failed to see that education can be used to spread ignorance and superstition as well as to spread enlightenment and scientific knowledge. Increased liberty included the liberty of the ignorant and the avaricious to propagate their superstitions among the populace.

With the publication of *The Age of Reason*, Paine's stature in this country plummeted from that of a national hero to that of "a dirty little atheist," as Theodore Roosevelt later referred to him. Of course, Paine was not an atheist, but a deist, as were many of the other fathers of our country. But Paine dared to criticize the people's sacred Bible.

Before the end came, Paine no doubt lost much of the optimism he expressed in the closing paragraphs of his book. Paine had greatly underestimated the stubbornness of the bicameral right brain.

Although Paine's book hasn't in 200 years been able to convince people that the Bible is a fraud and Christianity a hoax, there are a surprising number of atheists around who believe that they can. Their failure to, I have little doubt, is due to the Teflon nature of the right brain and to their battle tactics—the age-old negative approach that never has worked, of trying to undermine and destroy religion with reason. Atheists aren't very creative. You will recall that creativity is a feature of the right brain.

A few atheists and humanists have attempted the positive approach of creating a code of secular ethics and of developing an appealing life style to woo religionists away from their churches by offering them something better. The attempts haven't been very successful.

Most atheists flounder in the old argumentative approach of the past. One wonders when they will wake up to the fact that using the reason of the left brain against the heart of the right brain is futile. The Bible states as much in Romans 10:10: "For with the heart man believeth unto righteousness."

Believers are interested in fulfilling emotional and spiritual needs, not intellectual needs. In some cases one might as well try to use reason on a dog. For many people God is primarily a warm feeling. How can one argue with a warm feeling? Arguing with someone who places reason below faith and biblical authority is blowing against the wind.

I think of atheists as generally people of superior intelligence, but am frequently surprised at their lack of insight into the working of the religious psyche. They indignantly sneer at religion simply because they don't understand it.

Many atheists spend their lives pointing out the absurdity of religion and the contradictions and obscenities of the Bible. But for the most part they are just pointing them out to each other. Hardly anybody else is listening. The right brain is not interested.

We might say that atheists are barking up the wrong tree, or that they have a product nobody wants. Or how about that they are fishing with the wrong bait? No matter how good anglers they are, as long as they use the wrong bait they are not going to catch many fish. The Jerry Falwells, Oral Roberts and Robert Schullers succeed egregiously. They use the right bait.

In addition, too many atheist and humanist organizations are led and dominated by fossilized, ivory tower mentalities who fail to reach the populace.

Since most people have only a faint notion of what is inside the Bible, I will offer readers a few more tidbits from the Old Testament. The Old Testament God (Jehovah or Yahweh) is described as a murderer of innocent people, a jealous monster with no sense of justice, a sadist who orders the burning of helpless people and the raping of children.

God commanded Moses to order the Levi clan to murder all the other Israelites for worshiping a golden calf idol: "Slay every man his brother, and every man his companion, and every man his neighbor." (Exodus 32:27). And the children of Levi did according to the command of the Lord and slew about three thousand Israelites.

In another episode of pillage, slaughter and rape that might have made Adolph Eichmann wince, Moses, acting under God's order, commanded his victorious soldiers returning with their captives to "kill every male among the little ones, and kill every woman that hath known man by lying with him. But all the women children that have not known a man by lying with him, keep alive for yourselves." (Numbers 31:17)

The Israelite soldiers had already slain all the Medianite soldiers, burned their houses to the ground and stolen all their cattle.

Another delectable story that modern tabloids would have paid a pretty price for was that of the stranger and his concubine who had been given refuge by an old man in his house in Gibeah. As told in Judges 19:21-29:

> So he brought him [the stranger and his concubine] into his house, and gave provender unto the asses: and they washed their feet and did eat and drink.
>
> Now as they were making their hearts merry, behold, the men of the city, . . . beset the house round about, and beat at the door, and spake to the master of the house, the old man, saying, Bring forth the man that came into thine house, that we may know him [sodomize him].
>
> And the old man, the master of the house, went out unto them, and said unto them, Nay, my brethren, nay, I pray you, do not so wickedly; seeing that this man is come into mine house, do not this folly.
>
> Behold, here is my daughter a maiden, and my guest's concubine, them I will bring out now, and humble ye them, and do with them what seemeth good unto you: but unto this man do not so vile a thing.
>
> But the men would not hearken to him: so the stranger took his concubine, and brought her forth unto them; and they knew her, and abused her all the night until the morning: and when the day began to spring they let her go.
>
> Then came the woman in the dawning of the day, and fell down at the door of the old man's house where her lord was, till it was light.
>
> And her lord rose up in the morning, and opened the doors of the house, and went out to go his way: and, behold, the woman his concubine was fallen down at the door of the house, and her hands were upon the threshold. [Later her master cut his dead concubine up into 12 pieces.]

The Bible contains many such horrors, atrocities, cruelty, injustice and obscenity, yet this is the Book that is piously read at the convening of Congress and solemnly sworn before at the inauguration of our presidents.

We might also wonder if the biblical solutions described above were what former President Ronald Reagan had in mind when he said that the Bible has all the answers to all the problems man has ever known. I will be kind to Reagan and allow that he has never read the Bible.

(But our national lack of Bible knowledge will no doubt have been remedied by the time this book is published, as the result of Congress designating 1990 as the "International Year of Bible Reading.")

There are two different ways atheists may deal with the Bible: ignore it or attack it. Since most atheists view the Bible as a disgusting piece of absurdities, lies, contradictions, and forgeries embellished with lurid tales of atrocities, torture, murder and mayhem, why not treat the Bible at best as a questionable literary and historical document offering sociological and psychological insight into the ignorance, stupidity and criminality of the ancient Israelites? That should end it.

Why should atheists spend their lives trying to discredit a book that they have long since concluded to be an abominable, worthless fraud?

It would seem to make equal sense for an atheist to devote his life debunking Greek and Roman mythology, which are based on similar weird stories, violence and lies. Lot's wife wasn't any more turned into a pillar of salt than Venus was born from sea foam. But atheists waste their time arguing over such silly stuff.

But many atheists are hung up on the Bible. Even after dismissing it as worthless they proceed to treat it seriously, combing it for contradictions, absurdities, errors and forgeries.

These Bible-bashers devote their lives searching the big dumpster, the Bible, for putrid morsels to wave at Christians. One wonders why they waste their lives picking garbage out of a dumpster. But they do have a logic behind their zeal. Since the Bible is the foundation of Christianity, what better way could there be to destroy Christianity than by destroying its foundation? Destroy the foundation and the house falls. The Bible-bashers may have some method in their madness after all.

Some atheists, however, avoid such obsessions with the Bible, such efforts to convince believers that their God Book is just a bad fraud — believers who don't want to be convinced anyhow. These atheists believe that they can go on past the Bible and put their time in on more important and more positive ways to promote atheism.

The reader may wonder why the Bible, if it is such a horrible fraudulent book, is so popularly revered.

Here I will confess that, despite my vitriolic criticism of the Bible, I have a warm place in my heart for the Bible; I don't think my feelings are due entirely to nostalgia and the remnants of childhood conditioning.

The Bible seen as a book of folklore, creative literature and mythology is a wonderful book. I enjoy reading it; I like its quaint literary style (I detest most modern-language, bowdlerized versions). its tales, anecdotes and parables are inspiring; its lurid stories of sex and violence are a minor part of the Bible and no more obscene than much of today's television fare.

Taken as a whole, the Bible in my opinion ranks with the best of world literature. Isn't it too bad that Judeo-Christians, by promoting this book as the word of God, have turned it from a great historical literary masterpiece into an egregious fraud!

Religion has an organizational advantage over atheism. Despite their thousand-fold fragmentation, religions do have a central God (mystical or real doesn't matter) giving them psychological coherence and brotherhood that atheists don't have.

A more important advantage of religion is that religion is profitable.

You make money promoting religion; you only spend money promoting atheism. Even realistic presentations of Bible stories lose money for film producers. The past 10 to 15 years have seen a movement from idealistic, romanticized, profitable movies such as "The Ten Commandments," "Samson and Delilah" and "Ben Hur" to realistic, iconoclastic movies such as "The Last Temptation of Christ," "Monsignor" and "Salvation" — all money losers.

One of the creators of the iconoclastic, box-office loser "King David" explained the integrity of the producers, even at the cost of losing money: "We could have gone the easy way and played to the Bible belt, but we wanted to make a tough, honest film. We don't see David as a gung-ho, Praise-the-Lord kind of guy."

Religionists make a big point out of the fact that the pro-religion movies earned millions at the box office while all the realistic religious movies lost money. As if box-office receipts prove the existence of God. When you are catering to the 12-year-old movie-going mentality you don't smash the box office with irreverence.

Enterprising, charismatic personalities are drawn to religion where fabulous fortunes await them. The size of these fortunes was recently revealed by the series of televangelist scandals. It just makes good sense to go where the money is.

Appeals to the heart (right brain) loosen purse strings. It seems to matter little how crude and blatant such appeals are; some televangelists will stoop to anything to gain riches and fame. Oral Roberts distributed a letter to raise money for his Faith Hospital being built in the city of Tulsa. In the letter, Roberts claimed to have talked with a 900-foot image of Jesus, who assured him that He would speak to Roberts' followers about more donations for the hospital.

After succeeding with that stratagem, Roberts came up later with an even crasser claim that God had told him that if he didn't raise $4.5 million from his followers by the end of March God would call him home. Roberts' followers came up with the money and saved his life.

Without the enterprising, charismatic leaders that fabulous profits draw to religion, atheists and humanists remain bogged down in negative, profitless, defensive camps. Atheists and humanists have yet to learn that you don't succeed merely by being right.

Some atheists and humanists talk volubly about positive approaches, but seldom get beyond talking — which seems to be one of their chief characteristics.

Freethinkers may be right, but what good does it do them? Turns them into misfits, social outcasts. If not shunned, they are dogged, harassed, persecuted.

The use of reason in business, industry and science is advantageous, but in social life the use of reason is often detrimental. There are the usual exceptions: people like Robert Ingersoll, H. L. Mencken, Clarence Darrow and the Bertrand Russells road to fame and small fortunes astride the worthy steed of reason. But lesser people are quickly thrown into the ditch upon mounting, and remain in the ditch the rest of their lives.

There is a cultural compulsive that lends religion strong support. Almost everybody gives unhesitating approval of religion — no matter that they never pray, never step inside a church, poke fun at preachers and are totally skeptical of the Bible, or even are atheists — no matter if religion is completely divorced from their lives, from their behavior, from their value system — their reverence for religion is undiminished. Somehow, although they treat religion as of no good whatever for themselves, they are dominated by a compulsion to support it as good and necessary for society.

Writers and publishers are more likely to succeed by promoting religion, which has a tremendous following, than by promoting atheism and humanism, which have few followers. Little is to be gained by supporting losers.

Dozens of books have been written on "How I became disillusioned with religion" and haven't paid for the ink to print them. But books on "How I became disillusioned with atheism and found God" sell like hot cakes. In fact, such a book written by Bill Murray, son of notorious atheist Madelyn Murray O'Hare, made a pile of money.

Atheism does not necessarily imply a hostile attitude toward religion. There are all kinds of atheists. An atheist may merely not see any valid evidence for believing in God, so he doesn't. He may even see no reason to take people's comforting illusions away from them. But other atheists see eliminating religion as ending religious wars, pogroms, holocausts, bigotry, persecution of rationalists and scientists and a giant step of humankind out of the quagmire of superstition and ignorance.

Rare is the atheist who can graciously overlook the falsehoods spread by unscrupulous holy men over the millennia — phony gods, spirits, souls, heavens, hells, devils, angels, saviors, miracles, resurrections, scriptures, exorcisms and the transubstantiation of crackers and grape juice into Christ's flesh and blood — monstrous lies invented to dupe credulous people into humble submission.

Atheists surely must ponder the abject failure of communism to drive religion out of communist countries. With the backing of a totalitarian propaganda machine, state-controlled education, government-dominated press, laws suppressing religious activities and a state police system mandated to destroy religion, religion not only survives under communism, but the Soviet Union has apparently given up on destroying religion.

One has to conclude that 70 years of atheist propaganda and harsh religious repression in the Soviet Union have been in vain.

If religion is not instinctive, it is close to it. But to call it instinctive is to say that babies are born believing in God. Few psychologists would accept such a postulate. The fact that the particular kind of religion a child develops depends entirely on the kind of religion the child is inculcated with by its mentors pretty well proves that religion is a product of culture, not genes.

This is not to deny, though, that we may be born with certain nerve patterns developed over millions of years of religious belief and devotion that renders us highly susceptible to the enchantment of religion. This characteristic has been called the will or the need to believe.

Religion has been around as far back as archaeologists and anthropologists have been able to delve, and has demonstrated its tenacity by withstanding every known attempt to destroy it.

In view of this, it does seem a bit presumptuous for today's atheists to believe they can wean society from religion — that their 5 percent of humanity can convince the other 95 percent that the latter are wrong.

Their failure to may be seen as partly due to their negative approach — the old approach of condemning the brutality of the Bible patriarchs, of pointing out the Bible's contradictions, of blaming religion for the atrocities, social violence and wars of humankind, of criticizing the hypocrisy, dishonesty and avarice of religious leaders, etc. All valid arguments, but the right brain of religion has no interest in them. The problem has never been getting reason to religionists, but persuading them to accept reason.

I think it unlikely, in view of religion's demonstrated tenacity, that attacks on religion will gain much ground. Man is a coprophagous animal with a insatiable appetite for superstition, supernaturalism, mysticism and magic. It may take a hundred thousand years of evolutionary development and integration of his cerebral hemispheres before he can begin to act in a rational manner.

If this is true, atheists are not so much presumptuous and arrogant as they are foolish in fighting a battle they are foredoomed to lose.

About a decade ago I attended a dinner celebrating the birthdate of Robert Ingersoll, a popular 19th century American orator known as "the great agnostic."

The main speaker at the dinner was our town's atheist, a gaunt, 80-year-old gentleman who had spent his life fighting religion. He covered his customary agenda of criticism and castigation of religion, most of which his listeners had heard often before.

I felt mixed emotions as I listened. I had to admire this old man with his clear strong voice carrying on the fight against superstition and ignorance in the footsteps of our great forebears like Robert Ingersoll, Thomas Paine, Joseph McCabe and Clarence Darrow. He had consecrated his life to carrying on their struggle.

But as I looked and listened I was struck with sadness. He was ending where he had started—with a small motley group of followers, most of whom had grown old with him. He had never been noticeably effective against the immutable monolith of religion. A futile life endeavor that had ended back at ground zero—from which it had hardly ever risen.

Atheism has things to offer, but little the right brain wants. More often than not if atheists are successful in exposing the falsity of Christianity the result is to drive people out of traditional Christianity into Eastern religions, cults and New Age superstitions. Their hoped-for converts don't become atheists, but find new places at other swill troughs to slurp up transcendentalism, reincarnation, Scientology, astrology, channeling, crystal worship, witchcraft, parapsychology and so forth. This is just trading one bucket of slop for another. Irrationalism rules the world. Relatively few people are able to think critically. In the battle between reason and credulity, credulity seems to generally win.

Perhaps I have painted too dismal a picture of atheists. After all, preachers spend their lives trying to teach people to be Christians and invariably fail. Other good citizens spend their lives fighting to establish justice and they are doomed from the start.

No doubt many atheists are driven by the same proselytizing motive that drives many religionists — the illusory notion that the more people who believe something the truer it is. Psychologically, the more people you can convince to believe as you do, the more confident and comfortable you will feel in your belief. In addition, of course, numbers mean real actual power.

Most atheists, having a poor understanding of the right brain, live in a constant state of perplexity. They wonder how religions can go on thriving when historians have discredited their purported divine origins, when not one shred of scientifically acceptable evidence has been offered of their truth, when the many thousands of religions call all the others false?

Let's consider some of the reasons for the persistence of religion. First of all, we know that religion belongs primarily in the province of the irrational right brain and that the two hemispheres are not fully integrated. As a result they are able to harbor contradictory beliefs just as two individual people may hold contradictory beliefs. We know from experience that it is as futile to try to persuade the right brain to accept logic as to try to persuade the reasoning left brain to accept faith as a valid criterion for truth.

But this doesn't answer the question of why most people follow the urgings of their right brain, despite its irrationality.

Of course, there is the will or need to believe, but the deeper question concerns the origin of this will to believe. From whence comes the overwhelming will and need to believe, this easy acceptance of gods, of miracles, of poltergeists, of astral projection, of transmigration? Believing must have yielded a lot of payoffs over the millennia to have become so popular and deep-rooted.

Because religion lends itself to the exploitation of the masses, it has almost always been heavily supported by the establishments — economic and political as well as ecclesiastical. With such support, religion has been able to wield a dominant influence on the populace.

The interest of the establishments is to support religion, not atheism and humanism. In fact, the latter suffer from persecution, repression and discrimination.

Atheists in America are taxed both directly and indirectly to support religion; no religionists are taxed to support atheism. I could go on and on, but unless one is totally blind, one has to be aware that religion dominates America. Of our thousands of radio and television stations, how many are atheist stations?

The positive and negative reinforcements of religion versus atheism tell quite a story. First of all, most religions promise you Heaven and promise that your enemies will be punished in Hell. What these promises amount to is an assurance of justice, one of humankind's greatest longings. Atheism promises nothing.

Religion yields social status, respectability, economic advantages and the easier life of conformity compared with the ostracism, persecution and economic penalties suffered by atheists.

Religion also fulfills the emotional needs and pleasures of its parishioners: mysticism, ceremony, music, art, theater, brotherhood, entertainment, recreation, social involvement. About the only need fulfilled by atheists is intellectual stimulation. The will to be skeptical is rare. There would be no problem if it weren't, because there would be no religion.

Many atheists and humanists recognize the necessity for them to fulfill the many human needs that religions fulfill if atheism and humanism are to be able to compete.

Among other things they would have to develop a positive attitude toward atheism to replace their negative attitude toward religion. They would have to emphasize the glories of science and assume more credit for the fabulous world science has brought us.

They would have to get over their introspective, self-centeredness and develop an open, friendly attitude. They would have to learn how to appeal to the emotions. They would have to get over their hostility and resentment and offer joyful experience to newcomers. Humanist Frank Mortyn said, "Freethinkers need to develop in blood, in guts, in muscle, as well as in brains."

The fly in the ointment is, of course, that atheism and humanism *are* intellectual movements while religion *is* an emotional development. To suggest that atheists imitate religionists because that would lead to greater success is like suggesting that a chess champion play professional football because there is more money in it.

Few people get much pleasure out of intellectual stimulation, while most respond to the emotional appeal of superstition. So, being pleasure-seeking animals, most choose religion.

Born into a world of superstition, atheists can hardly avoid a negative stance. In addition, nothing succeeds like success. Religion is dominant; atheism picks up the crumbs. A thousand religious groups flourish for every atheist or humanist group.

One reason, as mentioned earlier, for this condition is that there is no money to be made promoting atheism, while fortunes are made from promoting religion.

Society always rewards its conformists, and in our society religious belief is conformity. Besides the rewards for conformity there is an equal array of punishments for nonconformity. It is perilous to swim against the current of tradition.

Social pressure for religious conformity comes from relatives, friends, neighbors, employers, lodge brothers, school teachers, business associates and customers. The only pressure on atheists is aimed at discouraging their atheism.

There seems to be no end to the reasons for the persistence of religion. Fear is certainly an important one. Not just fear of Hell for failing to live religiously, but fear of the dangers that imperil one in his daily life on Earth — sickness, fires, cyclones, earthquakes and mortal accidents. Help-less in the face of these countless hazards, people feel the need for a guardian angel or for a protective Savior and are more than willing to believe in them. Just feeling in this lonely, hostile world that one has a friend in Jesus is a great spiritual comfort in itself.

There are, of course, people with great self-confidence, feelings of inexhaustible resourcefulness and unquenchable egos, but most people feel weak and inadequate. They look for strong leaders for support and guidance. Feeling so unheroic themselves, they search for heroes to worship. The celebrity heroes of sports, entertainment, the military and government supply their need for secular heroes. Charismatic preachers, popes, saints, evangelists, ayatollahs and cult leaders supply their need for religious leaders and heroes.

We might note also that people's dependence on religious authorities for guidance relieves them of the often troublesome ethical decisions they would otherwise be called upon to make for themselves.

Religion gives people authoritative rules of conduct. It offers legalistic rules for behavior, such as the Decalogue. People love simple rules. Such rules not only relieve them of having to make ethical decisions, but allow them to feel guiltless while committing heinous acts so long as they don't violate any specific rule. They gladly assume that if an act isn't explicitly forbidden, it is all right. They learn to play the game of legalism with God.

And, of course, it is always nice to know that you have the truth while those around you are misled by false prophets.

It is natural to resist new ideas, and certainly religionists couldn't find a new idea more radical in relation to their present beliefs than atheism. A simple new idea can very easily be adopted to take the place of a current idea — if the current idea is separate and unconnected with all our other ideas. But it seldom is. And there lies the reason for the resistance. Most new radical ideas require an almost total alteration and restructuring of our present network of ideas. This colossal mental task we naturally resist. It's like adding a new page in the middle of a book we are writing. First we have to renumber the hundred or so subsequent pages of our manuscript. Then we have to reread the entire manuscript to make sure the new material is consistent with everything else in the book. If it isn't, we have to make a number of difficult changes to correct the problem. But a new idea in our thinking can be much more disturbing to the concept of the world we have developed over our lifetime than a new idea inserted into a book would be to the structure of the book. So we naturally resist new ideas.

Looking at the overall picture, atheists must sometimes wonder if religionists aren't better off than they themselves are, despite atheists' superior left-brain intelligence. Could it be that the right brain has an intelligence deeper than that of the logical left brain, a kind of pragmatic, subliminal voice that recognizes the advantages of religion for its host and overrules the left brain, directing its host to accept the irrational beliefs of the right brain? A super-intuitive guide that Blaise Pascal may have had in mind when he wrote: "The heart has its reason which reason does not know."

The pig that will not wallow in the muck with the rest of the pigs lives a lonely, self-ostracized life. Perhaps a person is better off to believe with the superstitious majority than to yield to the persuasion of reason and logic. Better to be wrong with the herd than right alone.

Atheists may just lack the intuitive, pragmatic guidance that unconsciously determines the belief systems of the conforming majority.

Maybe those who wallow in religion, superstition, supernaturalism, mysticism and magic aren't as stupid as atheists make them out to be. Maybe the lonely, bitter, resentful atheist is the one to be pitied. The poor fellow can't believe in superstitious rubbish, although he would be much better off if he could.

But the cultural compulsive in our country is not to feel pity for atheists, but contempt. The negative, dissident, anti-social and sometimes arrogant stance of atheists elicits little compassion for them even if they are a miserable segment of the populace. The fact is atheists are generally not nice people.

The reason they are not nice people is that they are a scorned minority, persecuted, dumped on and vilified by the vast majority, the effects of which renders many atheists ill-tempered, bitter, angry and sullen.

They are frustrated by their failure to have a significant effect on religion. They know that there is no evidence of a God that would be accepted by a scientific study or be admissible in an American court. They find ridiculous the biblical stories of God making light four days before He made the sun, Adam being made from a lump of clay and Eve fashioned from one of his ribs, Lot's wife being turned into a pillar of salt, Noah catching pairs of all the animals in the world and putting them in his little boat, Joshua commanding the sun to stand still, a holy ghost impregnating the virgin Mary, Jesus arising from his tomb and ascending to Heaven, dead people coming out of the graveyard and parading in the streets, etc.

It is not surprising that some atheists feel as frustrated as an innocent man facing a hundred lying witnesses in his trial for murder.

The resentment of atheists is increased by the jealousy felt by any minority without power toward a majority with power — especially when the minority, as is always the case, believes itself right and the majority wrong.

Adding to such resentment is the fact that religious shysters and ignoramuses enjoy high respect and veneration and live lives of wealth, power, luxury and joy while their glum, bitter atheist opponents, stuck with truth and personal integrity, attempt to eliminate superstition and ignorance in a struggle foredoomed to failure.

Then too, many atheists still resent the advantage taken of them in indoctrinating them with religion while children and their consequent later painful disillusionment.

Logically, the Christian majority being on top in our culture would be expected to be happier than the atheists, rationalists and humanists at the bottom. Sadly, that's the way it seems to be.

Let me interject here that from the viewpoint of religionists, atheists have no just complaint for the ostracism and political and economic sanctions they suffer from religion. Religionists don't forbid them from participating in religion. In fact, the religionists plead with them to.

The temperament of atheists is partly the reaction to the scorn heaped on them by religionists and the hordes of non-religious poltroons who take their cues from the religionists. The result is the resentful, mean-spirited atheist.

Atheists have valid grounds for opposing and fearing religion. Religion is a danger to personal freedom. No doubt if Christian fundamentalists came into control of the schools they would try to indoctrinate children with their religion and teach the children of atheists and humanists to hate their parents. Consider what has happened in Iran since the Islamic fundamentalist Shiites came into power.

Consider the historic role of religion in promoting wars, pogroms, torture, burnings, hangings and the church's support of tyrants, slavery and the degradation of women. The grounds for fearing the power of the church are real.

But little gratitude is shown atheists for their valiant stand to protect personal freedom from the encroachments of religion. In fact, they are more often criticized for it.

Nonbelievers are often disagreeable people not only because of their reaction to ostracism, frustration and persecution by the overwhelming religious majority they live among, but also because of the nonconformist, independent, skeptical nature that made them nonbelievers in the first place. Such independent thinkers don't get along well even with one another. Strong, cohesive organizations depend upon charismatic leaders and herd-minded followers. Nonbelievers significantly lack these elements. In addition, nonbelievers often turn their frustrations and mean-spiritedness on one another.

So, the failure of nonbelievers to develop happy lives independent of and oblivious to religionists is caused partly by the dissident natures and intellectual independence of nonbelievers. These are the characteristics that bring them together and these are the characteristics that hinder their binding into cohesive, effective organizations. Atheists and humanists may suffer less from persecution by religionists than from dissension among themselves.

Some of the ill-temperedness of atheists may result from discontent. This suggestion rests on the somewhat tenuous theory that religion satisfies a neuropsychological need inherent in our hereditary nerve pattern. Whatever the reason, atheists are a chronically discontented lot. Many atheists represent a break in their genetic line of hundreds of thousands of years of God-believing ancestors — a break that itself creates neurological discord.

One of the things that often exasperates, yes, infuriates many atheists is the presence of so many fundamentalist Christians around them stinking with ignorance and superstition but seemingly happy and vigorous, and getting along better in the world than the atheists are.

Everybody's life is a tragedy but the life of an atheist seems especially tragic. When the atheist dies he realizes that his whole life was in vain, that he entered a world that reeked with the stench of religion and leaves it still holding his nose.

The atheist cannot even look forward to being vindicated. Even if the atheist is right, religionists, after they are dead, will never find out that they had been wrong all their lives, that they had worshiped a God that didn't exist, that they had prayed to the wind, that they were mortal the same as a mouse — that the atheists were right all along. No, atheists know they will never even get this satisfaction.

For the person who takes everything lightly and conforms to herd behavior without giving it much thought, the question of religious belief is one of light concern. But for the earnest person indoctrinated with religion from early childhood, a loss of faith can turn out to be a traumatic experience that dominates the rest of his life. He is deeply stung by having been victimized by a hoax, and is consequently filled with resentment toward those who perpetrate the hoax.

Extreme cases of such reactions are Joseph McCabe who left the priesthood of the Catholic Church when he became disillusioned with religion and spent the rest of his life writing and lecturing in support of atheism, and Emmit McLoughlin, another ex-Catholic priest who devoted his post-clerical life to writing books denouncing the Catholic Church and religion in general.

These two are rare cases to be sure, but they may not be rare cases of priests who have lost their faith in the Church. They may be rare cases of priests who after losing their faith had the courage and the guts to leave the Church and the integrity to tell the world why—in the face of the loss of their means of livelihood, unmitigating public disapproval, excommunication, ostracism, and the concerted effort of the Church to shame them and humiliate them.

But we cannot expect everybody to be heroic. Ordinary atheists do not have positions of influence nor the literary, rhetorical or organizational ability to be effective promoters of atheism. The Miles Bjornstams of society succeed only in bringing massive opprobrium onto themselves while gaining few converts.

So, what is the wise course for the run-of-the-mill atheist? If he believes that religion, whether a mental disease or not, is practically instinctive to humankind and ineradicable, he would be foolish to dedicate his life to destroying it.

Atheists have been trying for centuries to cure the disease. They have used economic sanctions, even terror, but still religion persists.

Perhaps it is time for atheists to give up on eradication of religion and just learn to live with it as they have learned to live with other incurable diseases and as they have learned to accept bad weather, taxes, and inlaws as inevitable.

Perhaps it is time for atheists to accept the fact that most people are coprophagous animals born with a need to believe and should accept this fact as gracefully as they accept black pigmentation, red hair, corpulence, vanity, dishonesty and prodigality—characteristics one doesn't necessarily like but characteristics one doesn't allow to become the obsessive focus of his life.

There is always the nagging question of why atheists should care what anybody else believes. Why should they get upset because some (in the atheists' opinions) feeble-minded neighbors believe in ghosts, gods and poltergeists?

> Why should we strive, with cynic frown,
> To knock their fairy castles down?
> —Eliza Cook

SACRIFICE OF CAIN AND ABEL.

Many atheists spend their lives trying dissuade others from believing what others wish to believe, attempting to wrench their security blankets from them, trying to rob them of their comforting beliefs in a shepherding God, taking away their illusion of a Heaven where they will meet all their deceased loved ones. (The crowning blessing of these beliefs is that if they are false the believers will never find it out.)

Why should atheists be irritated by superstitions? If some people choose *in a land of freedom* to believe in such stuff, what business is it of atheists?

Atheists might answer that they feel compelled by their integrity to fight ignorance and superstition they believe are degrading our country. Probably more rhetoric than introspection.

But nonbelievers are not alone in being irritated and upset by the beliefs of others. Religionists suffer similar agonies over doctrinal differences. Does one earn his passage to Heaven by good works or by merely believing in Jesus Christ as his Savior? Does sprinkling water on the newborn cleanse them of original sin or must they be totally submerged? Etc.

Such differences of opinions, however trivial they may seem, have caused wars killing hundreds of thousands of human beings. Today wars based primarily on religious differences are being fought all over the globe, such as the Middle East war between the Israeli Jews and the Moslem Arabs, the presently suspended war between the Iranian Shiites and the Iraqi Sunnis, the war in Northern Ireland between Protestants and Catholics, the sporadic war in India between Hindus and Sikhs.

Perhaps atheists can take some comfort in the knowledge that Jehovah's Witnesses, Christian Scientists, Seventh Day Adventists, Mormons, Hare Krishnas, Moonies, Flat-earthers and other offbeat religions and sects experience from mainstream religions similar rejection and persecution.

The members of such groups, too, believe they are right. But the vast majority of religionists believe such groups are wrong and oppose them. The members of these offbeat groups generally spend their lives in the futile promotion of their unpopular doctrines. They apparently have a streak of masochism and a compulsion toward martyrism. Their situation is similar to but not quite the same as that of atheists. The followers of offbeat religions choose such religions. Atheists make no choice. Their belief is passive and no more chosen than a toothache. Their only choice is whether to be an active or passive atheist.

But the small, unpopular religions, nevertheless, seem to fulfill their followers' needs, needs for fellowship, transcendental dedication, emotional satisfaction, spiritual support, mystical experience, self-esteem and the security of belonging.

Although atheists cannot satisfy many of these purported human needs because of the religious nature of the needs, the few needs they could satisfy I fear they do a poor job of for the reasons covered earlier.

If atheists and humanists could do a better job of fulfilling people's needs within their own communities independent of religionists, if they could just ignore the benighted herd and develop close social relationships within their own groups—such relationships, after all, are the secret to happy joyful lives—they would not have the intense concern that they do have about what religionists believe—a concern that keeps many atheists and humanists upset.

I think that nonbelievers would surely do better by promoting a positive atheism than by wasting their time fighting religion. Gracefully ignoring religion is probably wiser for nonbelievers than is militant opposition. Too many atheists and humanists have enslaved themselves to Christianity and its Bible. Can we say of religion that the herd follows it, fools combat it and wise men ignore it?

One cannot expect every nonbeliever to be heroic. The ideal atheist is one who supports the positive presentation of atheism to a pragmatic public, while opposing religion short of bringing religious wrath onto himself and his family.

A wise atheist knows that it makes little difference, anyhow, what a person believes. When we're dead, believers are just as dead as non-believers — so what difference does it really make!

Isaac Asimov, scientist and author, writing in *the Humanist* gave an eloquent answer to the question of why atheists continue to engage in the never-ending fight with religionists with no victory in sight: "Because we must. Because we have the call. Because it is nobler to fight for rationality without winning than to give up in the face of continued defeats. Because whatever true progress humanity makes is through the rationality of the occasional individual and because any one individual we may win for the cause may do more for humanity than a hundred thousand who hug their superstitions to their breasts."

Chapter VII
THE WILL TO BELIEVE

Any discussion of nature (heredity) versus nurture (environment) leads to the question of man's origin. Since most people believe that God created Heaven and Earth, we cannot dismiss it cavalierly. According to biblical creationism, humankind was placed on Earth about six thousand years ago as a finished product complete with a soul and a conscience. This finished product was man's unalterable hereditary nature.

The presence of a soul in humankind greatly complicates the question of nature versus nurture. A soul, of course, presupposes an after life; otherwise there would be no point in having a soul. Atheists quickly dismiss the soul as an invention to shield man's ego from dreaded death and extinction. Most atheists accept their mortality with dignity.

The "wintry smile of truth," as Alfred Noyes called it, is frequently unacceptable, especially to people near the end of the road. The arch-skeptic Rousseau during his last years yielded to the palliative of an afterworld in a letter to his friend, Voltaire: "I have too much suffered in this life not to expect another one. All the subtleties of metaphysics will not make me doubt for a minute the immortality of the soul."

And more recently Henry Miller at age 88 said: "Death itself doesn't frighten me, because I don't believe it's the end. All my intuitive feelings are that this cannot be the only world. It's too damn short, too ugly and too meaningless. There's got to be something more to it."

The concept of soul has a rough time standing up under close scrutiny. As mentioned earlier the soul seems to be a redundant copy of the body and central nervous system. Perhaps this copy acts like the RNA genetic factor whose function is to duplicate DNA genes. The soul passes on to purgatory and recreates the trillions of body cells for which it contains the blueprints into a Heaven-bound duplicate of the deceased (or Hell-bound as the case may be).

This concept is a wee bit too fantastic to pass muster to the left cerebral hemisphere. Even if the soul is an ethereal duplicate of only the psyche, one wonders how the psyche could have any meaning separate from the body that created it—male or female, athletic or crippled, fat or slender, beautiful or ugly, sensual or frigid? Atheists, rejecting Christian dualism of separation of body from mind, of flesh from character, of blood from personality, see dualism as verbal nonsense, a semantic trick.

In describing and diagramming the course of human evolution from the simplest one-celled organism, to flatworms, to vertebrates, to reptiles, to lemurs, to pithecanthropines, to modern man, biological evolutionists significantly ignore the stage of evolutionary development at which the momentous innovation of a soul occurred. In taking their cue from evolutionists, atheists, with no great reluctance, disavow the soul.

The reincarnationists have a curious system in which souls are passed from one person or animal to another. When persons die their souls transmigrate to newborn babies. This makes some sense inasmuch as physical bodies do wear out, while souls, being made out of nothing, last forever because there is nothing to wear out. So souls can be recycled. But as cheap as they must be—made out of nothing—why should any baby creature have to take a hand-me-down?

To avoid confusion we will ignore the reification called the soul. A dictionary definition of nurture should be helpful at this point: "The sum of the influences modifying the expression of the genetic potentialities of an organism." Thus, nurture is the modification of nature.

Religion attempts to modify the nature of children by training and indoctrinating them, by suppressing their recalcitrant behavior, by filling them with guilt, and finally by scaring the Hell out of them with the biblical stories of burning for eternity in fires of sulfur and brimstone in the next world.

Atheists claim that we shackle children with religion while they are young and defenseless; if we waited until their brains were mature, it wouldn't be so easy to put religion over on them. Atheists see this indoctrination as based on the adult belief that children aren't able to think for themselves, so have to be told what to think; and by the time adults finish with brain-stuffing children, most children have been rendered incapable of thinking.

From the earliest days support of religion has been an economic imperative of the rulers of humankind. Whether secular or theocratic, rulers have used religion to maintain their power and ensure the subjugation of the populace. Under democracies, it is true there is sometimes a reversal of this power relationship. To some degree the people use their democratic franchise to protect themselves from power-hungry clergymen and their wealthy backers.

It is not difficult to see the advantages to rulers of indoctrinating children with the slave morality of Christianity; for example, making virtues out of meekness, patience, humility, obedience and piety.

Through their clerical handmaidens, the ruling element promise Heaven to the meek and obedient, and frighten the aggressive and disobedient with threats of Hell, while enjoying their power and wealth unchallenged. Persons who believe that salvation is in Heaven are little threat to the rulers of Earth. Persons who believe that the meek shall inherit the Earth have little cause to fight for a share of it today.

In addition, the success of the aggressive and greedy to achieve political and economic power rests heavily on their ability to fulfill people's need to believe. So establishments almost always give strong support to the churches.

The failure of communism is probably due as much to communism's policy of opposing religion as to the flaws of its economic system.

I suspect that many of our spiritual leaders are totally amoral, pragmatic people with superior charisma and business acumen. They see where the money and fame lie, and they go for them, experiencing no strong inhibitive, conscientious or other psychological barriers to such pursuit. It is the accepted American way.

Not being clairvoyant, I can only suspect that this is true. I have in mind such alleged charlatans as Oral Roberts, Billy James Hargis, Jimmy Swaggart, Pat Robertson, Garner Ted Armstrong, Shirley McLaine, Rev. Jim Jones, Mary Baker Eddy, Billy Sunday, Aimee Semple McPherson, Joe Smith, Bhagwan Shree Rajneesh and Sun Myung Moon.

The general public often recognizes the low integrity of charlatans while the news media in fear of offending the followers of charlatans speak of them gingerly; the common people sometimes display startling cynicism in their private assessments.

The Elmer Gantries promise their followers riches in Heaven while relieving them of the burden of their earthly wealth. Some Pentecostal sects promise health-and-wealth for the here and now in an implied exchange for monetary support. God will make you rich, they promise, if you give His vicars some money first as a token of good faith.

The money does roll in. Evangelist Robert Schuller collected enough donations to build an $18 million crystal cathedral in Garden Grove, California. Jim and Tammy Bakker's PTL television ministry came up with $100 million just to restore an 1851 English palace at their Heritage theme park in North Carolina. Oral Roberts collected enough money from his television evangelism to pay for a $250 million hospital — essentially a 60-story monument to himself because the area did not need another hospital.

Before his downfall in 1987, Jim Bakker raked in estimated revenues of $129 million a year; Southern Baptist Billy Graham, $55 million a year; James Kennedy, minister of a Ft. Lauderdale, Florida Presbyterian church, $27 million; Oral Roberts, $80 million; Pat Robertson, a Baptist who ran for president, $129 million; Jerry Falwell, founder of the Moral Majority and operator of the television Old Time Gospel Hour, $100 million; and Jimmy Swaggart of Baton Rouge, Louisiana Assembly of God, $142 million.

So we are talking about colossal sums of money, probably totaling for all the televangelists between $1 and $2 billion annually — from what atheists call swindling the gullible, and followers call donations for the glory of God.

At this point we must not overlook the collections of the Catholic Church that have made it the richest institution in the world.

So, what about the atheists and humanists with their bare treasuries and dingy little meeting halls. Unfortunately for them, money is made — piles of it — promoting religion, while money is only spent promoting atheism.

Atheists can make no promises as religionists can of a fabulous reward in the next world for supporting them. (What reward could be more fabulous than eternal life?)

In addition, there is an economic imperative to support religion in a religious society. Merchants, politicians, educators, publishers, broadcasters all support religion.

There is also a compulsion for those who do not even practice religion to support it. We have all been so thoroughly indoctrinated and conditioned in a reverence for religion that even most nonbelievers show respect for religion and contempt for atheism. It is the right thing to do; the good thing, the proper thing. They go right on showing the utmost respect for what they intellectually consider to be fraud, superstition and folly. Indifferent religionists and passive nonbelievers feel little compulsion to support atheism. Quite the contrary. The prejudice against atheism driven into their hearts from early childhood is not readily dislodged. So even nonbelievers often revere religion and scorn atheism. I have little doubt that atheists contribute more money for the support of religion than for the support of atheism.

According to science, after three billion years of slowly evolving step by step from a primitive microorganism, man had reached the threshold of civilization six thousand years ago. By then he had already developed a strong propensity for religion, whether it was built on superstition, magic, mysticism, fear, hope, ancestor-worship, pageantry or various combinations of them. He was deeply entrenched in religion. We can only speculate on the natural selection of religion over rationalism.

To understand evolution let us start out with what is, because everything that is is the result of evolution. Human beings have evolved from primitive forms. All the behavioral characteristics of human beings (such as selfishness, loyalty, competitiveness, dishonesty, cowardice, fecundity and the will to believe) have evolved along with biological evolution. These characteristics have been selected by evolution.

For clarification, let's look closely at the above sample listing. For brevity's sake I will loosely intermix characteristics conducive to individual survival with characteristics conducive to the survival of the group or of the species.

Selfishness (i.e., self-preservation) is often called the first law of nature. Its selection is too obvious to need further comment.

Loyalty is a trait that binds a group into a strong unit able to survive at the expense of opposing groups weakened by the fragmentation of disloyalty.

Competitiveness, like selfishness, needs no comment.

Dishonesty is ubiquitous because it gives an advantage in the competitive struggle. It pays to be dishonest.

The selection of cowardice is exemplified by the adage that he who fights and runs away lives to fight another day. Bravery is a rare characteristic because brave men are early eliminated.

Fecundity is often the top characteristic for survival. Some lower organisms depend almost entirely on fecundity for the survival of their species, being otherwise weaklings in the struggle for existence. It is also an important survival characteristic for humans. Sex has a preponderant, sometimes obsessive, interest to people. This is understandable because if there were no sex, there would be little life on Earth — certainly no human life. If sexual interest had not been selected by evolution, human beings could easily become extinct.

The will to believe, the fountainhead of religion, puzzles me. I can see no survival advantage in credulity to explain its evolutionary selection.

But the very selection of a characteristic is proof of its advantageous nature. I cannot argue against it. If a characteristic has been selected by evolution, ipso facto, it has been either conducive to survival or nugatory.

Credulity's offspring, religion, is an obsessive interest to many people and to whole societies. The search for an explanation of its evolutionary development is frustrating. I will suggest four tenuous theories to account for the selection of religion — after it once appeared.

(1)   Perhaps those societies survived better whose people were rendered docile and manageable by religion.

(2)   Perhaps those societies whose leaders could command the allegiance of their subjects by portraying themselves as God's emissaries were thereby able to muster armies that would fight and die for them, and thus prevail over enemy tribes whose soldiers felt no such divine, sacrificial allegiance to their leaders.

(3)   Perhaps, as in the modern world, the more ignorant and superstitious people are, the heavier breeders they are. Evolution would thereby select those prone to religion.

(4)   Perhaps leaders felt more secure with mindless, conforming followers and therefore eliminated from the gene pool intellectuals, rationalists, skeptics and atheists by execution or imprisonment.

Be that as it may, we are stuck with religion. Organic evolution by selected mutations goes hand in hand with the evolution of cultural practices — pageantry, art, theater, marriage, music, magic and religion. The two reinforce one another and become inseparably melded. Evolution selects people who accept and support religion and they in turn strengthen the institutions of religion by their support.

We should recognize that survival of the fittest as applied to societies and species does not always refer to physical ferocity, aggressiveness and ruthlessness. As mentioned above, such characteristics as high fecundity can aid survival.

In civilized human society, unlike the animal and vegetable kingdoms where the weak and maladjusted do not survive, the unfit often do quite well.

The less fit, the weaker have always been protected in many ways. This behavior is difficult to account for. Why should the strong and ruthless ever make any concessions to the weak? The only explanation I can find is in evolution. Societies in which the fitter eliminated all the weaker members apparently have been less viable societies and have not survived. They did not survive because once the weak members were eliminated, the strong ones began eliminating each other. There are always weaker members, so the process of eliminating the weaker members ends with the destruction of everybody but one survivor who can hardly carry on by himself.

So, human compassion for the weak and handicapped may be seen as advantageous to the survival of our species. Ayn Rand, however, took a dim view of such tendencies: "Today's mawkish concern with the compassion for the feeble, the flawed, the suffering, the guilty, is a cover for the profoundly Kantian hatred of the innocent, the strong, the able, the successful, the virtuous, the confident, the happy."

Some atheists do not see religion as an evolutionary selection, but as a genetic defect similar to sickle cell anemia or hemophilia that unfortunately got into the human gene pool and has contaminated it ever since.

There remains the great question of whether the will to believe should be called an instinct. Some scholars refrain from calling any kind of human behavior instinctive, although they acknowledge the inheritance of nerve patterns that render people more likely to behave in certain ways. They reserve the designation of instinct for the rigid behavior of lower animals, such as the singing, nest-building and migration of birds, the rigidly organized division of labor of ants and bees, and the spawning routines of whales and salmon.

The inheritance of instinctive behavior by lower animals is as certain and unalterable as their inheritance of legs, wings and fins. So, most behavior of lower animals is attributed to instinct, while the behavior of human beings is attributed to acculturation.

We get into a bucket of worms in calling widely observed human behavior instinctive. Are war, robbery, torture and murder instinctive?

Nevertheless, whether we call culturally inculcated behavior such as religion instinctual because human beings are readily amenable to it may be a matter simply of semantic choice.

Atheists wonder, if religion is instinctive, why they aren't religious. Atheists cite cases of infants imprisoned in attics and reared in isolation for their entire childhood and upon their discovery and release having no notion of God and a supernatural world.

No doubt ages of mutational selection have produced humans highly susceptible to religion, while at the same time cultural evolution has produced a religious environment highly appealing to believers—with its art, architecture, music, pageantry, ritualism, literature, mysticism and magic.

Religion fills a need in the human psyche, bringing pleasure and satisfaction. It fits Freud's pleasure principle that human behavior is determined primarily by seeking pleasure and avoiding pain. So as long as religion fulfills needs and enhances pleasure, it will persist until the crack of doom, regardless of how irrational, absurd or bizarre it may be. But in one sense, what could be more rational than seeking pleasure and avoiding pain!

Isaac Asimov writes: "All the ways of being wrong about the universe are more consoling than the ways of being right, because unfortunately to be right about the universe is very likely to end up with the decision that the universe doesn't give a damn about us and that a great many things that happen—if not everything that happens—is largely random."

Pride reinforces the will to believe. Pride suffers a heavy blow when a believer disavows his religious beliefs and admits he has been wrong all his life. The ego, being shaped by one's religious past, naturally is reluctant to be refuted, discredited and invalidated by having its very foundation kicked out from under it. For people to refute the very basis of their lives by declaring wrong and mistaken that which they have followed, defended and been guided by their entire lives, is a denial of themselves.

These considerations are constantly present on an unconscious level to suppress disturbing doubts.

Survival being the first law of nature, it is natural for human beings to wish to go on living in another world after death or to resume life on this planet in a reincarnated form. A lot of theology may boil down to the simple, crude, undignified reluctance of human beings to die and return to nothing.

So eager are people for immortality that they will believe any kind of malarkey that promises them guardian angels on Earth and eternal life in the hereafter.

Although born atheists, humans are readily indoctrinated with and emotionally attuned to religion during their impressionable childhoods. Their instinctive need to believe is readily encouraged in an environment rich with the manure of superstition, supernaturalism, myth and magic. They become coprophilic adults whose emotional health demands the continuous ingestion of religion.

Most people seem to have the neural structure of religion, just as they have the neural structures that can lead to phobias, anxiety attacks, delusions of grandeur, persecution complexes and so on. Whether they develop such tendencies depends chiefly on the experiences, influences and stresses of their lives.

The right brain has a need to believe in the fanciful, the irrational, the absurd and the bizarre. It scorns the rationality, reason, science and logic that appeal to the left brain. The God-worshiping 95 percent of people are turned on by fecal matter; they prefer falsehood to truth, hypocrisy to honesty, chicanery to integrity. Their need to believe is satisfied with supernaturalism, mysticism, superstition, obscurantism, religion.

It is easy to understand why older generations, who were steeped in religion before the explosion of scientific knowledge, would resist the avalanche of new information that refutes the religious beliefs around which they had built their lives. But it is not so easy to understand why so many youths of today with the advantage of more available knowledge than any generation ever, eschew that knowledge in favor of the teachings of Eastern gurus, charismatic cult leaders and Christian televangelist charlatans; why they are drawn to crystal worship, channeling, astrology, witchcraft and parapsychology.

We would expect as one after another scientific explanation of natural phenomena displaced the old supernatural explanations, as scholars found that Christianity was copied after older religions and its Bible is historically erroneous and mostly fraudulent, as astronomers discovered a universe the magnitude of which made ridiculous the concepts of the divinely inspired authors of the Bible, as archeologists increased the age of the world from the biblical five or six thousand years to five or six billion years — we would expect today's youth to scorn religion.

But the fact seems to be that despite this flood of knowledge, irrational bizarre beliefs persist, even among educated young people. The wonders of science do not stir up the passions that approach the zeal that supernaturalism does.

Such young people must think scientists are a bunch of dummies. Science, with its ability to carbon-date prehistoric bones, dissect the nucleus of the atom into its multiple parts, figure out the structure of genes, determine the composition of a substance to ten-thousandth parts, image stars billions of light-years away — surely if there is a god, a supernatural world, a spiritual entity, science would have by now found some evidence of it.

A Gallup survey found that 42 percent of college graduates are regular churchgoers compared with only 35 percent of those not going beyond elementary school.

Although the economic imperative in our culture encourages religion and suppresses atheism, as is apparent by library books, school books, the establishment press and radio and television broadcasts, a sizeable amount of atheist literature has been produced by non-establishment presses in the course of our free-press history.

I have before me a 1931 catalogue of books published by the Atheist

Book Company of New York. It lists 164 books and pamphlets exposing religion and arguing in favor of atheism, from a 5¢ pamphlet by Ingersoll, through a 20¢ one by Gauvin, through a 50¢ clothbound book by McCabe, through a 95¢ one by Anatole France, through a $1.25 book by Spencer, through a $5 book by Frazer.

In spite of all these books floating around for 60 years and hundreds of others published since, religion continues to predominate in our culture.

Humankind's will to believe coupled with the power of suggestion reveals itself in noxious eruptions around the globe. A great new interest stirred a few years ago over the Turin Shroud, even though on Jan. 6, 1390 Pope Clement VII issued a ruling that display of the Shroud should be accompanied by a public declaration that "it is not the true shroud of our Lord, but a painting or picture made of the semblance or representation of the shroud."

But Geoffrey de Charny, who displayed the fraud at his church at Lirey, continued to enrich his church from the tourists and pilgrims who would rather believe their swindler than the Pope. Today, 600 years later, gullible pilgrims are still paying to see the fake shroud.

In 1513 the Virgin Mary purportedly appeared to Juan Diego, a 55-year-old Indian at Tepoyac Hill near Mexico City. Mary gave Juan a life-size painting of herself. The coat in which Juan carried the picture to his church has been preserved and is now enshrined in the Church of Our Lady of Guadalupe. My source didn't say what happened to the picture.

In 1917 the Virgin Mary purportedly appeared to three children near Fatima, Portugal. Later the same year she appeared to 70,000 people assembled during a downpour of rain in the field where she had first appeared to the children. Surely, no one would question the witness of 70,000 people!

More recently an AP dispatch from Alice, Texas reported that a housewife had seen the image of the Virgin Mary (she gets around) on an old water tank. Within a month 19,000 persons visited the farm (at a charge of a dollar per car). Catholic clergymen in the area declined to comment on the matter.

The above examples of the will to believe, expressed in visions, are, of course, three out of thousands of their kind. But this will to believe has been cultivated since time immemorial and is to be found in more than the area of religion. Belief in magic, superstition and mysticism have spread throughout our entire culture and have become the chief ingredients of advertising.

The success of modern advertising of nostrums, foods, wines, cigarettes and cosmetics depends upon the belief in magic and miracles built up by thousands of years of religious conditioning.

The public buys billions of dollars worth of nostrums a year even though most of them are worthless. For example the government, the universities and the American Medical Association regularly report that there is no cure for the common cold, that nothing is to be gained by normal healthy people from vitamin or mineral supplements, that the effective analgesic in highly advertised super-aspirins is the same salicylic acid found in generic aspirins at a fraction of the price. Yet the public buys $1.8 billion worth of cold remedies alone yearly.

Food manufacturers commonly put out canned goods in two different price ranges whose only difference is in their labels. The higher-priced brand-name can has by heavy advertising been imbued with imaginative superior qualities.

A dozen years ago the major oil companies followed the practice of supplying gasoline to one of their service stations from another oil company's regional storage tanks if they were closer to that service station than their own storage tanks. The oil companies knew there was little if any difference in the gasolines, but the government saw the practice as fraudulent and stopped it.

Many a motorist who swore by Gulf gasoline was consternated to learn that he had been using Shell gasoline and couldn't tell the difference.

It has been averred that the only difference between Smirnoff vodka and many cheaper brands is Smirnoff's bigger advertising budget.

Most food faddists have a strong will to believe that there are some magical foods or diets out there that will make them into supermen.

The Federal Trade Commission had to crack down on the huxters of protein supplements, which had become a food fad. An FTC staff survey concluded: "In short, it is the opinion of the staff that for the vast majority of people, the purchase of these products is a total waste of money."

After the most comprehensive review to date (March, 1989) involving findings on nutrition and health, the National Research Council reported that "megavitamins" and supplements of calcium and fiber are apparently useless in maintaining health and some could be harmful. Yet Americans spent over $3 billion for such stuff in 1988.

All this shows how the will to believe affects our judgment. Advertisers exploit the will to believe by easily convincing consumers that their product is better than a competing product. Once convinced, the consumers will find the tomatoes in the chosen brand much tastier than those of other brands even if the only difference is in the label.

But in cosmetics we find the will to believe — especially in magic — exploited to its utmost. With a few pennies worth of ingredients and $10 worth of advertising, cosmetic manufacturers convince the public sufficiently of the magical properties of a product to pay $15 for it. The cosmetic companies are engaged in selling magic. Women spend $4 billion a year on makeup products. One wonders how much of that $4 billion goes for ingredients, production and distribution and how much goes for advertising appealing to women's Cinderella dreams and fascination with magic.

Consider this Avon appeal to the will to believe in magic:

AVON ANNOUNCES A BIOLOGICAL ADVANCE: NIGHT SUPPORT
A Skin Revitalizing Formula

Five drops are all you need for the most beneficial beauty sleep of your life.

Avon brings you a revolutionary biological advance that actually promotes and accelerates the skin's natural repair process at the cellular level. NIGHT SUPPORT is not a cleanser, not a toner, not a moisturizer or night cream. It is a nighttime skin *energyzer* — a way to a more beautiful you . . . overnight. Just five drops smoothed over face and throat tonight will give your skin a better tomorrow.

Or maybe you would prefer to celebrate spring in magic style with Elizabeth Taylor's Passion and receive a gift:

Embrace the stirrings of the season with the fragrance created for the passion in every woman: Elizabeth Taylor's Passion. And with any purchase from our provocative collection, you'll receive "Royal Majesty: as your gift, while quantities last. It's a glorious celebration of fragrance and body luxuries including a 1 oz. Eau de Toilette Spray and 1.25 oz. Pearlized Dusting Powder. For your purchase, may we suggest: Eau de Toilette Spray, 2.5 oz. $43.00, Perfume, 1/4 oz., $65.00 and Perfumed Body Lotion, 5.25 oz., $30. Also, look for the arrival of two new additions to the Passion collection: Shimmering Liquid Talc, 5.25 oz., $30.00 and an Eau de Parfum Refillable Purse Spray in a custom-designed flacon, 1/2 oz., $60.00.

But not just cosmetics are imbued with magic. Through heavy advertising and promotion the STP Corporation has convinced millions of motorists with a strong will to believe — that STP oil and gasoline additive will give their car superior performance, will put a tiger, or at least a wildcat, into their tank.

But the Federal Trade Commission ordered STP to cease making false and misleading claims. The FTC chairman said he has reason to believe that STP Oil Treatment "is of no significant value to the majority of cars which regularly use the proper grade of oil."

The will to believe sometimes leads to bizarre conclusions. A 29-year-old Ann Arbor Yoga instructor was found dead in his room. There was speculation that he might have died while in a deep self-induced trance that slowed his heart to a point where his brain received too little blood. A spokesman for the Integral Yoga Institute said the instructor may have projected his soul from his body through astral projection. Examination by pathologists showed that he had overdosed on cocaine.

Humans are distinguished from other animals primarily by their superior intelligence. The greatest products of that intelligence have been scientific achievements. One would expect that the unique ability to think, to reason, would be revered, respected and loved above all human attributes. But it doesn't seem to be the case. Too many people hold science in disdain.

The majority of people on Earth dislike science and the other products of the intellect; they prefer the superstitions, supernaturalism, mythology, mysticism and magic of the right brain. Their love is for religion, astrology, witchcraft, palmistry, yoga, pyramid power, psychic phenomena. But, nevertheless, they don't pass up the material goodies produced by science—radio, television, compact disc recorders, VCRs, computers, automobiles, airplanes, automatic washers, microwave ovens. They seek wonder drugs and high-tech surgery that extend their life spans. They enjoy the abundance of food resulting from scientific animal breeding and improved fruits and vegetables. They covet their high wages and affluent living standards attributable almost entirely to science. But they don't love science; they tolerate science for the goodies it produces for them.

They are like a wife who although her husband feeds her and adorns her with furs and jewels sleeps with her paramour.

The will to believe overwhelms all. After 70 years of communist determination to erase religion from the culture of the Soviet Union, religion remains stubbornly intact in the hearts of the majority of Soviet Citizens. Russian satellite Poland is as deeply embedded in Catholicism as ever.

Abominable Islamic fundamentalism, the fastest growing religion in the world today, is sweeping over the Mideast, Africa and Asia.

In our own country, our fastest growing religious sect is the Latter Day Saints, with one of the most fantastic theologies and incredible origins of all the denominations in America.

Atheists despair of humankind when they see that great growth in scientific knowledge is accompanied by concomitant great growth in religious superstition. It seems that the greater our knowledge becomes, the greater our irrationality.

The failure of powerful Marxist governments to eliminate religion casts the feeble efforts of American atheists and humanists into the category of Don Quixotes.

Atheists worldwide have used reason, economic sanctions, political pressure, even terror, but still religion persists. The will to believe overwhelms all. No wonder some atheists have given up on religion as an incurable, chronic disease.

It is interesting to note that in America with its potpourri of religions, switching among religions is common. Not just among Protestant denominations, but between Catholics and Protestants, Christians and Jews, Christians and Islamics, cults and mainstream religions.

Some well-known switchers were John Wayne and Kate Smith to Catholic, Dwight D. Eisenhower to Presbyterian, Charles (Peanuts) Schulz from Lutheran to Church of God, Elizabeth Taylor from Christian Science to Judaism, Mohammed Ali to Muslim, Sammy Davis Jr. to Judaism, guitarist George Benson to Jehovah's Witnesses, Sonny Bono to Scientology, Omar Sharif from Catholic to Muslim, Tina Turner to Buddhism, Abdul-Jabbar from Catholicism to Islam, Clare Booth Luce and Heywood Broun to Catholicism.

The associate director of the national Office of Evangelization reported that 95,000 people in 1985 switched into Catholicism. Religionists will switch from one denomination to another but will not give up religion.

As suggested earlier, the tenacity of religion in the face of the insurmountable adverse facts of science may be attributed to religious instincts, using a loose definition of instinct. We must speak of instincts, however, in the plural because we cannot very well conceive of a religious instinct as a discrete unit, since religion itself is no definite entity. Religious instincts include belief in God and an afterworld, a feeling of righteousness, a need for a transcendental ideal, fear of the supernatural, a sense of the mystical belief in magic, a felt need for a protective guardian and loyal friend, the need to serve and worship a higher being, and many other components.

Even if we look upon religion as a cluster of instincts we still must wonder how instincts develop. Physical attributes evolve from the natural selection of mutations. It is reasonable to believe that instincts evolve in a similar fashion. Religion may be seen in such a light.

Loneliness seems to be a fortifier of religion. Most animals seek companionship as a sexual necessity or because of the need for mutual protection and the advantages of cooperative hunting techniques.

Humans certainly show evidence of a very strong need for companionship, and since such desire is a recurring and persistent thing which cannot once and for all be satisfied, most of us live with an unsatisfied hunger for companionship — a condition we call loneliness.

Gnawing loneliness is not an affliction of only the aged. It seems to be a normal condition of human life.

During the 60s the youth counterculture fought loneliness with drugs, dogs and religion. Being the first generation brought up on television, they were accustomed to instant gratification by pressing a button and turning a dial. But overcoming loneliness through social relationships was not so instant. Drugs were. A high was an immediate escape from gnawing loneliness.

And dogs became popular, the non-discriminating, loving dogs, succor for the desperately lonely.

Then there was religion. The Jesus freaks and the various cultists found in a personal savior what lonely people always have found down through the ages — a trustworthy and compatible friend, because that is the savior that has been created.

Loneliness is surely one of the principle drives behind religions which involve a personal God. Imaginary companionship with a Deity is the only kind which is always available to lonely people for which they do not need to depend upon others.

The prayers and supplications of religious seekers, the imaginings and visions of prophets, the metaphysical and transcendental meditations of philosophers and mystics — all these activities may be just the agonized writhings of loneliness.

The spiritual or emotional void that people try to fill with religion may not be an instinctive need for religion, but a natural loneliness misinterpreted as a need for religion. If it really is a need for religion, it may be more the product of religious nurturing since childhood rather than an instinctual need. After a person has been addicted to religion since childhood, he cannot fare well without it. Heroin addicts, alcoholics and tobacco smokers feel similar voids inside them when deprived of their addictive substance.

Whether religion is instinctive, a hereditary nerve pattern, a product of nurturing or a combination of them, people often find great solace and contentment in religion.

When people feel that they have "found God" and offer testimony to their experience, they are most sincere. They feel they have been redeemed, are now on good terms with God, have been "born again." After years of secular living, they slip back into the niche in harmony with their instincts, their inherited nerve pattern, their childhood nurturing and conditioning. Their newfound harmony they interpret as "finding God."

Such experiences of contentment are a perfectly reasonable phenomenon. The contentment might be compared with the contentment a bird would experience in migrating as compared with the discontent and restlessness of a caged bird unable to migrate.

Contentment results from the harmony between one's life and inherited nerve pattern. The discontentment and vexation of atheists is partly the result of a break from their nerve pattern deeply ingrooved by tens of thousands of generations of superstitious ancestors.

At any rate, we have to be cautious in the use of the term "instinct." Even some behavior characteristics of lower animals generally thought to be instinctive, such as the herding or flocking tendency of sheep, turn out to be adaptations to environmental conditions. In New Zealand the sheep tend to scatter widely since they have no predators in their environment to induce them to flock together for mutual protection, and so an extraordinary number of sheep dogs are needed to round up the sheep on vast open ranges. So much for the herding instinct.

Someday neuroscience will come up with more concrete explanations of religion than my loose speculations and theories. In the meantime we have to live with the conflict between religion and science and choose our side.

I call it a conflict although many wimpish liberals and conciliatory scholars maintain there really is no conflict, a popular Pollyannish view that I suspect comes from the Machiavellian insight of some religionists that it is wise to associate themselves with the exploding wonders of science.

Should the will to believe be encouraged or discouraged? Sincere believers, of course, think the will to believe should be nourished above all.

Many liberal religionists, not too certain about the inerrancy of the Bible or anything else about Christian theology, nevertheless believe that religion is an absolute necessity for civilized society. Moreover, they see the need for religion irrevocably woven into the cultural fabric of our society, and perhaps even woven into our genetic structure.

Atheists, of course, think it is immoral to teach children that any religion is true when, as they believe, all religions are man-made and without a shred of proof. Atheists wonder how a good society is possible erected on a foundation of myths, lies, deceptions and superstitions.

Atheists think truth should be easier to swallow than lies and myths. But it doesn't seem to be so. Their best explanation of the embarrassment is that religion takes advantage of vulnerable, intellectually defenseless children by brainstuffing them. Atheists would like to see children taught truth in the first place rather than be nurtured in superstition and myth. This would spare many children later disillusionment, bitterness and cynicism.

Finally, one might wonder if religion is peculiar to Homo sapiens or if religion would evolve in any intelligent life anywhere in the universe.

One is rightly puzzled by the triumph of religious irrationality over reason and logic down through the centuries. One is puzzled by the belief in medicine men in the face of their general failure to cure, by the belief in prayer and sacrifices to propitiate the gods in view of consistent failure to bring any benefits; by the sadness of Christians over their loved ones' departure to Heaven, by the resolute belief in God without any evidence for His existence acceptable by American judicial standards or that would pass the test of scientific scrutiny.

In relation to the bicameral brain, religion, nurtured by social rewards and moral approval, grows with the development of the right brain into firmly-rooted, pre-rational, a priori assumptions. Because of the separate bicameral nature of the brain, the irrational beliefs of the right brain aren't subjected to review by the rational left brain.

Of course, there are many reasons why an institution like religion, once developed, enjoys the support of society to perpetuate it. By then the establishment, as well as most of the population, has developed a vested interest in its perpetuation.

Mothers and fathers, kings and dictators, politicians and preachers all fear change, especially from the enlightenment of the younger generation, that might adversely affect the status of elders. After all, what has modern literacy and religious freedom done but tear up feudalism, destroy colonialism, bring politicians into disrepute, lower the respect for clergymen and question the impeccability of mothers and the infallibility of fathers!

Mistakenly, most atheists believe that truth will win. This is their blind faith similar to a blind religious faith and every bit as unsupportable as belief in God.

Truth may well be on the side of atheists, but so what? In human affairs truth and justice are seldom winners. Belief that they automatically win is the false faith of atheism. How many more eons must nonbelievers struggle through before discovering the facts of life?

In view of the real world around them, atheists must accept that either truth is impotent and irrelevant or that religionists possess the truth.

The will to believe impels otherwise sensible people to believe in such absurdities as gods, angels, devils, ghosts, Heaven, Hell, souls, apocalypses, Adam and Eve, the Second Coming, the star of Bethlehem, Noah's Ark; it induces people to believe in miracles, which require the suspension of natural law upon which all science is based. The will to believe predisposes people to believe in poltergeists, astrology, palmistry, fortune telling, crystal worship, pyramid power, ESP, mental telepathy, clairvoyance, precognition, astral projection, reincarnation and more.

Most people willingly accept such unfounded beliefs, while in the case of scientific beliefs, they demand irrefutable proof. One puzzles over falsehoods being so eagerly accepted, while truth is accepted so reluctantly.

What if none of science's inventions of the prolific 19th and 20th centuries ever worked, or at the best *only once*. Telegraphs wouldn't work, radios wouldn't play, televisions wouldn't produce pictures, airplanes wouldn't fly, guns wouldn't shoot, cameras wouldn't take pictures, automobiles wouldn't run, antibiotics wouldn't cure diseases, vaccine wouldn't prevent diseases, refrigerators wouldn't freeze, calculators wouldn't give correct answers.

Would the public go on buying them anyhow? That's what the public does with astrology, parapsychology, faith healing, prayers, crystal power and Jean Dixon! No wonder many of us are puzzled.

The Bible writers really stretched their imaginations to come up with the fantastic, bizarre and incredible. But nothing they could think up was beyond the right brain's credulity. A talking snake, an insolent fig tree, parting seas, a flood inundating the Earth under 50 feet of water, a homemade boat that would hold pairs of all the animal species of the world, dead people arising from their graves and parading in the street, God creating light before He made the sun, turning a woman into salt, a cuckling Holy Ghost, a three-headed Deity, a stream of blood as high as a horse's bridle and 200 miles long, a woman made out of a man's rib, the sun and moon standing still on order from Joshua, Samson slaying 200 men with the jawbone of an ass, ad nauseam.

Despite the vivid imaginations of the Bible writers, their wildest fantasies (with the possible exception of John) fall far short of what science has actually produced. Compare the invisible spirits of biblical days with the invisible radio and television signals present in every palace, house and hovel in the world free for the tapping! What is a flaming bush compared with a nuclear bomb capable of destroying New York City!

Well, I must admit that John was one up on the nuclear bomb in his Revelations account of the coming Apocalypse: "Hail and fire mingled with blood appeared, and were hurled upon the earth. One-third of the earth was burned up, one-third of all the trees was burned up, and every blade of green grass was burned up. Something like a vast mountain blazing with fire was thrown into the sea. A third part of the sea turned into blood, a third of all living creatures in the sea died, and a third part of all shipping was destroyed."

To convince people of his divinity, Jesus turned water into wine, raised the dead, put a curse on a fig tree, cured the lame and the blind, walked on water, cast the devil into some pigs. Our own magicians, faith healers and other shysters today could put the pedestrian, amateurish Jesus to shame with their highly sophisticated and polished performances.

Even so, one wonders why Jesus, if really the Lord of infinite power, shuffled around the countryside on a donkey performing purported miracles to convince people He was the son of God. If He had really been the earthly incarnation of the omnipotent God of the universe, would He have had to compete against the sleazy charlatans of his day with tricks and sleight of hand to convince people that He was the Lord God! If He really wanted to convince people, He could have done something more spectacular than turning water into wine. Say, like moving a couple of mountains.

Miracles depend on the violation of natural law and the abrogation of cause and effect logic. Atheists don't accept such a possibility so atheists don't believe in miracles.

Although the left cerebral hemisphere is the locale for the mental functions of reason, logic and linear thinking, each hemisphere seems to have some ability to perform the functions that are predominant for the other hemisphere.

Thus the right brain is capable of what we might call a low order of reason and logic. The right brain begins with conclusions and then searches for evidence to support its conclusions. If evidence doesn't fit, the evidence is ignored. We find abundant illustrations of such weak and skewed logic expressed by religious minds.

Religions from time immemorial have indulged in skewed and undisciplined logic. If a taboo was violated and the next day a windstorm blew down the meeting house, the disaster was attributed to the violation of the taboo. If the windstorm didn't ensue, the priests would find some lesser misfortune to blame on the violation. There were always ample violations of taboos and evil sorcerers to blame misfortunes on.

If rain is prayed for and it rains, the praying is accredited. If it doesn't rain, the explanation is that a witch has interfered with the rain (so an old woman is scourged) or that God is testing their faith or that they are being punished for impiety, sacrilege or infidelity.

Believers wear charms (St. Christophers?) for safety from disaster. If the charm fails to protect them from disaster, they're usually not around to protest its failure.

The news media makes much of cases where a tornado destroys every home and building but the church in a small town. (Usually the church is the only building constructed of solid stone.) What is such skewed logic really saying, that God cares about His house and the hell with the houses of his parishioners? But religionists never seem to think of it that way.

I have an AP wirephoto of the Pilgrims West Baptist Church in Jackson, Tenn., or what was left of it after hit by a tornado. This is a reversal of the usual news media bias. Only a few pews remain standing after the church literally exploded when hit by the tornado. Religious sophists must have experienced considerable chagrin in explaining this one. The Devil did it?

One may search in vain for the logic behind New Hampshire's annual observance of Fast Day. It commemorates the death of John Cutts over 300 years ago. Cutts was chosen by Charles II to be president of the Royal Province of New Hampshire. But shortly afterward, he took ill and a day of fasting and prayer for his recovery was declared by the Colonial Assembly. But Cutts died three weeks later. Apparently, New Hampshire annually celebrates the failure of prayer.

Faith healers are generally accredited with a small number of successes resulting from the psychosomatic emotional effects of the experience, but hardly enough successes to balance the damage done by such charlatans in dissuading supplicants from seeking legitimate medical help, by traumatic disappointment of the incurable, by swindling sick people with false assurances.

A remarkable phenomenon of faith healing has taken place during the past 15 years in Poland. A Canadian faith healer named Clive Harris became famous in that solidly Catholic country by conducting twice-yearly healing sessions in Church refectories.

Harris started out small, but in a few years his supplicants grew to 30,000 a day. Thousands waited in the bitter cold as long as five hours for that moment when they would file quickly past Harris for the touch of his hand.

Faith healing in that form was new to Poland, but struck a responsive chord. It seemed a misfit in a society that is a mixture of atheism and

NOAH'S SACRIFICE AFTER THE FLOOD.

Catholicism. In the course of several weeks' stay that took him to all major cities, Harris touched as many as 450,000 persons.

People offer various theories about Harris's purported powers: that his fingers emit radioactive rays, that he employs biomagnetism, that the effects are merely psychosomatic.

Does anybody still believe that the communists will root religion and superstition out of Poland!

Religionists are adept at crediting God with the accomplishments of science. They prefer crediting the hand of God rather than the hand of the surgeon for the healing of a sick child. They pray to get well, and when wonder drugs make them well, they thank God instead of medical science.

The first Morse code was transmitted by Samuel F. B. Morse 150 years ago. Not surprising, Morse credited God with his invention of the telegraph: "What hath God wrought?" tapped Morse for his first telegraph message.

Since then God hath been so busy wroughting that telephones, radio transmission, microwave, FAX and satellite systems have replaced the telegraph.

Religionists, relying on their right brains, fall victims to weak, skewed and convoluted reasoning. A social worker related the story of an un- employed Jewish taylor during the Depression. The man had a large family and the usual accompaniment of illness. He was relating his financial distress to the social worker when his face suddenly brightened. "We know," he said, "with all our trials, that the Lord has not forsaken us, for we are going to have another baby."

In Seattle the pilot of "God's Balloon" during a promotional flight for a Christian radio station drifted into the radio tower leaving him dangling helplessly in the gondola. Involved in the ensuing rescue were the coast guard, state patrol, county police and the fire department. After the rescue a witness was quoted as saying: "The lord was watching him."

If the Lord was watching him, why did the omnipotent Lord not shift the winds a little so the Christian balloonist would miss the radio tower? What ingratitude that the Lord would stand by and watch him get perilously tangled with the radio tower when the balloonist was doing a promotion job for the Lord Himself!

Nevertheless, God was credited with saving the life of the balloonist.

When a small plane carrying Mother Teresa skidded into a crowd of well-wishers in Tanzania, two young boys and three adults, including a nun, were killed. Mother Teresa called the accident "the will of God." The cause could have been a slippery runway or pilot error, but Mother Teresa put the blame on God. Christian logic is often baffling.

Nine people were crushed to death and about 60 were injured in a stampede to see Pope John Paul II when he made an address in Kinshasa, Zaire.

Two months later in Fortaleza, Brazil, a similar stampede to see the Pope took place in the early morning darkness at a soccer stadium. Three people were trampled to death and more than 30 were injured.

A mother and her young daughter there for a glimpse of John Paul described their ordeal: "We had arrived early hoping to get to our seats quietly before all the others. . . . A guard slid open a gate and then tried to shut it again. It was too late. Everybody surged forward. Lots of people were pushed to the ground and the others just climbed over them."

The lady concluded: "I know the Pope saved me. It was a miracle." But what about the three killed and the 30 injured? Maybe they were sinners. And how about giving God a little credit for saving her and her daughter? Actually, the Pope was partly to blame for not having enough security police there to control the crowd of 100,000 worshipers who had come to see him. But such is Christian logic.

At the holy city of Mecca, 52,000 Moslem pilgrims were gathered to celebrate the feast of Id Al-Adh marking Abraham's sacrifice of the lamb on nearby Mt. Arafat, when a fire broke out burning to death 138 of the pilgrims.

One can only speculate about skewed Moslem logic. No doubt some blamed the fire marshal, or Mohammed, or Allah, or Abraham. Would they blame Allah for the deaths of these good Islamic pilgrims who traveled from far and wide to worship at His prophet's shrine? Or would they thank Allah that only 138 out of 52,000 pilgrims died?

At Sao Paulo, Brazil 176 persons perished when a 25-story bank building was ravished by fire. Many caught in the upper floors jumped to their deaths. The AP report spoke of a Roman Catholic priest on the street raising a rosary toward people in the burning building and crying: "My children, don't jump! God is with you." God apparently wasn't with the 176 who perished.

In Toccoa, Georgia, a dam broke and flooded the Toccoa Falls Bible College, killing 37 persons. After the tragedy a common chant was heard among the survivors, "We still believe in the goodness of God."

One student who had lost several friends in the flood stated emphatically that there was no way his faith had been undermined. "The Lord has me in his hands. I don't know why the Lord has spared me, . . . but the Lord had a purpose in all of this, . . . the glory still goes to God."

Another student referred to the dean of men, who three times nearly lost his two children in the flood: "Three times he lost his children, a little boy and a girl, but he got them back. Praise the Lord."

Other students granted that the flood was God's will and hard to accept because they couldn't understand it.

One student quoted Romans 8:28: "And we know that all things work together for good to them that love God, to them who are called, according to his purpose."

In an interview with two couples who survived the runway crash between a KLM Boeing 747 and a Pan Am 747 in the Canary Islands which killed a total of 577 persons, one of the wives said: "The Bible says there's a time to live and a time to die, and it just wasn't our time to die. We praise the Lord we were able to escape."

The wife of the other couple reflected: "When I think of all those hundreds who died and why we are alive, I just say "thank you, Lord, thank you, Lord."

Did the Lord really deserve any thanks when he allowed 577 innocent people to be killed?

Supplying logic to God's mysterious ways is certainly a task beyond the ability of either cerebral hemisphere. Were the 12 million Jews, Poles and Gypsies killed by the Nazis guilty of mortal sin? Were the 20 million killed under the Stalin dictatorship part of God's plan of punishment?

What were the millions of Chinese executed under Chairman Mao's regime guilty of? Or the million Cambodians killed by the Khmer Rouge? Or the estimated 800,000 Chinese victims of the Japanese atrocities committed at Nanking?

How to explain the drowning of 1500 persons in 1987 aboard a passenger ship and tanker that collided south of Manila? The 1700 people killed by poisonous gas expelled by Lake Nios in the Cameroons? The 242,000 who died in an earthquake that destroyed Tangshan, China in 1976? The 1985 Mexico City earthquake that killed 25,000 people?

How explain the 1974 Honduras Hurricane Fifi that left 8,000 dead and 100,000 homeless? The 1988 Bangladesh flood that submerged three-quarters of the nation and left over a thousand dead?

Religionists who believe that God controls and intervenes in nature and human affairs (and that includes everyone who believes the efficacy of prayer) have a big job explaining the mysterious ways of their just God.

Atheists believe that millions of years of superstitions have mired the right brain in a sea of irrationality; bent it, polluted it, compromised it, imprisoned it, crippled it, infected it, truncated it. One can hardly expect much sense from such an impaired brain.

The admitted frauds and miracles promoted by religion have added to the pollution. About 20 years ago the Vatican did some reshuffling of its saints to give them a more universal appeal. In doing so, the Church cast serious doubt that 46 of its saints had ever existed at all, citing "grave historical difficulties" of proof, and dropped them.

Of course, when atheists speak of the frauds of religion they are speaking of the whole caboodle, lock stock and barrel.

Thomas Moore succinctly expressed his view of religion in his "Veiled Prophet":

> Yes, too, believers of incredible creeds,
> Whose faith enshrines the monsters which it breeds;

> Who, bolder even than Nimrod, think to rise,
> By nonsense heaped on nonsense, to the skies,
> Ye shall have miracles, ay, sound ones too,
> Seen, heard, attested, everything — but True.

Our society, nurtured in religion and superstition, is wont to embrace every fraud that comes down the pike: crystal worship, channeling, reducing diets, food fads, flying saucers, weeping Marys. Surrounded by scientific inventions a thousand times more fantastic than the Bible writers could even imagine, most people are still looking for magic and miracles.

Many health-seekers reject the advice of scientific professional nutritionists and medical doctors with their six to eight years of university training in favor of the advice of ignorant gurus who haven't been through the sixth grade of grammar school.

Lottery players buy dream books to help them pick the winning lottery number, palmists are still being paid for stock market advice (it's probably as good as that of professional advisers in an efficient market), astrologers are sought for advice even by one of our First Ladies.

The will to believe is probably greatly reinforced by the implications of not believing.

Not believing means acknowledging that human beings have been the victims for thousands of years of the monstrous fraud of religion. Not believing means acknowledging that Heaven is a myth, Hell the dream of sadistic brutes, the Bible a compilation of lies and forgeries, and Pope John Paul II the head of a worldwide parasitic hoax. Not believing means acknowledging that the Eucharist is gruesome symbolic cannibalism, the Jews are afflicted with delusions of grandeur believing to be God's chosen people, all holy men and women are witting or unwitting criminals promoting an enormous con game. Not believing means acknowledging that souls, spirits, ghosts, angels, demons and redeemers are all right-brained inventions and fabrications infesting the minds of 95 percent of the people of the world.

Not believing means acknowledging that the killing of hundreds of millions of human beings in religious wars down through history was a ghastly mistake; that the hundreds of thousands of people tortured, beheaded, burned alive, mutilated and imprisoned for religious reasons were the result of disputes over bogus gods; that the Christian Crusades resulting in the horrible deaths of millions of Christians and Saracens in a search for a non-existing Holy Grail illustrated what fools religion makes of people.

Not believing means acknowledging that the Hindus and Sikhs, the

Irish Catholics and Ulster Protestants, the Armenian Christians and Islamic Azerbaijanis, the Israeli Jews and Palestinians, the Lebanese Christians and Shiite Moslems are today shooting, stabbing and bombing one another over religions that are hoaxes, shams and frauds from the beginning.

JOSHUA COMMANDING THE SUN TO STAND STILL.

Chapter VIII
CULTS AND NEW AGE RELIGIONS

There have always been cults. All religions, including Christianity (a cult of Judaism), started as cults. When they started they were the New Age religions of their day. The new cults of the latter part of the 19th century were called New Thought.

Throughout history cults have sprung up by the thousands, most of them short-lived. Among the relatively few that have survived, the less successful are still thought of as cults while the more successful have become our established religions and denominations. Many cults were brought to America by immigrants, others introduced by gurus from Asia, others native-born.

Cults are often spinoffs from old established religions. Being unorthodox and rebellious, cults ask for the role of persecuted minority. Such a role inspires the characteristics of zealotry and loyalty. Cults become aggressive seekers for converts because from their early days they face the imperative to proselytize or perish.

Cults are generally started by charismatic leaders, the cult soon becoming as much a devotion to the leader as to the new theology. An ambitious person thirsting for power, recognition, fame and fortune faces the choice of studying many years in a dreary seminary followed by a lifetime struggle to reach the top of the crowded hierarchy of a mainstream church or starting a new religion of his own, in which he *starts* at the top.

Among past and present cult leader-originators were Jesus Christ, Mohammed, Martin Luther, John Calvin, Joseph Smith, Mary Baker Eddy, Charles Taze Russell, Mrs. Ellen White, Maharishi Mahesh Yoga, Sun Myung Moon, David Berg, Bhagwan Shree Rajneesh, L. Ron Hubbard and Jim Jones.

There must be a widespread spiritual discontentment among religionists that explains their constant search for new religious devotions, a search that renders them easy prey for every charlatan coming down the pike with a newfangled faith, however irrational and bizarre.

Often atheists, rationalists and humanists play a part in disillusioning people with Christianity. It must be discouraging for them to then see such people turn to unorthodox cults, New-age religions, astrology, witchcraft, channeling or parapsychology. It's like after rescuing a child from drowning in a lake to see the child run off and jump into a river.

Take away his Christ and he worships Buddha; take away his Christian mysticism and he turns to parapsychology; take away his angels and he looks heavenward for flying saucers; take away his crucifixes and he worships crystals; take away his Bible and he reads Shirley MacLaine.

One may view this phenomenon of switching to flying saucers or parapsychology by former religionists as a symptom of the disease. Something like a leather fetishist switching to rubber.

Some of today's newer religions, such as Religious Science, Unity and those centered around channeling and crystal worship are grouped under the name "New Age" religions. However, their theologies vary greatly; some employ the power of religion as an aid to achieve health, wealth and happiness; some are oriented toward the monism of Eastern religions; others are involved in channeling, crystal worship, reincarnation and the blending of parapsychology and spiritualism.

The decline in membership of most of the mainstream religions has been due partly to the growth of cults and New Age religions. The result has been a constant flow of congregants from the mainstream churches to their new competitors. The world beats a path to the religion that best fulfills people's needs.

The preachers of traditional churches make labored, dry, thoughtful appeals while their competitors combine emotionalism with new theological grotesqueries in an overwhelming appeal to the right brain. And the humanists and atheists with their narrow intellectual appeal, are left in the dust.

SEASONED CULTS

MORMONS

The Church of Jesus Christ of Latter Day Saints (Mormons) is one of the early spinoffs from the Christian religion in this country. The cult was founded by Joseph Smith, an upstate New York farmhand.

Smith grew up in a rural area of belligerent Protestants whose religious quarrels resulted in so many burned-down churches, houses and barns as to earn them the epithet "the burned-over district."

In such an environment, Joseph Smith naturally developed an intense concern for religion. While still a boy, Joseph was approached out in the woods one day by God and Jesus standing above him in the air. God told the boy that all the churches were wrong and an abomination in His sight.

Joseph's family accepted his vision but the community scoffed at it. He continued working in the area as a farmhand. When 18, Joseph had another vision. This time the angel Moroni appeared and told him about a book written on gold tablets hidden on a hilltop near Joseph's house at Palmyra. But Joseph was not to remove the tablets for four years.

When the time came Joseph dug up the gold tablets and took them home and by some magic deciphered the hieroglyphics into English. The translation became *The Book of Mormon*, a complement of the Bible.

The book recounts Mormon history from 600 B.C. to 421 A.D. in which a small group of Hebrews sailed to America, were later visited by Jesus Christ and eventually split into two warring factions. The one faction (ancestors of American Indians) annihilated the other faction. A few survivors of the defeated group buried the gold tablets that Joe Smith dug up 14 centuries later.

Hearing about Smith's gold tablets, shysters tried to get their hands on them. They searched the Smith home and ransacked it. But Smith had done a good job of hiding the tablets.

In 1830 Smith had translated the gold tablets and had *The Book of Mormon* printed. By then he had a motley following whom he formed into a church. Through proselytizing, baptizing and performance of healing miracles by Smith, the church grew rapidly. But not tranquilly. Other churches resented the Mormons, and a pattern of persecution began that soon resulted in numerous arrests of the Mormons and threats of mob violence.

There was even a case of deprogramming in which a Presbyterian minister attempted to abduct a young woman sympathetic to the Mormons and prevent her conversion. But the attempt failed.

Taking their cue from Smith, many other Latter Day Saints began having visions and revelations. To stop such a divisive plethora of revelations (some contrary to Smith's), Smith put an end to the revelation frenzy by receiving a revelation himself that instructed the church that only Smith's revelations were genuine.

To escape persecution, Smith moved his flock from the East to the more hospitable location of Kirkland, Ohio. Later they migrated to Independence, Missouri to found their New Zion.

But anti-Mormon resentment grew in Missouri. Armed clashes between Mormons, mobs, police and state troops were frequent.

The governor proclaimed: "The Mormons must be treated as enemies and must be exterminated or driven from the state, if necessary, for the public good."

There were twelve thousand well-armed Mormons in Missouri. A war ensued. Smith and other leaders were captured and sentenced to be shot, but the order was never carried out.

Smith gave up on Independence and moved his headquarters to Commerce, Illinois, renamed Nauvoo by the Mormons. In seven years the Mormons built Nauvoo into a major city. But Nauvoo turned out to be no Shangri-la. Adding to the harassment by non-Mormons in the area was the church's internal disorder and factionalism. Smith's revelation allowing "plural marriages" didn't help matters any.

Finally, the situation in Nauvoo became intolerable. Smith was charged with several offenses, among them an attempt to shut down a newspaper published by a rival Mormon group.

Hostile citizens in Nauvoo and the surrounding countryside vowed to drive out the Saints. The governor had Smith arrested and jailed. The next day a mob broke into the jail and murdered Joseph Smith and his brother Hyrum.

With Joseph Smith dead, the Mormon battle over his successor was furious and divisive. It split the Mormons into several different factions still extant today. The most successful faction, led by Brigham Young, eventually migrated to the valley of Salt Lake, Utah. There the Mormons built their famous tabernacle around which grew Salt Lake City.

The main theological theme promulgated by founder Joseph smith is that the original Christian church was perverted by the Roman Catholic Church, which built its power through totalitarian devices such as the brutal Inquisition to stifle dissenters and the sale of indulgences and granting of patronage to gain supporters. According to Mormons, the Protestant revolt was an attempt to *reform* the Church. But the Mormons have gone a step further: they have purportedly *restored* the original Christian Church of Jesus.

Most Mormons believe in the Second Coming of Christ, the gift of tongues, baptism, faith healing, continuing prophecy, visions, resurrections of the dead, continuation of marriage in the afterworld.

But Mormons are best known for their early practice of polygamy, a practice that kept them embroiled with neighbors and the legal authorities until they finally gave it up.

Brigham Young, who led the main branch of the Church after Smith was murdered, practiced polygamy, having 17 wives and 47 children. Young based his authority for polygamy on a revelation Joseph Smith had from God advocating plural marriages. (Joe purportedly had 27 wives.) Plural marriages generally meant one man with a harem of wives. History is sprinkled with cults and religions whose male god has sanctioned the males who created him to have all the women their lustful hearts desired, even if the Mormon elders in Utah did admonish their followers that polygamy was not meant to "gratify the carnal lusts and feelings of men," but to be practiced in holiness.

But a small dissident group of Joseph Smith's descendants say it ain't so — Joe Smith never practiced nor advocated polygamy and there is no authentic document proving he did.

All that controversy notwithstanding, the Latter Day Saints are one of the fastest growing sects in America and have surpassed the Presbyterians and the Episcopalians.

The Mormons have a strong appeal to the right brain (could the left brain swallow Smith's story?), and they draw to their religion the lonely and alienated with an offer of group mutual security and a convincing dedication to caring. They emphasize family values, entrepreneurism and morality that includes specific rules of health.

Mormons have an organizational framework that strongly encourages socialization among the members. The Mormons also have going for them taboos against alcohol, tobacco, coffee and even Coca Cola. These taboos confront Mormons daily, keeping them constantly reminded that they are Mormons. This not only builds up their religious consciousness, but reinforces the feeling that they are different (better).

Mormonism is just more evidence that the coprophagous right brain doesn't care how absurd, ridiculous, patently fraudulent, irrational, contrary to reason and totally without proof a religion may be, it can enlist the enthusiastic support, belief, commitment and faith of millions of people even in a supposedly enlightened nation like America.

JEHOVAH'S WITNESSES

The Jehovah's Witnesses were earlier known as Russellites after their founder, Charles Taze Russell, an Allegheny, Pennsylvania haberdasher. Their official name is the Watchtower Bible and Tract Society. They are one of the fastest-growing sects in the world; only about a third of Witnesses are in the United States. Their phenomenal growth is largely a result of their zeal for evangelism.

The Witnesses are a spinoff from Christianity but have a distinct theology of their own. They believe in imminent doomsday. They regard the Bible as the infallible word of God, but call their God only by the name Jehovah. They do not believe in Hell, but they believe in a Heaven reserved solely for 144,000 elite Witnesses selected by God for that prestigious penthouse.

The Battle of; Armageddon between the forces of God (Jehovah's Witnesses) and the forces of Satan (the rest of us) "will make atomic explosions look like firecrackers." (They've been reading Revelations.) The only survivors will be Jehovah's Witnesses, who, after cleaning up the toxic ashes and burying the dead, will enjoy a trouble-free eternal life on Earth.

The Jehovah's Witnesses, unlike the Mormons, who are highly patriotic, have brought considerable denunciation upon themselves by their disrespect for government — such as their refusal to salute the flag or pledge allegiance. This attitude is based on their belief that governments are tools of Satan. (Many libertarians would agree.)

The approach of Jehovah's Witnesses to religion is a kind of pseudo-intellectual one. They go in for carefully analyzing the Bible and coming up with strictly Jehovah's Witness interpretations and conclusions. They deal heavily with biblical arithmetic, from which they predict future events, particularly the time for the return of Christ and the ensuing Armageddon. Such intellectualizing goes on in the right brain of Jehovah's Witnesses, where logic is weak and skewed, where evidence that doesn't accord with preconceptions is ignored, where scientific discipline is unknown.

Founder Russell accepted the earlier prediction by Second Adventist William Miller that Christ would return in 1844. But 1844 came and went and no Christ. Russell then studied the Bible again and came up with 1874 as the year for the Second Coming. But nothing happened in 1874 — so back to the drawing board. This time Russell came up with 1914. The Jehovah's Witnesses were certain that 1914 was the right year; but it too came and went with no appearance of Jesus and no explosions that would make atomic bombs look like firecrackers.

With the embarrassment of striking out a third time, the Witnesses came up with the explanation that the Second Coming really did happen in 1914. Jesus was around but hadn't revealed himself and hadn't yet started up the pyrotechnics. Witness theologians explained that 1914 only marked the beginning of an invisible struggle in Heaven which will culminate in the fiery battle of Armageddon on Earth — any day now.

After Russell's death in 1916, Judge Joseph F. Rutherford became head of the Witnesses. He prophesied that "millions of Jehovah's Witnesses now living will never die." That prophecy has fallen short, too. There aren't a million Witnesses alive today who were living at the time of Rutherford's prophecy.

The attempts by the Jehovah's Witnesses to predict the time of Armageddon seem a bit strange in view of Matthew 24:36 where Jesus says of the time of His Second Coming: "But of that day and hour knoweth no man, no, not the angels of heaven, but my Father only."

But then, this was the same Jesus who told people that He would return and Armageddon would transpire during the lifetime of His listeners.

Rutherford reigned during the First World War, and because Witnesses believed worldly governments were more Satanic than Christian, Witnesses refused to support the war effort. Rutherford and seven other Witnesses were arrested and jailed on various charges relating to their disloyalty to the United States. Rutherford received eighty years, but all were released at the end of the war.

The cult grew even more rapidly after the war. The Witnesses went in heavily on publishing and distributing Witness literature, and began broadcasting worldwide over radio, owning as many as six of the broadcasting stations. But legal pressure brought against them, mainly by the Roman Catholic Church, resulted in their withdrawal from radio broadcasting.

The Jehovah's Witnesses seem to bring on the wrath of mainline churches; in fact, the wrath of the public at large. It is probably due to their aggressive, obtrusive proselytizing and to their elitist stance: they are the anointed emissaries of God out to save the rest of us, who are dupes of Satan.

Every period of history appears to its contemporaries as the final days — with its wars, floods, earthquakes, famines, revolutions, rampant crime, sexual sin, political corruption and breakdown of morality. Today we can add acid rain, pollution, deforestation, nuclear accidents, mutual assured destruction, ozone depletion and international terrorism.

It is easy to persuade frightened, insecure people that doomsday is imminent. Cults exploit the public's apprehensions with offers to save people from the worst of the coming holocaust.

Millenarians are still at it. Edgar Whisenant, a retired NASA rocket engineer from Arkansas, published a book (4.5 million copies) in which he prophesied the Second Coming of Christ for September, 1988.

When Christ failed to show up, Whisenant wrote another book, *The Final Shout: Rapture Report — 1989*, explaining that he was off a year because he overlooked the fact that the calendar counts only 99 years in the first century. So Whisenant moved the new end date ahead to September, 1989. Whisenant said he was 99 percent certain.

At that time, according to Whisenant, 40 million born-again Christians will undergo an instantaneous chemical body change, their new bodies able to appear and disappear and pass through walls.

I can neither affirm nor refute this prediction because I am not a born-again Christian. But surely there are enough born-again Christians in our prisons to have solved the overcrowding, but the problem continues to worsen. I must conclude that Whisenant is a false prophet.

CHRISTIAN SCIENCE

Mary Baker Eddy, the cult leader-originator of Christian Science was born Mary Morse Baker in rural New Hampshire in 1821.

Her fantastic unbelievable life full of tragedy, sorrow, betrayal, invalidism, failure and finally fragile success was as much the result of her religious ideas as the molder of them. She was the sole originator of Christian Science, the author of its bible, *Science and Health*, and the driving spirit behind the greatest faith-healing movement in history.

Mary was one of seven children of a Congregationalist couple. Her father was a hard-shelled, authoritarian predestinationist who had little sympathy for Mary, a near-invalid who spent most of her time at home in a rocking chair reading the Bible and listening to voices. She suffered from "nervous ailments" and from a spinal condition that prevented her from regular school attendance. But with the tutoring help of her brothers and sisters and some formal schooling, she attained literacy and even became a skilled published writer.

Mary's strong compassion, which led her to hope for everybody's salvation, was in conflict with her father's belief in the selective grace of predestination.

After a courtship primarily by correspondence with a South Carolina gentleman of some means, Mary accepted his proposal of marriage and began a new chapter in her life at age 22 by becoming a Southern lady of leisure. But it was an unhappy marriage marred by Mary's strong compassion, which led her to sympathize with the movement to free the slaves, an affront to her Southern-reared (or Southern-bred) husband. Then a year later Mr. Grover died of yellow fever.

Mary returned home, six-months pregnant with George. Because of her feeble health and the grief from her husband's death, Mary gave up for the time the care of her son to a local nurse.

Five years later Mary's mother died and her father remarried the next year. The stepmother didn't want Mary or her son. Mary retrieved George from the nurse and moved in with one of her sisters. But the sister's husband didn't want the boy around so Mary returned George to the nurse.

Mary became more and more absorbed with religion and had more problems with spinal weakness and nervous ailments. But she apparently appealed strongly to men despite her fragility (or because of it); she soon married a second time. Her new husband, Dr. Daniel Patterson, was a dental surgeon. He had promised to take George into his home, but later changed his mind.

While living with Patterson, Mary renewed her interest in the emancipation of slaves and wrote numerous articles on it for a local newspaper.

Eventually, son George at age 16 was forcibly taken away from his mother and sent away to Minnesota to live. Mary's explanation of the separation in her autobiography was that "a plot was consummated for keeping us apart."

In time the dashing, dapper Dr. Patterson grew tired of Mary and began engaging in extra-marital affairs.

Mary began experimenting with freak diets, esoteric religions, spiritualism and hypnotism to restore her health, for she was still a near invalid.

Then Mary Baker Patterson met Phineas P. Quimby, a charismatic charlatan, magnetic healer and hypnotist. She went to Portland to visit him with the hope that he could cure her. After one session with him she claimed she was cured. She stayed on in Portland for three weeks, visiting Quimby daily. He had a profound effect on Mary's life and thought.

After she returned home she had a partial relapse and visited Quimby again. She continued to correspond with him until he died five years later.

Shortly after recovering from the news of Quimby's death, Mary fell on an icy sidewalk in Lynn, Massachusetts and was knocked unconscious. She was carried to a house nearby and visited by a Dr. Cushing. His diagnosis was "concussion of the brain and spinal dislocation with prolonged unconsciousness and spasmodic seizures." She remained unconscious all night. In the morning she was semi-conscious and Dr. Cushing carried her by sleigh to her home in Swampscott.

She remained in bed, cared for by her friends, who believed she surely was going to die. But on Sunday (significantly the third day after her accident), Mary asked her friends to leave the bedroom. Mary said she wanted to be alone with her Bible. Her friends despairingly left the bedroom, feeling that this was the end.

But with proper supplication a miracle of divine intervention instantly healed Mary. She arose, dressed and walked out into the parlor to the astonishment of all. She had arisen on the third day as Jesus had.

This was the culmination of all those years of study of the Bible. She attributed her healing to following the method of Jesus Christ. Mary Baker Patterson had now mastered the secret of divine healing. Eureka!

Not long after Mary's remarkable healing, Dr. Patterson ran off with a female patient. The husband of the patient with the help of a policeman found his wife and took her home. According to Mary's autobiography, Dr. Patterson was properly punished for his despicable act of deserting his wife, for thereafter Patterson wandered about New England, lost his medical practice and finally died in the poorhouse.

In the meantime, Mary obtained a divorce and began living in boarding houses. She survived on a meager two hundred dollars that Dr. Patterson sent her.

At the boarding houses she told about her cure and about her new science of healing. She explained that sickness, disease and death are "the false testimony of false material sense, of mind in matter."

Mary not only preached her healing science, but practiced it on the boarders and neighbors. She cured a small boy of brain fever, she cured a man of acute constipation. She cured a consumptive, she restored sanity to a madman, she restored to physical wholeness a teamster who had been crushed by a wagon.

Mary acquired a reputation in the Lynn area as a new kind of faith healer. But her success was slow and laborious. It was ten years before she had accumulated enough money from her healing to buy a house in Lynn. She hung out a sign "Christian Scientists' Home." That was the formal beginning of her movement. She was then 54 years old. She published her book *Science and Health* the same year.

Two years later she married one of her pupils, Asa Gilbert Eddy. She continued to gain followers and to build up her reputation as a healer. It is interesting to note that Mary's original intent was to work through the established churches, but she found she was not welcome by them, so she established her own church.

Mr. Eddy died after five years of marriage, but Mrs. Eddy continued with her fast-growing organization that was expanding nationwide. She now ran a college for practitioners, charging them an exorbitant fee of three hundred dollars for a three-week course. In today's money that would be about six thousand dollars.

But the road of Christian Science leader was a rocky one. Dissidents challenged her authority and her doctrines. Law suits were threatened and attempts were made to oust Mrs. Eddy. But she hung in there.

Before Mr. Eddy died she had called in a doctor at the last moment. This indicated that Mrs. Eddy had lost her faith in Christian Science and damaged her reputation.

As the years came upon her, Mrs. Eddy gradually retired from control of the Church. She suffered more ill health in her old age.

Even with only a sickly, nervously-impaired body to start with, Mrs. Eddy outlived most of her detractors, critics and competitors, so there must have been something to her science of health ideas.

Mrs. Eddy possessed an intuitive mastery of human gullibility combined with superb business acumen. Her will indicated she had acquired an estate of two million dollars, in today's dollars about 40 million.

A rival, Mrs. Josephine Curtis Woodbury, wrote an article in 1899 entitled "Quimbyism, or the Paternity of Christian Science" in which Woodbury said of Mrs. Eddy: "What she has really 'discovered' are ways and means of perverting and prostituting the science of healing to her own ecclesiastical aggrandizement, and to the moral and physical depravity of her dupes."

But what was Mrs. Eddy's opinion of Mrs. Eddy? In a 1910 letter she wrote: "Jesus was called Christ, only in the sense that you say, a Godlike man. I am only a Godlike woman, God-anointed, and I have done a lot of work that none others could do."

Mrs. Eddy fared much better than the men in her life. Her first husband died in less than a year; her second husband, whom she divorced, ended dying in the poorhouse; her friend and collaborator Quimby died after a five year acquaintance; her third husband died after five years. But Mrs. Eddy went on to celebrate her 90th birthday.

Today, Christian Science is slowly declining. Does it need another valetudinarian, an invalid suffering from nervous ailments and spinal condition?

SEVENTH DAY ADVENTISTS

The millennium movement inspired by Revelations has pulsated sporadically since the beginning of Christianity. In fact Jesus led his followers to believe that the millennium would arrive in their lifetime. Briefly, the millennium is the thousand-year period of peace to follow Christ's return to Earth.

The temptation to prophesy the time of Christ's advent seems to have been irresistible to the self-deluded and to charlatans. In the 17th century millennialism pulsated strongly in Europe and twenty thousand peasants burned themselves alive in anticipation of the Second Coming.

Millennialism swept America in the early 19th century, with various dates predicting the return of Jesus. Even the mainline churches joined in the fandango.

A young farmer, William Miller, became famous for his prediction that the Second Coming would occur between March 11, 1843 and March 21, 1844. Miller calculated the time from the Bible. Believers moved to the tops of mountains to be the first to greet Jesus as He descended from Heaven.

But Jesus failed to appear in accord with the predictions, as He had dozens of times before. The failure this time became known as the "Great Disappointment." Miller was excommunicated from his church and died five years later, glum and woebegone.

But Millennialists are not easily discouraged. One Millerite, Ellen Gould Harmon, continued to promote the Second Coming, maintaining that the problem had been merely one of miscalculation. She explained that Christ's tardiness was due to the time it was taking Him for investigative judgments of individuals in preparation for His return. Even an omniscient, omnipotent God needs a little time to investigate the lives of everybody on Earth.

Ellen had many visions and talked with angels. She gathered together new groups of millennialists. She married a fellow millennialist, James White, and became Ellen Gould White, the matriarch of today's Seventh Day Adventists.

Ellen Gould White was remarkably similar in many ways to Mary Baker Eddy. Ellen also as a teenager was in poor health and "in constant bodily suffering, and to all appearances had but a short time to live." Nevertheless, she lived to be 88, just two years short of Mary Baker Eddy.

Seventh Day Adventists believe they have a duty to warn humankind that the end of the world is at hand. They send about 40,000 missionaries abroad, preaching millennialism in over five hundred languages.

Adventists are known for their Saturday Sabbath, health discipline, missions, vegetarianism, medical colleges and hospitals, and the expectation of the imminent coming of Christ.

The Adventists, similarly to the Mormons, appeal to the lonely, the alienated and offer the security of a caring minority group. They also have stringent health rules which, along with their Sabbath Saturday, keep Adventists constantly conscious of being Adventists, a consciousness that grows deeper daily.

Recently an Adventist brouhaha raged among the members over the question of Mrs. White's plagiarism, some maintaining that most of her writing was copied from others. But she had become so idolized by the Church that critics of her risked being defrocked. Several of them were.

The curious thing about millennialism is that many modern-day biblical scholars don't believe in it. They say that Jesus never promised to return and usher in a new age, a millennium. The Second Coming was fabricated by later followers and the Gospel writers. Millennialists argue over when Christ is going to return, when apparently He has no intention of returning—and nobody can blame Him for that.

FAITH HEALERS

Obviously, if faith healing really worked we would need only enough doctors and hospitals to accommodate atheists and other people God didn't care about. We wouldn't need to spend billions of dollars on medical colleges, hospitals, pharmaceutical manufacture and health insurance.

There is an irony in faith-healer Oral Roberts' building a multi-million dollar hospital when he can cure people merely by the laying on of hands.

Atheists, of course, grant the possibility of an occasional cure of an illness by the psychosomatic effect of the laying on of hands, but believe that such cases are inconsequently rare.

If actual healing by faith were not extremely rare, the charlatans who operate the racket would not have to resort to deception and trickery to delude the public into believing in it. All too many faith healers have been exposed as common charlatans exploiting the hopes of the incurable and terminally ill.

Investigators discovered that one notorious faith healer, Peter Popoff, carried a radio receiver in his left ear during his healing services. From the pulpit he would hold forth a half hour giving names, addresses, illnesses and other information gathered by his wife before the show and now broadcast to him from back stage. Giving the audience the impression through facial gestures and tone of voice that he was receiving the information directly from God, Popoff readily won the trust and confidence of the faithful, who were there in the first place because of their will to believe. The electronic swindle helped Popoff rake in millions of dollars a year.

James Randi, a magician dedicated to exposing the false claims of magicians, faith healers and paranormals, teamed up with Joe Barnhart, a professor of philosophy at the University of North Texas, to investigate the performance of faith healer W. V. Grant.

They discovered that the wheel-chaired people in the healing line were not crippled and had received their wheel chairs beforehand from the Grant organization.

As Grant moved down the healing line and healed the phony, chair-ridden cripples, they stepped out of their wheel chairs to the amazement of the audience and walked up and down the aisle to demonstrate the power of divine healing.

The investigators were puzzled why these seemingly sincere people, without pay, would willingly participate in such a fraud. After interrogating a number of them, the investigators concluded that the wheelchair participants saw themselves as heroes and heroines in a holy drama designed for good purposes: to increase the faith of the audience and to coax the Holy Ghost to come down and heal the really sick and crippled. And of course, from W. V. Grant's viewpoint, the performance had another good purpose — it filled his collection buckets.

Faith healing is supported by the sloppy logic of the right brain, which is predisposed to believe in the healing power of the Holy Spirit. This phenomenon is not surprising, though, when similar sloppy logic credits medical doctors with far more healing than they produce. Franz J. Ingelfinger, former editor of *The New England Journal of Medicine*, estimated that 80 percent of patients are unaffected by treatment, that only 10 percent actually experience "dramatically successful" medical intervention, while nine percent are made sicker by the cure than by the disease.

When we consider that the body does 99 percent of its own healing and that we almost always get well whether we go to a doctor or not, it is easy through careless reasoning to mistakenly credit cures to medical intervention as well as to the intervention of faith healing.

Faith healers, we must admit, get a disproportionately large number of incurable, hopeless, terminal cases. But a heavy dose of chicanery boosts their results.

According to a humorous account, even the Pope can't always be depended on for healing. A fellow was telling his friend about the trip he and his brother had taken to Europe. "We went to see the Eiffel Tower in France and I climbed to the top."

"How about your brother, did he climb to the top?"

"No, my brother didn't climb it; my brother is a cripple. Next we went to Italy to see the Leaning Tower of Pisa, and I climbed to the top."

"How about your brother, did he climb to the top?"

"No, my brother didn't climb it; my brother is a cripple. Then we went to see the Pope at Rome. The Pope blessed my brother, and told him to throw away his crutches. So my brother threw away his crutches."

"Then what happened?"

"Why, he fell down; I told you my brother was a cripple."

Charlatans and those suffering from delusions of divine calling profess to other magical powers besides the power of healing; powers that mark them as fortune tellers, seers, palmists, soothsayers, astrologers, chicken-gut divinators, clairvoyants and channelers. Atheists put them all into the same box—conscious or unconscious frauds.

If there were any way of predicting the future outside the intermediary of natural laws, science—that has produced radio, television, fiber optics, laser technology, moon flights, outer-space probes, nuclear energy, computers and genetic engineering—would surely have discovered it by now.

Right-brained fools pay a palmist $50 for stock forecasts. Fools should wonder, if the palmist can foretell stock prices, why she is sitting on that dirty rug inside a crummy tent at the edge of a dusty highway. If she can foretell the stock market she can start out with his $50 and in a few years *own the world!* The right brain is not very skeptical.

CULTS OR NASCENT RELIGIONS?

There have been in this country, starting with the 60s, a resurgence of religious cults. Because the mainstream religions of today started as cults, Christian parents whose children have joined cults are embarrassed when it is pointed out to them that their children's cults are more like early Christianity than their own traditional churches.

But the definition of cult is fuzzy and debatable. Since cult carries a pejorative connotation, cultists reject the term as applied to themselves, but use it in referring to competing non-orthodox sects. Cultists are the other guys; we are the possessors of the true religion.

Since cults differ so radically in their theology, practice, rituals and social attitudes, we are left with a definition of a cult as any group that most people call a cult.

Nevertheless, cults do exhibit some similarities. Most cults are founded by charismatic leaders calling themselves gurus, swamis, masters, fathers prophets; some cult leaders even claim to be the Second Messiah or to be God Himself. Assuming such grandiose stature, they reign over the flocks autocratically.

Their opposition to and expressed scorn for mainline religions brings onto the cults reciprocal hostility and persecution. Such persecution, both real and imagined, is exploited by the cult leaders to bind their followers more closely together and induce their surrender of individual freedom for the good of the group, now seen as a victimized minority.

Most cultists identify with the persecuted Christians of early Christianity. The leaders assure them that they are among the few righteous people of Earth in possession of the truth, a conviction that frequently leads to arrogance toward outsiders.

Most cults attempt to control members' life styles as well as their theological beliefs. Clothing and hair style are often dictated. Allegiances to family and former friends are transferred to the cult. Sex life is circumscribed and controlled. Members are pressured to turn all their money and possessions over to the cult.

To avoid critical thinking and dissension, cults keep their followers occupied with praying, chanting, meetings, proselytizing, soliciting funds, domestic cult duties and operating cult-run industries. Such a frenzied life, along with a near-starvation diet, insufficient sleep and constant immersion in cult doctrine has the effect of maintaining the zombie-like state of the members and making leaders rich.

There is, however, a democratic aspect to cults. Cult founders need no credentials, no ordination, no license. Anyone has the right to become a cult leader. But their followers are another story.

Said one former Hare Krishna: "You become non-thinking. You accept the leaders as God and do anything you're commanded to without question."

Moses Berg, leader of The Children of God, instructed his followers: "Instant obedience is imperative; you must obey, implicitly, quickly and without question, your officers in the Lord."

In looking over the hundreds of cults, we find a wide diversification, from secular cults, through Christian cults, through cults based on Eastern religions, to Satanic cults. Then there are also the Seventh Day Adventists, Mormons, Christian Scientists, Jehovah's Witnesses, which have most recently graduated from the status of cult to established religions.

A good example of a secular cult is est, founded by Werner Erhard, a Philadelphia high school graduate, born John Paul Rosenberg. During varied occupations of selling encyclopedias and minor management jobs, Erhard became involved in many of the new psychotherapeutic and growth experience movements of the dynamic 60s, such as human potential, Scientology, sensitivity training, encounter therapy, psychic powers, Zen Buddhism, Yoga, Gestalt and psychocybernetics. Out of these experiences,

Erhard developed his own self-improvement or self-transformation system of psychotherapy called est (Erhard Seminars Training). He structured his program around two consecutive weekends totaling 60 intensive hours of training.

Erhard was a dynamic promoter who understood the times. The seminars cost $400 each and were usually held in hotel ballrooms. He and his helpers trained up to three hundred people at a time. Erhard enticed many celebrities to his seminars, aiding his rapid renown and business success.

The seminars were rough encounter-type meetings in which the object was to arouse, infuriate and humiliate the clients in order to shake them free of their normal selves so that the vacuum remaining could be filled with est principles. One est trainer said: "We're gonna throw away your whole belief system. . . . We're gonna tear you down and put you back together."

Long exhausting hours of continuous encounter were employed to render the trainees more amenable to what some critics called brainwashing (a tactic similar to that employed by North Koreans and by many religious cults).

Est training is obviously pitched to the right brain. Intellectuality is disparaged; objective truth is called an illusion; est puts its truth beyond the realm of rationality and reason. Incidentally, this is what religion does too.

As to the question of God, Erhard said: "There isn't anything but spirituality, which is just another word for God, because God is everything." But if God is everything, God becomes a meaningless word.

Est groups are treated as mobs, the training effectiveness depending on the infectiousness of herd emotional behavior. The experience is in this way similar to the emotionalism of Pentecostal revival meetings that depend on herd amplification of emotion for their profound effect on participants.

Thousands of est graduates continue with advanced seminars, volunteer their time for the cause, and recruit friends and relatives with evangelistic zeal.

THE UNIFICATION CHURCH

The Unification church, founded by Sun Myung Moon, son of a North Korean farmer, is more religious oriented than est. It could be described as a cult splintered from Christianity.

Following a common pattern of cult founders, Moon came across Jesus on a mountaintop, and Jesus told Moon he had been chosen to finish the work Jesus had begun.

During World War II, Moon studied electrical engineering in Tokyo, Japan. After returning to Korea, Moon joined a community in South Korea where he studied under a mystic who claimed to be the long-awaited Messiah.

Inspired by this experience, in 1946 Moon returned to North Korea and established a church of his own. Moon claims he was later tortured for three years in a communist prison, comparing his suffering for his faith to the suffering of Christ. After his release he was beaten unconscious and left to die, but some of his disciples retrieved his body to give it a Christian burial. But to their surprise, Moon recovered and in three days began to preach again (shades of Mary Baker Eddy). Rev. Moon claimed that his imprisonment was for anti-communist views. But others have said it was for adultery and bigamy. At any rate, Moon made his way back to South Korea. He became associated with a paralyzed former medical student, Hye Won Yoo, who developed most of the Divine Principle upon which Moon based his new Unification Church (although Moon claimed the book was based on revelations Moon received from God). Yoo also invented an air gun which Moon developed and promoted to get his start as a businessman.

Divine Principles is an innovative interpretation of Christian theology beginning with Adam and Eve — twisted, convoluted, inventive, alien. With a theology so at odds with conventional Christian theology, one is puzzled by Moon's hope to join the fraternity of mainstream Christian churches.

Rev. Moon's activities in Seoul after his wife left him in 1954 raises the eyebrows. In 1955 Moon was imprisoned for adultery and promiscuity. Most of his followers at that time were men. Students and faculty accused of taking part in "the scandalous rites of the Unification Church" were dropped from universities.

A few years later Moon married again and vowed to have twelve children, one for each of Christ's disciples. Lo and behold, in February, 1981, their twelfth offspring was born.

Moon started a recruiting tour in the United States in 1971. With plenty of money, he made rapid progress in gathering converts to his new cult. He came at a very ripe time for cults.

Moon predicted that the year 1981 would be the year the New Kingdom of Heaven on Earth would begin and the world would recognize Rev. Moon as the Second Advent. Of course, Moon failed as had all the Adventist prophets before him, and like them he had to come up with an excuse: The world was not yet ready for the new age because of the failure of faith; the Apocalypse would not arrive until 2001.

To bolster his Messianic claim, Moon interpreted the reference of

Revelations 7:2-4, which describes an "angel descending from the rising of the sun" as meaning that a new Christ would be born in the East — specifically in Korea. However, Moon's claim to be the new Messiah has been low-keyed to avoid the angry reproach of orthodox Christians.

"Moonies" have developed a clever system of proselytizing involving what critics call brainwashing and mind-control. Recruiters prey on lonely, alienated youths, many at college campuses, "love-bombing" them with pretended overwhelming concern for them, a false concern justified as "heavenly deception." Gradually, the prospect is persuaded to accept an invitation to a Moonie center for dinner. All the while, members are "working" on the prospect to break down resistance with love — hugs, hand-holding and the undying Moonie smiles.

Young people particularly are attracted by the ideological appeal of the Unification Church's purported purpose to unify the peoples of all races and religions around love and fraternity.

Eventually, through pleading, begging and the shedding of a few tears, the recruiters pressure the prospect into yielding and joining.

Why do recruiters work so hard and prostitute themselves to gain new members? Among other things, Moonies are taught that in order to become perfect and receive Rev. Moon's blessing, they must bring in three new members. And they must become perfect before the Church will assign them a spouse.

Moon has an obsession with marriages. On one occasion in New York's Madison Square Garden, he united over two thousand couples paired by the Church in a mass marriage ceremony.

The Unification Church is rich. Moon and his church have over the years acquired a financial empire. How much of the wealth comes from the surrender by new members of all their possessions, how much from the street solicitations of thousands of Moonies and how much from Moon's and the Church's enterprises is uncertain.

One notorious source of Moonie money — hundreds of millions of dollars — has been Japan, where Moonies have bilked the Japanese with an illegal, high-pressure scheme to sell them religious talismans, stone urns and other charms to ward off evil spirits. Most of the victims were widowed or divorced or had suffered a miscarriage.

Although the sources of Moonie money remain somewhat mysterious, there is no mystery about the amount. The Unification Church spreads money around like fertilizer, and I presume as with fertilizer, the spreading pays off well.

Through heavy contributions to various conservatives and organizations they are connected with, the Church does all it can to influence American politics and public opinion. Beneficiaries of the largess have been: Christian Voice (a Washington lobby), the American Freedom Coalition (Richard Viguerie), Coalition for America (Paul Weyrich), the Global Economic Action Institute (former U.S. Treasury Secretary Robert Anderson), National Conservative Political Action Committee (the late John T. Dolan), and evangelical Christian churches.

In addition, and surprisingly, Eugene McCarthy was an interim chairman of the Moon-backed Global Economic Action Institute, and civil rights leader Ralph Abernathy served on two Moon-dominated boards.

Hundreds of journalists, academics, state legislators, retired military officers and other respectable leaders have attended expense-paid conferences on anticommunism and Unificationism at luxury hotels in such places as Paris, London, Tokyo, Seoul and Miami financed by Moon interests.

"Anybody influential can get money from them at any time in virtually any amount," said Howard J. Ruff, founder of two powerful PACs. "The Moonies scare me," continued Ruff, "because, clearly, they have become the most influential group in the New Right in terms of political power, influence and money."

Lastly, the Unification Church bought the conservative *Washington Times*. The *Times* was then-President Ronald Reagan's favorite newspaper. "We now have direct influence on Ronald Reagan," boasted Moon. The newspaper proceeded to lose about $200 million. A rather heavy cost to catch Ronald's eye.

THE HINDU RAJNEESH CULT

Bhagwan Shree Rajneesh, a Hindu guru, was graduated from an Indian college in 1957, and then taught philosophy for several years. While in college he had become "enlightened."

After quitting his teaching position, he became a public speaker and convener of religious seminars. Finally he settled in Poona, India where he organized an ashram. Although his ashram had room for only a few hundred resident members, the Bhagwan (meaning "God") became famous enough to attract thousands of Westerners who, to be near their guru, lived in the Poona area. In addition, the ashram in time began receiving as many as several thousand visitors a day.

And what was there about this guru that he could attract ultimately hundreds of thousands of worshipers? Outside of his long beard and hypnotic brown eyes it is difficult to find anything.

Rajneesh demanded complete surrender to himself and unquestioning acceptance of his word. He dictated the behavior of his devotees in every area of their personal lives. Followers were asked to give up their families and jobs as well as their minds. They were to become zombie, mindless followers of the Bhagwan.

This guru claims to have lived seven hundred years earlier when his mission was to enlighten humanity. Now he had returned as Rajneesh to finish the job.

The Rajneeshees believed in the therapeutic benefits of the release of suppressed emotions and sensual desire. The result was considerably rough and violent encounters, physical abuse and even rape at the Poona ashram. Bones were broken, personalities destroyed, minds deranged. Finally, in 1979, physical violence in the workshops was forbidden, but verbal abuse continued.

After seven years of operations at Poona, the Bhagwan had become a rich man, thanks mostly to Western dupes who streamed to his ashram. In 1981, after a lifetime of lecturing, the guru stopped talking. He felt that only through silence could he communicate his ultimate message. With thirteen tons of personal luggage, Rajneesh took a Pan Am flight to New York, leaving his abandoned disciples dismayed and hurt. One suspects he was searching for even greener pastures.

That same year the Rajneeshees bought 100 square miles of lowgrade land near Antelope, Oregon for $6 million. They proceeded to build a rural Shangri-la. American patrons with loads of money beat a path to Antelope.

With all-volunteer labor, religious and ideological zeal and millions of dollars, the ashram, named Rajneeshpuram, rose in short time from the semi-desert: two-story town houses, A-framed houses, shopping mall, university, greenhouse, disco nightclub, boutique, two restaurants, bookstore, ice cream parlor, Chamber of Commerce building and a 145-room hotel.

A dam was constructed to create a lake for recreation and water storage, a paved airstrip was built and 35 miles of roads laid.

Farm operations included 550 head of beef cattle, 4,000 hens, 50 cows, 100 bee hives, 11,000 grape vines and a 60-acre irrigated garden. A veritable utopia — especially in the eyes of city people with their romantic back-to-the-land notions about self-sufficient farming. Rajneeshpuram reached a population of four thousand permanent residents.

Although credited with writing 350 books explaining his philosophy, the Bhagwan was no stickler for consistency. He was given to contradicting himself or giving two people different answers. Understanding was to be gained by experience, not by words, so verbal communication was not important. As a result one cannot be very sure of his philosophy.

The guru says that God is everything, similarly as did Werner Erhard. But, again, if God is everything, God becomes a meaningless word. God is beauty, God is ugliness, God is a swan, God is a rattlesnake, God is love, God is hate, God is the vaccine against polio, God is the AIDS virus.

The Bhagwan seems to see the mindless man as the enlightened man. The brain stands between man and his enlightenment. God has to be experienced, and the mind is in the way. Rajneeshism seems to be an attempt by the irrational right brain to subdue and destroy the rational left brain.

The Bhagwan teaches that our struggle is with the ego, which is always thinking—seeking purpose and meaning to life. The guru says, "The self is not something to be protected; it is something to be destroyed."

According to atheists and humanists, of course, life's purpose is the fulfillment and survival of the ego, not the destruction of it. Rajneeshees aren't really too far from Christians, though, who believe in humility, self-sacrifice, self-flagellation and spiritual enslavement to the clergy and God.

Nevertheless, the residents of Rajneeshpuram loved their guru, worshiped him and enjoyed the euphoria of living in an earthly paradise. Said one female devotee of the Bhagwan: "I was struck by the beauty of this man. He was in touch with the essence of life. It was a miracle to me that he was willing to help me reach the same state. We call him our beloved, our lover. He has 400,000 lovers [worldwide]. And each one of them very satisfied. What a man!"

Said a new convert: "I'm the most drastically changed person I know. I couldn't believe there was a place like this. I'm never leaving." Another male convert spoke of the effect on him of just seeing the Bhagwan: "It's not that the Bhagwan just passes by. He looks into everyone's eyes. One day he hesitated and looked into my eyes for the longest time. When he looked into my eyes I knew that he was what was important."

Said a disciple with the Sanskrit name of Swami Kurim Govind: "His presence was total and all-consuming. It was like being in a deep, hypnotic trance in which I was suddenly freed of all my troubles, all the depressions, all the hate, spite and jealousy that afflict people. . . . In my mind, he is godly. I would go anywhere any time to sit at his feet."

"There is something real, something authentic, something honest about him I nave never experienced in another person," said a 40-year-old male follower. "Whenever I was around him I felt an immense amount of bliss and energy like nothing that I'd ever felt before."

A female tour guide Rajneeshee explained the hostility toward the ashram. "Everyone told us what we were doing here was crazy. They said we couldn't make vegetables grow, that the dam wouldn't hold water. They were hoping we wouldn't succeed. And now they are angry at us because it worked. Here we are working together in a cooperative way, as society outside becomes more fragmented. Outside there is the generation gap, the threat of nuclear war. And here we are creating an oasis in the desert."

The high point of the day at the ashram came in the afternoons when the bearded Bhagwan went for a short drive in one of his Rolls-Royces. The road would be lined with orange-clad worshipers joyfully dancing and singing and playing tambourines and sitars. The Bhagwan would move his bejeweled hands up and down in a saintly fashion in recognition of their devotion, but never murmur a word because of his vow of silence before he came to the United States.

Who were these worshipers of the guru from India? By and large they were the Yuppies of the Baby Boomers—the flower children of the 60s. They were the better-educated and wealthier remnants from the counter-culture of that era. They still had an unfulfilled desire for community, a felt need for spiritual commitment, an ideological dedication to save the environment and promote world peace, as well as a positive attitude toward money, sexual freedom, self-illumination and enhancement of human potential. Rajneeshism was a designer religion for Baby Boomers.

A 1983 study by professors of the University of Oregon found that 97 percent of the Bhagwan's followers at his Oregon ashram had incomes over $20,000 a year before joining. The study also found that 64 percent held bachelor's degrees. (What this says about our colleges I leave to the reader.)

Rajneesh was capable of talking in a very down-to-earth manner during his less-spiritual moods. In a post-Rajneeshpuram interview, the guru pontificated: "Jesus Christ was a crackpot. He was trying to save the whole world. He couldn't even save himself."

Rajneesh blamed world poverty on religions that praise the poor and exacerbate overpopulation by opposing birth control and abortion. "Stop giving Nobel prizes to criminals like Mother Teresa," said Rajneesh. "These priests and politicians are responsible for keeping poverty alive."

But all good (?) things must come to an end. After four years of existence, Rajneeshpuram began to disintegrate. From the outside the ashram was attacked by native Oregonians who resented the Rajneeshees' life style, feared the growing population of these strange outerspace aliens in their midst and fought against the Rajneeshees' attempts to take over the town of Antelope and the county.

At the same time from the inside, corruption, discord and dissention among the ashram leaders were tearing its guts apart.

Ma Amand Sheela, the guru's personal secretary, left the Oregon ashram for Europe in 1985 with 15 other top Rajneeshees after a bitter power struggle.

The Bhagwan accused Sheela of making off with $55 million, of poisoning restaurant food, of setting a fire, of tapping phones and of attempting to murder the Bhagwan's doctor and dentist.

Sheela denied the charges, but confirmed that the $55 million had vanished. She alleged that the guru allowed drug trafficking in Rajneeshpuram to raise money for Rolls-Royces for him. She said that the guru once threatened to commit suicide if his followers didn't buy him another Rolls-Royce. By the end he owned a fleet of 93 of the luxury cars his devotees had bought him to express their love for him; the Bhagwan had graciously accepted them to validate his teaching that the spiritual life shouldn't mean discomfort and unhappiness.

Sheela said she had fled for her life because she knew too much about the Bhagwan Rajneesh. When learning of her charges, Rajneesh called them nonsense. "There are no drugs whatsoever in this community. Drugs are against awareness."

Eventually the Bhagwan pleaded guilty to charges of violating immigration laws and was deported after paying a $400,000 fine. Ma Amand Sheela and two of her Rajneesh cohorts were jailed in Portland to await trial on a variety of charges. The Rajneeshees at the Antelope ashram packed their bags and went home.

The Bhagwan, upon being order deported, returned to Poona, India, where he died of heart failure at age 58 in January, 1990 and was cremated by his disciples in a riverside funeral pyre in the traditional Hindu manner. A little Hindu charlatan whose spectacular success was a humiliation to supposedly enlightened America, attested to by 93 Rolls-Royces.

THE PEOPLE'S TEMPLE

The People's Temple was started in 1952 by the enigmatic guru, Jim Jones, in Indianapolis, Indiana. Jones began as an unordained faith-healing minister with a combination of fiery sermons, psychic revelations and miracle healing.

Ever seeking greater opportunities, Jones moved his church to Ukiah in Northern California and then a decade later to San Francisco. There he became politically involved and was appointed to the city's influential Housing Authority. He soon became a highly respected community leader and champion of the underprivileged, but he violated the trust placed in him by looting the public treasury under the pious guise of feeding the hungry and clothing the poor.

In addition, Jones inveigled many people to sign their properties over to him and live in the People's Temple commune. The value of such properties ran into millions of dollars.

Rev. Jones ruled his sizable flock in an imperious manner. He demanded sexual favors from his female followers, both black and white, and even from some of his male followers. Such unscrupulous activities were bound to arouse resentment among his flock. Insiders began defecting and talking.

In addition, some years earlier Jones had been arrested for lewd conduct in a theater restroom. The judge had dismissed the case and ordered records of the case sealed and destroyed. There were rumors of a bribe. Jones may have later feared an exposé of this segment of his past life. Jones also was developing a fear that the government was after him. And on top of that Jones had become convinced a nuclear holocaust was imminent.

Maybe all four of these factors contributed to Jones' growing paranoia. At any rate, his fears spurred him to flee with his flock to a jungle in Guyana, South America. There the People's Temple built their Shangri-la. And if it had not been for the growing mental derangement of its charismatic leader, Jonestown, as it was named, might have been just another utopian dream that failed, after which its disappointed communards packed up and went home — as happened seven years later with Rajneeshpuram in Oregon.

But a few years of isolation in the jungle seems to have driven Jones over the edge. At the end of an investigative visit to Jonestown by Congressman Leo Ryan, prompted by complaints of corruption and abuse at the Temple compound, Jonestown guards fired on the visiting group as they were boarding their plane to depart. Ryan was shot to death along with three newsmen and a Temple defector.

Jones then urged his flock to kill themselves before they were killed by their "enemies." Most of them drank willingly from a vat of cyanide-laced grape Flavor-Aid. The drink was forced down reluctant members and children. Jones died of a single gunshot by an unknown hand.

The mass suicide-murder claimed the lives of 913 men, women, children and babies. Thus the spasmodic story of the People's Temple ended in a mass death orgy.

We can attempt to explain the mass-suicide by attributing it to the charismatic, hypnotic power Jones wielded over his followers, to the terror instilled by the Temple guards, to the jungle isolation from normative society and to the previous conditioning rehearsals of ritualistic drinking of non-poisonous Flavor-Aid.

All these factors were designed to overcome the rational left brain, the total paralysis of which is a necessary condition for mass hysteria.

Jim Jones didn't believe in Christianity or God. His church was a fraud. But Jim Jones wasn't like the run-of-the-mill charlatans of the sawdust trail who exploit the gullible to enrich themselves. Jones was a sincere ideologue so fanatically dedicated to communism that he was willing to use any means however immoral or ruthless to the end of glorious communism. He was a Marxist-Leninist Communist, and set about to establish a communist colony in Guyana. He idolized Mao Tse Tung, Josef Stalin and Fidel Castro.

In early 1978 Jones initiated the compulsory study of Russian at Jonestown. He offered the colony's $10 million treasury to the Soviet government, but the Soviets refused it. His will left all his property to the Communist Party USA.

What drove Jim Jones? My guess is, angered by failure, frustration and futility in his efforts to significantly promote communism, Jones went over the edge of sanity into a prolonged madness that ended with the oft-rehearsed mass suicide.

The story of the People's Temple is a good example of the ability of the bilateral human brain to harbor diametrically opposing beliefs concurrently. There were Rev. Jones propagating fundamentalist Christianity and atheistic communism from the same pulpit and his congregation assimilating the incompatible philosophies with no insurmountable difficulty.

Dr. Lowell Streiker, Ph.D., executive director of a group in San Francisco which counsels former cult members, claims that what he calls dangerous cults are at an all-time high despite the horror of Jonestown. Jonestown, instead of discouraging cults, opened the eyes of potential cult leaders to the enormous power a leader can wield over is followers. "There are other Jonestowns just waiting to happen," said Dr. Streiker.

NEW AGE RELIGIONS

Among New Age religions are probably many frauds designed to gain fame and fortune for their promoters or to enhance the careers of entertainers. Many are orchestrated by PR professionals, employing the latest techniques of advertising and promotion, using direct mail and the free publicity of press, radio and television.

Channeling is one of the current New Age religious fads. One successful channeler, F. V. Night, enjoyed a big boost by actress Shirley MacLaine, who identified Night as her spiritual guide.

Ms. Night, who goes by the channeling name of Ramtha, a former male incarnation of 500,000 years ago, charges $400 to attend her meetings and $1500 for a weekend retreat. The Ramtha organization can earn up to $200,000 for one appearance.

Night goes into a trance and turns into the male Ramtha. She changes her facial expressions and her voice and proceeds to talk as Ramtha.

Ramtha predicts that a series of national disasters will destroy America — earthquakes, droughts, tidal waves and more. Ramtha says the Northwest is safe. As a result, hundreds of people have given up everything and moved to the Northwest, abandoning friends, neighbors and sometimes even families.

Ramtha has a hypnotic effect on her/his listeners. Getting hooked by Ramtha sometimes destroys people's domestic lives and professional careers. One devotee said, "When Ramtha speaks there's such love in his voice. You can see the love coming out of his eyes."

Is it love or greed coming out of Night's eyes? A former advance man for Night now says that greed is the motivation for Ramtha.

Not content with raking in millions of dollars from her followers for her meetings and retreats, Ms. Night had a stable of Arabian horses and sold shares in them to her devotees. As Ramtha she would advise them to invest in Night's horses. Finally the government investigated and ordered her to stop. Many of her investors lost a lot of money on Night's horses.

One observer suggested that Ramtha followers are transfixed by a blend of Eastern mysticism and Western pop philosophy with a large dose of theatrics. Score another for P. T. Barnum.

Nevertheless, according to Maria Donato writing in the *Chicago Tribune*, "Just look around. There are now New Age churches, radio programs, stores, tapes, newsletters, magazines, seminars and classes. Jewelry, featuring quartz crystals and other healing stones, is in vogue."

New Age religionists illustrate the boundlessness of right-brain fantasy, delusion and absurdity. They go for such things as trance channeling, reincarnation, extraterrestrial communication, astral projection, pyramid power, quartz crystals, telepathy, clairvoyance, astrology, precognition and psychokinesis — you give it a name: they'll buy it.

Much of it is patterned after Eastern religions. Actress Shirley Mac-

Laine, a New Age exponent, let the cat out of the bag when she explained: "Eastern systems of thought tend to be . . . more capable of absorbing many contradictory concepts. . . . Eastern systems find it easier to embrace perceptions that are not logical." So that's it! Rationalists couldn't agree better with MacLaine.

Instead of thinking, you depend upon your right brain's intuition, which is dipped in a reservoir of supraconscious Ultimate Reality and always readily available to guide you in your decisions. The corrupting left brain must be kept subservient. Intuition and spiritual insight, not reason, logic and rationality are the key to success.

Most Christians, appalled by the injustice, cruelty and suffering in the world, hope through prayer, religious devotion and righteous living to induce their Lord and guardian angels to spare them from the worst of it.

New Age religion, ignoring Christian theology, has developed a do-it-yourself approach. Through their right hemisphere, the New Agers seek spiritual and prenormal powers that connect them to the indestructible universal life force that is coextensive with their own psyches. Access to this Ultimate Reality is achieved and maintained by meditation, yoga, music, chanting, fasting and proper breathing.

In the New Age view the intuitive right brain is superior to and transcends the pitifully deficient left — so, take that, you lame-brained rationalists. Well, at least, the right brain can't be accused of lacking imagination.

Cults keep abreast with technology. UFO lore and a U.S. landing on the moon inspired a frenzy of right-brain activity that spawned a number of space-age cults. Guru charlatans popped up all over the country claiming to have traveled by flying saucers to various extraterrestrial worlds. Some even claimed to have come from other planets.

George Adamski, an Englishman who ran a hamburger stand in the Arizona desert, claimed to have been on spacecraft trips to Mars, Saturn and Venus. Adamski took a photograph of one of the flying saucer space ships, a photograph that became famous. Skeptics believed the picture was of the beverage bottle cooler at his hamburger stand.

Adamski wrote a book on flying saucers that sold over a million copies. He became a cult figure and famous lecturer on UFOs. Adamski revealed a line of quasi-religion he received from extraterrestrial men of advanced ages and great wisdom. The line included the suggestion of transmigration to other planets for those who work for the good of the universe. Planetarians were spoken of reverently as space brothers.

The religious tinge of those revelations was enough to attract tens of thousands of followers, those people with a strong need to believe — the spiritually starved, the mystically inclined, the seekers of truth, the alienated.

Adamski's followers demanded no proof other than his word for his story of having traveled to other planets, along with the photographs he took of flying saucers — photographs that U.S. Air Force investigators suspected were closeup shots of a vacuum cleaner.

Although Adamski never personally founded a space cult, his followers founded a number of them. Adamski made his money from his book and from lecturing — no more hamburger grilling.

The groups inspired by Adamski showed all the characteristics of cults. They demanded loyalty of their members, communal living, volunteer labor, total commitment, alienation from parents. There were even cases of parents hiring deprogrammers to kidnap their children from UFO cults. It is significant that most of the followers of UFO cults were from 18 to 24. Most of the leaders were middle-aged.

A clue to the degree of Adamski's sincerity may be found in his attempt in the 1930s to start up a mystic occult group called the Royal Order of Tibet. But people just weren't interested in Tibet. Flying saucers, however, went over flying.

A middle-aged couple in 1975, known as Bo and Peep, represented themselves as two heavenly messengers with the power to prophesy as foretold in Revelations. They concocted a fantastic story that they would be killed by disbelievers, but would arise from the dead after three days and lead their followers aboard a UFO and take them to Heaven.

Many of their followers gave up families, homes and jobs to await the flying saucer to whisk them to Heaven. But Bo and Peep never got killed by disbelievers and no space ship came to pick up their followers. Bo and Peep left a videotape of their "final statement on earth" and disappeared, leaving about a hundred followers holding the snipe-hunt bags.

It seems that UFO buffs will believe anything. Another Englishman, George King, moved to the United States in search of more gullible prospects than he could find in England. He claimed to have ridden in flying saucers with Jesus and the Virgin Mary, and that Jesus, Saint Paul, Krishna and a Venusian master all speak through him. He established a center in Los Angeles and soon had a considerable following.

Cults cover the full range of extremism from compassionate reverence for life to devil worship. The Jainas monks of India gently sweep away insects on the path in front of them to avoid crushing them. They wear shields over their mouths to prevent germs from being drawn to their death; they sponge themselves lightly instead of bathing so as not to kill small organisms on their bodies; they eat only in the daytime to avoid insects being drawn to their lamps and accidentally getting into their food and being killed by the eating.

The Jainas sect has been around since before Christ and has 10 million followers. At the other extreme are the devil worshipers, who kill animals and even sometimes humans in their sacrificial rituals.

In 1988, talk show host Geraldo Rivera featured United States devil-worshiping cults in his usual sensational manner. For that he was severely criticized for having indulged in gross exaggeration for the sake of TV ratings. His critics said that he had picked up on a current fad of a few young skinheads and tried to turn it into a grave threat to the nation.

Less than six months later, though, Geraldo was partially vindicated by a horror story from Matamoros, Mexico, across the Rio Grande from Brownsville, Texas.

The scenario began with the disappearance of a 21-year-old University of Texas premed student, Mark Kilroy, while on a late-night outing in Matamoros with friends during a spring break. A $15,000 reward had been offered for information concerning the student's disappearance.

Kilroy had been lured to a pickup truck on a Matamoros street, according to cult members, grabbed and forced into the truck and driven to an isolated ranch 20 miles out of town. Twelve hours later Kilroy was ritualistically hacked to pieces with a machete by Adolfo de Jesus Constanzo, the leader of the black magic, voodoo cult.

Kilroy had been selected at random for ritualistic slaying by the cult, slain in a shed, then buried in a shallow grave nearby.

The cult was involved in drug trafficking and Adolfo had convinced his followers that the sacrificial slayings and mutilations would magically protect them from the police and render them bullet-proof.

About a month after the slaying of Kilroy, Mexican police found the killing shed. In the surrounding area Kilroy and 15 other victims were unearthed, most of them too mutilated for immediate identification.

Inside the shed was a satanic altar littered with candles, broken glass, chili peppers and bottles of cane liquor that cult members offered to their gods. Cauldrons held chicken heads, goat heads, animal bones, human blood and human brains. A sheriff said that the place was like a slaughter-house.

After the discovery of the graves, Adolfo with several other members of the cult including his female satanic associate, Sara Aldrete, a 24-year-old Texas college student known as the witch of the cult, fled to Mexico City. Later, as police closed in on their hideout, Adolfo ordered a subordinate to shoot him and his male lover. Sara and the other fleeing cult members were arrested and jailed.

After the arrests in Mexico City and the arrest of several other cult members in Matamoros, authorities were amazed by their light-hearted attitude. They showed no remorse or shame over the slayings, but laughed and joked about them.

And what kind of person could mastermind and promote such ghastly, grizzly, macabre "religion"? Constanzo, known as the godfather to his followers, was born in Miami, Florida to Cuban refugee parents in 1962. His mother reported that her son began to have out-of-body experiences when about 14. He also began healing the sick and predicting the future. Adolfo's mother, who practiced *Santeria*, a mixture of African religion and Christianity, no doubt gave Adolfo his original nudge into occult religion.

In time the boy grew into a very attractive young man. In reference to his appearance and charisma, Adolfo's mother said, "People were always asking, 'Who's that?' — everybody believing he was somebody and asking if he's a movie star." Adolfo moved to Mexico City where he became an astrologer for popular entertainers as well as for top-ranking police and government officials.

Through his charismatic charm and ruthless manipulation he organized a secret society that practiced black magic and human sacrifice, as well as drug smuggling. The latter became a necessity to support Adolfo's lavish life style. To entice drug dealers to favor him he promised them magical protection against arrest. Like the Bhagwan, Adolfo wore rubies and diamonds on every finger, but Adolfo owned only one Mercedes-Benz — not 93!

Adolfo was unquestionably a homosexual, having two lovers in his cult; one was his "lady" and the other his "man."

CULT POTPOURRI

The extremely bizarre, aberrant behavior found in cults and religions illustrates how far the right brain, unrestrained by reason and rationality, can lead people astray. Cult gurus recognize the threat of the rational left brain to their control over their devotees. In the Divine Light Mission cult, followers are taught to accept the opinions of the pure light of their spiritual master, Maharaj Ji. They are constantly warned against having any opinion of their own — in cult jargon "being in your mind." Or, in the terminology of this book, using your rational left brain.

We should not be surprised at the frequent appearance of new cults. Even the Bible predicted them. Apostle Paul wrote: "The time is coming

ABRAHAM OFFERING ISAAC.

when people will not endure sound teaching, but having itching ears they will accumulate for themselves teachers to suit their own likings, and will turn away from listening to the truth and wander into myths." (2 Tim. 4:3-4)

Jesus said: "For many shall come in my name, saying, 'I am Christ'; and shall deceive many." (Mark 13:6)

Covering such a wide expanse of theologies, practices and objectives, cults and religions are difficult to categorize. Their theologies range from animism to monism, to polytheism, to trinitarianism, to monotheism to secularism.

The practices of some religions are concerned mostly with rites and rituals, chanting and ceremony, pageantry, pomp and power. Other religions involve a more private, personal relationship between the followers and their God.

The objectives of religions can differ greatly too. For example, the

Christian religion believes in a personal God and an afterlife and generally perceives the object of religion as earning passage to Heaven through moral living and the acceptance of Christ as Savior. But most Eastern religions see ethics and morality as irrelevant. The objective of religion is to become spiritual by merging into the divine.

Then there are the secular cults dedicated to self-improvement and success. They too, generally have little concern for ethics and morality. Many such cults are open ego trips for their followers, who hope to achieve superiority through learning the psychology of success, or to become physical supermen through health food fads, or achieve superiority through harnessing the powers offered by parapsychology. Adherents seem to be seeking any easy, magical way to the top short of tedious academic training and hard work.

Some of the New Age religions are exploiting a swing away from the materialistic, self-improvement cults and away from objective traditional religions into the subjective fantasy and mysticism of Eastern religions. They seem to find new satisfactions in quartz crystal power, reincarnation and pantheism (God is in everything).

A description of cult leaders helps in the understanding of cults. Most religious cults are started by weird characters who have a private mystical experience or prophetic dream which they take seriously enough to believe that they have been chosen by God and invested with divine authority. The common garden variety of such experiences are the calls that send young men to divinity school.

But the person destined to become a successful cult leader must be charismatic, aggressive and adamantly convinced of his God-given authority. Obviously, he has to be an egomaniac to believe that he alone in all the world possesses the truth and has been selected by God Himself to disseminate it. (There is, of course, one other possibility: the all-out charlatan, a master of deception, promotion and showmanship and possessor of extraordinary business acumen.)

In due time the money comes rolling in to the successful cult leader along with adoration and fame. It is not surprising that even for the sincere man, the profits, perquisites and adoration showered on him sometimes corrupt such a morally ordinary mortal.

Cult leaders gain members by washing the brains of the prospective members clean of their old religious ideas and then indoctrinating them with the cult's theology.

The prospective members are often lonely, alienated, unhappy young people seeking answers to their problems. The cultists overwhelm them with love, attention and companionship and offer them direction for their lives and easy solutions to their problems.

After joining the cult, still innocent of what is happening to them, the new members are kept mentally fatigued with long hours of intense cult activity. Such fatigue renders the neophytes more amenable to brainwashing and indoctrination. In addition, they are now living in a cult commune, a closed society that insulates them from outside influences. Their religious beliefs are changed, their value systems are inverted, their ties with friends and family are broken, their personalities are lost in robot-like conformity to the group. They stay, nevertheless, because they find their new life self-fulfilling — even if it is at the cost of self-surrender.

They now need to be deprogrammed. Deprogramming is the term that has come into use to signify the deliberate attempt to reverse the brainwashing process of the cult and restore the members (victims) to their original condition. Professionals engaged in deprogramming are usually hired by parents to "rescue" their children from the influential clutches of the cults and return them to their homes.

Deprogramming runs into many legal problems such as the necessity sometimes of kidnapping the cult initiate, violation of the First Amendment freedom of religion and the fact that the object of deprogramming is a legal adult with whom parents have no legal right to interfere.

The view of parents and deprogrammers is, of course, that their own religion is the true religion while cults are propagators of false religions. They feel morally justified in rescuing children from false prophets.

Atheists view deprogramming as an attempt within the right brain to wrest control of it from the seduction of cult nonsense and return it to its former subjection to traditional nonsense. To condemn cults is to condemn religion. (Some truths can't be admitted.)

In studying cults, one must face the nagging question of whether the cult leader is a charlatan or a sincere believer. Or as an atheist might put it, whether a charlatan or a self-deluded nut. Or, could it be in between: their left brain being a charlatan and their right brain being sincere?

Short of the ability to read minds, one must judge the best he can from the behavior and statements of cult leaders. But even these are not reliable when we consider the contradictions between the right and left cerebral hemispheres — when we consider that a person can believe and not believe something at the same time.

We also must recognize that the judgment of thousands — even millions — of followers is that their cult leader is sincere.

The leader of the Renters, a cult of 17th century England, claimed to be the divine incarnation of the Biblical prophet Melchizedek. He named certain cult members as incarnations of Cain, Judas and Jeremiah, whom he had raised from the dead. The people so-named vigorously affirmed the truth of Melchizedek's claims. Was this a conspiracy to deceive their followers?

Quaker apologist Robert Barclay believed that "those persons were mad, and had a singular power of producing a kind of sympathetic madness or temporary aberration of intellect in others." So, apparently, Barclay didn't consider them charlatans, but rather self-deluded.

The long-suffering from persecution, rejection and isolation of many cults may produce emotional sickness and mental aberrations that account for some of their bizarre beliefs and behaviors. We must conclude that just because a theology is unbelievable doesn't mean it's not believed; just because a religious practice is inconceivable doesn't mean it's not practiced.

No doubt such modern televangelists as Oral Roberts, Jim Bakker, Jimmy Swaggart and Pat Robertson would argue that the millions of dollars they take in from their evangelism is well-deserved. And they would vigorously affirm their honesty and sincerity. But one may still wonder about the 900-foot Jesus that Oral Roberts claimed to have talked with.

There are such vast differences between mainstream religions (Catholic, Jewish, Protestant) and seasoned cults (Jehovah's Witnesses, Seventh Day Adventists, Mormons), and newer cults (Unification Church, Bahai, Hare Krishna, Scientology) that it is difficult to find any common denominators.

An atheist would say that they are all false. (This, of course, is what each one says about all the others.) But one wonders how such a diversity of theologies, practices, liturgies, organizations, moralities, life styles and value systems could arise out of belief in the same God.

One is left in total confusion pondering the far-ranging bizarre beliefs, rituals and customs of religion: The Quakers, Shakers, Ranters, Jumpers, serpent handlers and Drano drinkers; the speakers in tongues, swooners, faith healers, psychic surgeons, animal sacrificers, resurrecters of the dead, genuflectors, Second Comers and God impersonators; the transmigrators, astro-projectors, prophets, clairvoyants, celibates and eunuchs; the collectors of Rolls-Royces, New Age space people, love bombers, circumcisers, flagellators, total immersionists and the eaters of Christ's flesh and drinkers of His blood.

Every religion, sect and cult thinks it has the answer to life, it has discovered the way, it has received the revelation of divine truth, it has been anointed to be God's earthly viceroyalty. Such claims might be attributed solely to the irrationality and creativity of the right brain if it weren't for the array of left-brained secular groups making similar claims to having the answers: pragmatists, objectivists, empiricists, materialists, rationalists, scholasticists, psychoanalysts, rational emotive therapists, Gestaltists, human potentialists, biofeedbackers, technocrats, Marxists, general semanticists, humanists. So, even left brainers demonstrate a compulsion to find simplified answers to the problems of life; their conceit often leads them to believe they have.

Both hemispheres seem to be potential dupes of eternal hope, and fearful of facing the truth of the human predicament.

Notwithstanding the common characteristic of both hemispheres to believe they have the exclusive answers, right brainers have proved to be a drag on human progress with their fraudulence, denunciation of reason and fight against science and education, while left brainers have pulled us out of savagery and raised the common man's living standard above that of ancient kings — even if he does take it all for granted.

There is hope that perhaps through the corpus callosum the left brain will eventually be able to sterilize the right brain of its virus of religious superstition, allowing it to continue to function as a valuable generator of the imaginative and creative — art, architecture, music, theater, literature, folklore, pageantry.

Chapter IX
MORE GOOD THAN HARM?

The public accepts it as axiomatic that religion does more good than harm. Even some credible atheists agree that religion is necessary to a civilized society. And all religionists seem to believe that without religion morality, compassion, justice, cultural arts, government and even science could never have developed. We would still be beasts of the jungle.

General Hugh S. Johnson, a New Deal administrator, wrote: "Man may have arisen from the lower animals but the thing that set him apart was that there was within him a germ of the divine intelligence which grew to fight and partly overcome that savage animalism from which he set out. Religion, and that almost alone, has nurtured that advance."

Dostoyevsky went so far as to say that "if God does not exist then everything is permitted."

Skeptics who support religion take a pragmatic view, believing it is best for society to promulgate myths and imbue the masses with religious morality backed by fear of God and the belief in an afterworld of atonement. Some people believe that if the world is not constantly raised by religion, however false and flimsy, crass materialism would destroy us.

Voltaire said, "If God did not exist, it would be necessary to invent him in order to keep the peace and order in our society." Of course, Voltaire, being a skeptic, believed that that was what had been done.

Napoleon Bonaparte also thought religion a necessity: "How can you have order in a state without religion? For, when one man is dying of hunger near another who is ill of surfeit, he can not resign himself to this difference unless there is an authority which declares, 'God wills it thus.' "

Will Durant said, "We shall find it no easy task to mold a natural ethic

171

MOSES DESTROYING THE TABLES OF THE LAW.

strong enough to maintain moral restraint and social order without the support of supernatural sanctions, hopes and fears."

John Stuart Mill also took the pragmatic view: "It is conceivable that religion may be morally useful without being intellectually sustainable."

The humanitarian fruits of religion are many. Religionists engage in charitable and humanitarian activities as an expression of their faith. They support hospitals, children's homes, summer camps, homes for the handicapped, old people's homes, private charities for the poor, soup kitchens and shelters for the homeless.

Religions teach morality, instill compassion, encourage kindness, comfort the grief-stricken, practice humility and inspire hope.

Religions sustain peace of mind and contentment in a chaotic world, provide stable moorings in a choppy sea, invest lives with meaning and purpose, raise self-respect and inspire to higher goals; religions offer joyful emotional experiences and the soul-enrichment of mysticism, give the lonely and alienated a personal friend in Jesus and put beauty into drab lives. Religions offer social opportunities to the isolated and provide recreational opportunities to the inactive while fulfilling the need to believe. So how could anyone do other than affirm the inherent goodness of religion?

So far as the question of the truth of religion is concerned, it is merely academic in relation to the good or harm religion does. Religion should be judged by its practical, pragmatic effect on society, not by its truth. There is no conclusive evidence that societies based on rationalism fare any better than those based on religion. Of course, such comparisons are extremely difficult to make because of the many other highly variable factors.

Believing the truth doesn't mean that you are any better off (although most people assume this without question).

Blaming wars and other atrocities on religion is seldom justified. One could well argue that if there were no such thing as religion, humankind's aggressive, predatory nature would have used nationalism, racism and manifest destiny as excuses and fought just as many wars and committed just as many atrocities. But atheists are wont to list the atrocities committed by religionists down through the centuries. Rulers (the successful), how-ever, use any ideology available as an excuse for committing atrocities. Do the atheistic Soviet Russians commit any fewer atrocities than did the Orthodox Czarist Russians? (Actually, the Soviet Russians have committed more and worse atrocities.)

The United States' recent cold war with the Soviet Union was very slightly due to the conflict between atheism and Christianity, but primarily due to the conflict between two different socioeconomic ideologies.

We can't say that without religion we would have a peaceful world. Fascism and nationalism, along with the antagonism between the capitalist and Communist ideologies, would doubtless fill any void left by religion. Humans will always find reasons for forming antagonistic, murderous, marauding groupings — always formed and manipulated by the shrewd and ruthless. Thousands of years ago the Essenes lamented humankind's propensity for evil: "Where in the world will you find a people that has not plundered the property of another?"

While we have made relentless progress in the physical sciences — heliocentrism, relativity, quantum physics, nuclear science, computer tech-nology and genetic engineering — our sociopolitical ideas and our religious ideas have changed very little since the time of Christ. Marxism and Nazism are about the only radical ideas that have taken hold, and I hesitate to call them progress.

How do we explain this? Perhaps evolution has selected societies that were conservative in the sociopolitical sphere and in the religious sphere. If sociopolitical progress had taken place at the same fast rate as scientific progress, human society might have by now disintegrated from the resulting progressive explosion.

Religion may be a governor that slows down progress—progress that would only hasten the explosion in the sociopolitical sphere and in physical science that would inevitably lead to destruction.

I would prefer a governor based on something besides dishonesty, hypocrisy and fraud. But, nevertheless, religion may contribute a pragmatic function.

Religion really needs no defense, no exposition of its beneficence nor elaboration of its goodness, so I will go no further into that. Evolution has selected religion and who can argue with evolution!

I will, though, in view of the overwhelming belief that religion does more good than harm, assume the role of devil's advocate and point out some of the unfavorable aspects of religion.

As devil's advocate, let me offer the opinion of H. L. Mencken: "I believe that religion, generally speaking, has been a curse to mankind—that its modest and greatly overestimated services on the ethical side have been more than overcome by the damage it has done to clear and honest thinking."

While rationalists view all religions as limiting humankind's mental development by filling children's heads with superstition, mythology and other humbug, rationalists do recognize a distinction between relatively harmless nonsense and beliefs that lead to mutilation, mayhem and murder.

Praying may be psychologically beneficial to many people, belief in a higher being may inspire transcendent behavior, humbleness may be conducive to peaceful social order, religious pageantry may be harmless enjoyment, religious art and music may enrich cultures, fear of Hell may have minor inhibiting effects on criminal behavior, heavenly rewards may motivate charity and good works. Saint Christophers hung on a dashboard can't hurt anything, the sacrament of eating Christ's flesh and drinking His blood is not much worse than repulsive. The love potions, black magic charms and gris-gris of voodoo are no more harmful than astrology charts in our daily newspapers.

But on the negative side rationalists see religion as chiefly responsible for the massacres among Old Testament Jewish tribes, the Christian

Crusades that wantonly slaughtered thousands of Moslems and stole their land, the medieval and Spanish Inquisitions that imprisoned and tortured tens of thousands of heretics and burned many at the stake.

The Holy Crusades of the Middle Ages are dramatic examples of the injustice, bigotry, zealotry, fraudulence, crime and brutality that have been committed in the name of the Prince of Peace.

Crusade organizers recruited followers by kindling religious hatred against the Saracens whom they described as an accursed race of Satanic infidels defiling the holy land of Christianity. But more often the Crusade organizers were landless feudal princes more interested in seeking kingdoms than in protecting holy land from desecration by Saracens or in retrieving the Holy Grail.

To facilitate easy enlistment, the pope granted the Crusaders special indulgences, the effect of which was to give them permission to sin all they wished while on the Crusade.

Such an enticement drew together much of the worst human scum of Europe into marauding mobs that rolled over the land like a flood, torturing and plundering Jews on their way to massacring the Saracens.

On the First Crusade many died on the great march, and when food ran out in Byzantium the Crusade leaders traded thousands of their followers into slavery in exchange for food.

Of the seven thousand who reached Asiatic soil, four thousand were slain by the Turks at Nicea. Many lives were lost by disease, internecine fighting and debauchery. The one force that unified them was their hatred of the infidels, which they vented in the massacre of men, women and children after capturing a city. Besieging Antioch, they shot heads of slain Turks into the city with their catapults.

When Crusaders took Jerusalem they burned all the Jews alive in their synagogues. Onward Christian soldiers!

The crowning glory of the series of Crusades that strung out over two centuries was the last one, the Children's Crusade. Among many of the misadventures of the children, about five thousand of them were offered free passage by ship to the holy land "for the cause of God." But they never reached the holy land; they were shipped to Algiers and Alexandria and sold as slaves.

All told, an estimated nine million human beings lost their lives in the attempts to retrieve the Holy Grail. Then it wasn't even found. In the light of the subsequent Crusades, John's First Epistle 2:8 seems a bit premature in announcing: "The darkness is past, and the true light now shineth."

In more recent times we have seen the Holocaust—the Nazi attempt to extinguish the Jews and Judaism. Soon after World War II, the Zionist Jews fought three wars with Islamic Arabs and Egyptians over the Zionist attempt to reclaim land the Jews say God had promised them.

In Northern Ireland we have witnessed a seemingly endless war between the Catholics and Protestants over political control of Northern Ireland.

In India the Moslems and Hindus are still slaying one another. Since the British government agreed to the partition of Pakistan and India in 1947, more than two million people have been killed there in interreligious massacres.

In Lebanon the horrible consequences of religion can be seen today where its capital city, Beirut, once known as the Paris of the Middle East, has been reduced to rubble by fighting among Israeli Jews, Palestinian Moslems, Shiite Moslems, the Christian Phalange and other religious factions.

Many religious virtues upon closer examination lose much of their sheen. Religious people act kindly and charitably not solely from a selfless desire to help the needy but also, of course, from a selfish desire to help themselves into Heaven.

Humanists and atheists, not expecting any heavenly reward, would seem to be doing good solely for the benefit of others. But I suspect that they too enjoy the warm feeling resulting from giving to the needy. In addition, such virtuous behavior is rewarded by the heightened respect shown them by friends and neighbors.

To be cynical, probably the greatest amount of private charity in America comes from corporations and individuals motivated by public relations considerations — the ultimate aim being greater profits.

The God factor in religion produces an unhealthy mental attitude toward life. The religionist is led to believe that his health is in the hands of God, rather than his own responsibility. He prays instead of jogging, he drinks holy water instead of mineral water, he goes to a faith healer instead of a medical doctor. He believes that sickness is punishment for wrongs against God rather than for his own wrongs against himself. He fails to take the responsibility for his own life and suffers for it. He is a victim of the false cause-and-effect logic that religion teaches. In addition, he suffers from religion-induced fear, guilt, self-denial and sex repression.

Although religion has fostered altruism, charity, kindness, love, compassion and brotherhood, much of these have been outweighed by its concomitant fostering of superstition, religious bigotry, hatred, sexism, dogmatism, intolerance, persecution, cruelty and war.

Religionists probably do engage in more charitable and humanitarian activities than do rationalists, atheists and secular humanists. But, of course, the greatest humanitarian largess for the poor and unfortunate comes from politicians and bureaucrats — if one considers their magnanimity in passing out taxpayers' money as acts of compassion and philanthropy.

A common belief is that goodness, compassion, love and honesty were created by religion and would vanish if religion were given up. The fact is most Eastern religions are concerned primarily with spirituality and see virtue and morality as much less important. Atheists believe it to be possible to carry on a decent and well-ordered world by means of a system of secular ethics and morality without a religious foundation. They see good behavior as primarily the product of education, training and conditioning along with good role models and a just system of reward and punishment.

In addition, there are certain views and attitudes already established that one picks up from his environment — views determined by nationality, race, social position, economic interest, sociopolitical ideology, taboos and cultural compulsives. Such views are taken as granted by both oneself and his neighbor, and often are treated as sacred and taboo and rarely discussed.

Also, more of our behavior than we probably realize is fashioned by our unconscious respect for subtle, unwritten rules such as returning greetings, answering a question rather than ignoring the questioner, maintaining a respectable distance from strangers, willingness to lend a reasonable hand to someone is need, holding an entrance door open for the person behind you, etc.

After you add to all those molders of behavior the fear of personal revenge for wronging others and the fear of embarrassment and punishment from legal sanctions, we end up with little need for the influence of religion.

Good behavior in children is produced by operant conditioning — the reward and punishment system — not by theological considerations. We train our children to behave well in the same way we train our dogs to behave well — by operant conditioning. Dogs never heard of the Bible.

We should ponder a quotation from the 18th century naturalist, John Burroughs: "You confound our ethical system, which we all accept, with Christianity. Our civilization is founded upon reason and science. Our civilization is not founded upon Christianity."

Religion may benefit society as a whole by indoctrinating people with honesty induced by fear of Hell and by charity induced by the selfish desire for eternal life and by humility induced by the desire to emulate Jesus. But the individual victim of such indoctrination is often crippled in our competitive world. And, in the view of atheists, he has been lied to about the reward he is counting on in an afterworld.

It is obvious that the goodies of Earth go mostly to the selfish and ruthless. People with strong consciences, those who take moral, ethical and religious teachings seriously, are crippled. As writer Budd Schulberg expressed it: "That's what you get for being a rabbi's son, a conscience. Going through life with a conscience is like driving your car with the brakes on."

It is both wise and cowardly to preach ethics and morality to other people. It makes the human environment safer for you and cripples competitors. The successful, the establishmentarians, with their Machiavellian wisdom, are great supporters of churches.

The term "religious hypocrite" is almost as common as "wicked witch" or "crooked politician." This results from the inhuman moral demands made on the private behavior of ministers and their flocks in a competitive milieu in which they are expected to succeed, or at least survive. The demands for success have forced clergymen down through history to support the ruling establishments. This often required that they preach love, compassion and mercy while supporting slavery, sexism, racism, witch-burning, Medieval torture and war. But such requirement makes them no less hypocrites, even if it does elicit some forgiveness born of understanding.

So, ministers and their flocks are perhaps more to be pitied than censored. They are the victims of the evils of religion, as well as the perpetrators of them.

John Stuart Mill described his father as regarding religion not as a mere mental delusion, but as a great moral evil. His father saw religion as the greatest enemy of morality. It fosters belief in creeds, devotional feelings and ceremonies not connected with the good of humankind. Finally, Mill's father took a dim view of the Christian God, who would make Hell and create the human race with the foreknowledge and intention of consigning most of them to the horror of burning forever in Hell.

Charles Darwin wrote in a similar vein: "I can indeed hardly see how anyone ought to wish Christianity to be true; for if so the plain language of the text seems to show that the men who do not believe, and this would include my Father, Brother and almost all my best friends, will be everlastingly punished. . . . And this is damnable doctrine."

The religious right brain has been warring against the rational left brain since time immemorial. Thousands of rationalists, scientists, philosophers, educators and writers have been opposed, persecuted, imprisoned, tortured, burned at the stake by religionists.

Fearing exposure of its frauds, curtailment of its power and loss of credibility, the church has always curried the favor of the ruling establishment by preaching humility to the potentially truculent masses and keeping them mired in enfeebling ignorance.

From the atheist's viewpoint, every segment of society suffers harm from religion, even the religionists themselves. The more devout they are the more tragic their lives. They plan their lives in accordance with their sect's theology—lives of piety, devotion and holy obedience. They attend church, they pray, they bless every meal, they tithe, they do charitable work, they renounce many earthly pleasures, they follow the commandments, they do good deeds, they turn the other cheek, they humble themselves to their church superiors. They do all these things believing that God is watching them and will reward them handsomely in the next world. But the atheist, believing neither in God nor a next world, sees the religious game as a cruel hoax, a grand swindle.

Theodore Dreiser wrote in "The Color of a Great City": "Of all pathetic dreams, that which pictures a spiritual salvation elsewhere for one who has failed in his dreams here is the thinnest and palest."

Atheists see the billions of dollars spent on religion as not just wasted, but doing great harm to society by promoting ignorance and superstition. If taxes were collected on presently tax-exempt church property and collected from tax-exempt church income, the amount of money available for education and other benefits to society would double.

Millions of priests, nuns, ministers, holy men and church janitors could give up their useless occupations and be reeducated and rehabilitated to lead productive lives contributing to our national affluence. Without the parasitic burden of religion we could all be rich.

James Madison, the paradigm advocate of freedom and democracy, described the fruits of Christianity: "More or less in all places, pride and indolence in the Clergy; ignorance and servility in the laity; in both, superstition, bigotry, and persecution. . . . What influence in fact have ecclesiastical establishments had on Civil Society? In some instances they have been seen to erect a spiritual tyranny on the ruins of Civil authority; in many instances they have been seen upholding the thrones of political tyranny; in no instance have they been seen the guardians of the liberties of the people."

The harm that religion has perpetrated on one-half of society since ancient times is now being slowly (too slowly) recognized. Almost all religions have treated women as sub-humans. Preceding the Judaic culture, pagan religions treated women with no less contempt than did the succeeding Judeo-Christian religions. Priests arrogated to themselves the sacred duty of acting as surrogates of God in deflowering all the virgins within their domain. Holy men created the institutions of temple priestesses to ensure themselves an ample supply of girls to fulfill their sexual desires. Temple priestesses were also exploited as prostitutes to enrich the male-dominated temples.

The succeeding Hebrew religion found it necessary for its ascendancy to discredit the sensuality of the old phallus-worshipping temple religions. Sex was declared to be original sin, and Eve the original sinner. Eve had disobeyed God and ruined all mankind.

The Hebrew religion viewed women as sinful and unclean. Bearing a child was a sin that had to be expiated either by the mother being ostracized for eighty days or by the alternative of making a sin-offering. The Talmud declared three cleansings were necessary for leprosy and three for childbirth, thus placing childbirth on the same plane of defilement with a hideous disease.

The new Christian sect continued the same theme: God had to sacrifice his own son to save the world from the plight into which woman had plunged it.

St. Paul said: "How can he be clean that is born of woman?" St. clement said: "Every woman ought to be overcome with shame at the thought that she is a woman."

How did women come into such disrepute in the new religion? Once the new religion took a stand against sex, women, whose whole lives revolve around the functions of copulation, impregnation, gestation, parturition, lactation and menstruation, were bound to be scapegoats. To treat the natural functions of women as nasty, obscene and sinful was to relegate women to the barnyard manure pile.

The Islamic religion has been no better in its treatment of women. Mohammed veiled women and barred them from social, economic and cultural life. "O true believers," said Mohammed, "when you prepare yourselves to pray, wash your faces and your hands unto the elbows ... but if any of you cometh from the privy, or if you have touched women, and you find no water, take fine, clean sand and rub your faces and your hands therewith."

The popularity of the Iranian fundamentalist movement initiated by Ayatollah Khomeini is apparently a backlash of Moslem men against the modernization reforms of the Shah — reforms that were liberating Moslem women from domination and exploitation by Moslem men.

Our negative attitude toward women accompanies our negative attitude toward sex. If sex is evil, then women, whose lives are totally involved physiologically with sex, are inextricably evil.

Most of our laws, customs, morality and attitudes have come to us from patriarchal Judeo-Christian theology. In supporting Judeo-Christian religions, women are supporting their chief oppressors.

In the past, men were able to do very much as they pleased with women. Men were masters because of women's relative physical weakness and because of women's dependence on men resulting from continual pregnancies.

Men used these advantages to enslave women just as militarily strong nations have reduced weaker nations to bondage and more advanced races have enslaved more backward races.

Three of the great religions of the world—Jewish, Christian and Islamic—have promoted the fiction of the intrinsic inferiority and lesser value of women. Not until the 585 A.D. council at Macon were European women granted souls. And not until about 1700 were women counted in the census of the Greek church, because only "souls" were counted.

Saint Paul said that a husband is supreme over his wife. "A man has no need to cover his head," said Saint Paul, "because he reflects the glory of God. . . . But woman reflects the glory of man. . . . Nor was man created for woman's sake, but woman was created for man's sake. . . . Therefore, a woman should have a covering over her head, to show that she is under her husband's authority."

There you have in a nutshell Christian theology regarding women. Women are chattels of men, property similar to cattle and she-asses, merchandise, male playthings, domestic slaves; also semen bags and incubators to extend the immortality of the male ego.

The false doctrine of male superiority proclaimed by religion has been built into our educational system, our politics, our cultural arts, our legal and medical professions—even into our languages.

When I was a child I was mystified by nuns in their black and white vestments whom I occasionally passed on the street. I did not know then that they lived cloistered lives in prison-like convents nor that there were similar religious places where celibate men lived.

Had I known this, I might have wondered what possible good monasticism could be—to the Church, to society, to the martyred inmates.

One wonders, is monasticism religion for religion's sake? Maintaining such mental sinkholes of ignorance, superstition and gloom costs churches heavily and appears to benefit no one—least of all the poor dupes accepting such a doleful substitute for living.

Joseph McCabe, a former priest turned atheist, exposed the evils of monasticism, which nearly ruined his life: "The monastic system is a fraud and hypocrisy from beginning to end. . . . Almost half are immoral . . . and their life would be intolerable but for the generous supply of liquor, the possession of each of money (in defiance of their vows), and the incessant visitation of their lady parishioners. Their long religious ceremonies are an empty and a dreary formalism."

The shabby Christian treatment of love and sex probably shouldn't be blamed on Jesus, but on whoever authored the term "conceived in sin." As a result of this precept, sex is treated as dirty and sinful — something to do behind closed doors. How much more sensible it would be to take the same wholesome attitude toward sex that we take toward eating. The one is just as necessary and natural as the other. If the church taught that eating was a sin, you know people would eat anyhow. They'd eat in dark corners, sneak their food away, and lie about it all. And that's just what happens when we try to prohibit love and sex — we make people into sneaks and hypocrites.

Of course, sex can be unhealthy and dangerous — imprudent sex can lead to unwanted pregnancy, disease and even death. But so can eating. The wrong kind of nutrition can lead to an early grave. Poisonous and tainted food can lead to an even earlier grave.

But the Bible writers centered in on sex as their prime sin. That unfortunate choice has resulted in ceaseless damage to society and to individual humans. The very promoters and enforcers of this pernicious rubric are more often than not its chief victims.

Priests, preachers, deacons, nuns, monks and holy men earnestly try to abide by their sex-renouncing vows that demand behavior in violation of nature and detrimental to emotional, psychological and physical health.

Their attempt to lead such unnatural lives inevitably results in violation of their vows, coverup deceit, hypocrisy, criminal behavior, humiliation, defrocking and sometimes imprisonment.

William Lecky, a famous British historian, refers to the Catholic convents of the Middle Ages: "The writings of the Middle Ages are full of accounts of nunneries that were like brothels, of the vast multitude of infanticides within their walls, and of that inveterate prevalence of incest among the clergy, which rendered it necessary again and again to issue the most stringent enactments that priests should not be permitted to live with their mothers and sisters."

What seems to happen as a result of the attempts of religious men to deny themselves normal sexual outlets is that the buildup of their testosterone hormones creates overcharged sexual desires that warp their judgment, twist their thinking, weaken their inhibitions and overpower their resistance to temptation.

In many cases their moral attention is focused on normal heterosexual desires, to which they build up a willpower of resistance. But so strong is their sex drive that they glance off the highly resisted target into periphery sex perversions — masturbation, homosexuality, child molesting, sexual fetishes, bestiality.

A typical modern (1988) example of crime perpetrated by men of the cloth concerns a roving evangelist Mario "Tony" Leyva, his organist Rias Morris and business manager Rev. Freddie Herring. Leyva, a smooth-talking, charismatic preacher, persuaded his audiences to give him money and lend him their sons for what was called "special religious instruction."

The latter instruction consisted of molesting the boys by the three conspirators. The boys were kept quiet by showering them with gifts and money and by taking them on exciting and adventurous travels around the country to revival meetings. The flamboyant Leyva swept the boys, 13 to 16, off their feet by dressing up in a Superman costume and portraying himself as "Super Christian." The boys idolized him.

Leyva and his associates molested dozens of boys for a period of over four years before being caught.

The mother of three of the boys said: "I was a widow at the time and was happy about the attention he paid to my boys because I felt they needed a good, strong Christian father figure. I thought Tony Leyva was what he claimed to be — a man who had been anointed by God to preach the gospel. I thought he was above suspicion."

Tony Leyva, reacting indignantly to the charges against him, told supporters that Satan was trying to wreck his ministry. Rev. Herring told reporters that he felt "in the same position as Jesus was when he was on the cross. Right now it's open season on ministers."

Leyva claimed that Jesus appeared to him at age 12 and anointed him to preach the Gospel. And there is no reason to believe that Leyva didn't start out as a sincere Christian believing he had received the call to spread the Word. But years and years of sex starvation can twist one's thinking to the point where one condones his own reprehensible behavior. The demands of the libido can mold one's morality.

The above example is not rare. The December 1986 issue of "Freethought Today" listed two dozen recent cases of the sexual misdeeds of men of the cloth. Among them were Roman Catholic priest Andrew Christian Anderson, 34, who received a five-year probation for 26 counts of molesting four altar boys; Rev. David Boyea, 38, of the Green Bay

Catholic Diocese, who was sentenced to ten years in prison for first degree sexual assault involving a young boy (other charges of fondling nine other boys were dropped as part of a plea bargain); Rev. Gilles Deslauriers, 49, of Cornwall, Ontario, a Roman Catholic priest who offered to help young men with their sex problems, was sentenced to two years probation after pleading guilty to four counts of gross indecency; Fred Beihl, 43, former employee of the Oklahoma Conference of Churches, sentenced to a 240-year prison term for first degree rape, forcible oral sodomy, indecent exposure and lewd acts against four girls ages 8 and 9; Thomas C. Konopka, 40, a member of Community Chapel and Bible Training Center in Burien was sentenced to ten years in prison for taking indecent liberties with a teenage relative; preacher Nicholas Hatcher, 46, was charged with repeatedly raping and molesting two girls under 12 at the Taft Pentecostal Church of Christ. The Roman Catholic Diocese of Orlando agreed to pay $490,000 to the family of one of four altar boys sexually assaulted by priest William Authenrieth; ex-priest Gerard Vesnaugh, 47, wanted by Michigan authorities since he jumped parole in 1985 following child molesting charges, has been convicted of additional charges of sexual assault and perjury; pastor Bob Walton, 42, of St. Paul United Presbyterian Church, Mecklenburg, S.C., pleaded guilty to misdemeanor sexual assault of a high school student at his church, and was sentenced to 30 days in jail; Rev. Clyde Johnson Sr., pastor of First Baptist Church of Petersburg, Va., upon being indicted on 39 counts of sexual abuse of five female juveniles from ages 10 to 15, asked his congregation to march to the jail in a show of support and 100 showed up; a Seattle woman has filed a $16 million suit against Trent Rogers, 69, convicted of molesting her four-year-old daughter, and against the Mormon Church, which appointed him as a "home teacher" to watch over the family; Mormon parishioner Steve Paris, 34, was arrested and accused of engaging in sodomy and oral copulation with seven boys ages 5 to 11; Hare Krishna handyman Kenneth Capoferri, 38, received a 50-year prison sentence in Los Angeles for molesting two girls and two boys, ages 2 to 4, at the sect's child care center; Poway, California church youth counselor Lionel P. Jacques, 31, pleaded guilty to engaging in oral copulation with one of the youngsters he was counseling; a Spokane Bible instructor, Mayor J. Baker, 64, who calls himself "Jesus Christ reincarnated," was charged with rape, statutory rape and indecent liberties against three girls, ages 9, 13, and 16 during private Bible study sessions over a period of six years; Jeffrey Bart Schreck, 30, a Sunday school teacher, has been charged with multiple counts of sexual assault involving four boys aged 9 to 12 during youth group meetings for the God's Covenant People, a church in Aurora, Colorado; Rev. Altha Baugh, 59, former executive of Valley Forge headquarters of the American Baptist Churches of the USA was sentenced to three to ten years in prison for sexually assaulting young boys, including sodomy, between the ages of 9 and 12.

It is common knowledge that down through Roman Catholic history since the Lateral Councils of the 12th century demanded celibacy of priests, the Church has been plagued by homosexuality, child molestation and incest among its priesthoods and monastic orders. Today it is additionally plagued by AIDS.

The number of members of the Catholic priesthood across the country who have contracted AIDS is unknown, the Church having worked to keep the problem secret because of its stand against homosexuality and its prohibition of any sexual activity for priests.

One of the few priests whose AIDS has been publicized is Benedictine Brother Mario Riveccio, 37, of Washington. "I'm willing to go public," said Riveccio, "because I don't think the Church is dealing with reality."

Until recent years police and prosecutors seem to have been glad to let the Church handle the messy business of priestly sex crimes. The Church's main concern has not been to punish the errant priests but to cover up their transgressions in order to protect the Church from scandal. The common practice has been to transfer pedophilic priests from one diocese to another when their sexual involvement with children became known. And the Church has been very successful until the recent popular concern over child abuse, a concern that has reached hysterical heights reminiscent of the McCarthy era.

Today priests (as well as Protestant ministers) are being arrested right and left and sent to prison for their sexual crimes. No more verbal scoldings from bishops and transfer to other dioceses where they can resume their mischief. In addition, the Church is being successfully sued for hundreds of millions of dollars for damage done by priests to altar boys and other Catholic children. The game seems to be over.

One of the most egregious cases of priestly pedophilia took place in the Lafayette, Louisiana diocese. One priest, Rev. Gilbert Gauthe, 41, pleaded guilty in 1987 to molesting 11 altar boys. Gauthe received a 20-year prison sentence. Gauthe had been confronted with allegations of child molesting in 1974 and 1976, but after counseling was allowed to return to duty.

Another priest from the same church was sentenced on sex charges, and lawsuits were instigated against a third priest. One church official said about 20 priests in the diocese have been accused of or counseled for sexual misconduct. Lawyers say the church has paid $10 million in out-of-court settlements to at least 18 children sodomized by Gauthe, and at least 22 more alleged victims have lawsuits pending.

Priest Ronald Fontenot, a youth leader, was removed from the diocese in 1983 after a family threatened to bring molestation charges. Fontenot later worked at a Church-run teenage drug abuse center in Spokane, Wash., where he was arrested for molesting five boys there.

After years of coverup, the Lafayette scandal was finally broken open in 1986 when the parents of one of the victims chose to fight their suit in public rather than accept an out-of-court settlement as other families before them did. Their victimized son testified that he thought the priest was doing the right thing. "He was a priest." The jury awarded the family $1.25 million.

Thomas Doyle of Washington, D.C., a canon lawyer who investigated the Lafayette case for the Vatican, said: "I do think this is the single most dangerous problem facing the Church today."

One would think that the Catholic Church could not be blind to the connection between the deviant behavior of its priests and its demand of unnatural celibacy, as well as the connection between its sin-prone laity and the Church's demand of proscriptive sexual behavior.

But the Church may not be blind at all. The demands of the Church for the celibacy of its clergy and the constrained sexual behavior of its members are beyond the ability of most humans to obey. This assures the Church of guilt-ridden priests and laity whose guilt keeps them ashamed and subservient. They are forever at the mercy of the Church because only the ordained can forgive Church members for their sins and relieve them of their guilt, and only superiors in the Church hierarchy can forgive the priests for their sins and relieve them of their guilt. The Church gathers much of its power from the inhuman demands it makes on its clergy and laity.

But sex is not intrinsically ugly. Various sex-denouncing religions have crushed the beautiful potential of sex. They have condemned whole civilizations to sex-sin-guilt pathology, and turned the miracle of procreation into a dirty, ugly thing.

The treatment of sex by most religions is contrary to nature, unwholesome, neurotic and imbecilic. Sexual perverts are mostly the victims of our deplorable religious attitude toward sex — more to be pitied than censored.

In every direction atheists look, they see harm done by religion. I think it is much more than a case of seeing what one believes.

Religion has inveterately opposed science and free inquiry. It has skirted learning by equating education with religious indoctrination.

The function of the Church of the Middle Ages was to curry the favor of the secular rulers by keeping the peasants and workers illiterate and ignorant: An uninformed commonality poses little threat to rulers.

Up until the 16th century the Catholic Church told the people what to think. In fact, the Church even forbade the laity to read the Bible. Martin Luther and other dissidents then began to do a little thinking for themselves and ushered in the Reformation. The only trouble was that their minds remained enslaved by the superstition and mythology of religion. They had broken out of their cells but were still surrounded by the walls of the prison.

C. E. S. Wood, in his *Heavenly Discourse* makes a cogent point concerning religion's opposition to science and learning. Wood has God address Peter: "You might convert your church back to Christ. Do you realize, Peter, that your church in all these years has never once led human thought or stood for any rebellion toward freedom and progress, but has steadily supported power, tyranny, authority, the old against the new, and has tried to shut out every new ray of light? Do your realize that your church is founded on ignorance, superstition, and blind obedience, that it puts the mythologies of the Jews, old and new, above the living truth voiced by me in the tongues of rocks, the sea, the golden pollen of plants, the egg and the spark? These and such as these are the Book of Life which I myself have written."

Atheists don't believe that the evidence of supernaturalism could be supported in either a scientific laboratory or a court of law, and that supernaturalism is an institutionalized anachronism of our age, a hideous millstone around our necks supported by the hypocrisy of the educated, the greed of vested interests and the will of the herd to believe.

Some atheists, including Freud, see religion as something that has grown in the human brain like a cancer until it has become the most widespread mental disease afflicting humankind. The sad part is that religion is probably no more necessary to us than are the diseases of tuberculosis and leprosy. Viewed as a cancer, religion makes absurd the frequent question about what one would replace religion with if it were abolished. One does not ask a surgeon with what he is going to replace a malignant tumor.

If not a mental disease, religion has certainly retarded mental development. When a person is convinced that his Bible contains the absolute truth, the stimulus for him to think any further is removed. When you find the ring you were searching for, you stop searching.

People, upon finding the "truth," spend the remainder of their lives defending it. Christianity protects itself against the doubting of its theology by making doubting one of its greatest sins. By contrast, doubting is the greatest virtue of science.

Specific harms done by religion are common stories. Faith healing, including Christian Science, teaches a false reliance on divine healing power. The result is sometimes death to believers as well as to their children resulting from refusal of medical treatment. In 1984 the four-year-old daughter of a Sacramento Christian Science couple died of acute meningitis 17 days after being taken to a Christian Science healer instead of to a hospital. The parents of an 11-year-old Barstow, California boy who had been a diabetic for five years threw away his insulin after a faith healer of an Assembly of God church had purportedly cured him. The boy died.

The Jehovah's Witness prohibition against blood transfusions has resulted in the unnecessary deaths of uncounted numbers of Witnesses and their children.

The most widespread harm to health results from the carryover of the superstition and magic of religion into the realm of medical quackery. The quackery includes practitioners and clinics that claim to cure anything from an ingrown toenail to cancer. They employ ridiculous diets, senseless fasting, wheatgrass and coffee enemas, laetrile, snake oil, psychic surgery, magical radiations, iridology, reflexology and any other humbug a gullible coprophagous public will swallow.

Witchcraft and exorcism, direct derivatives from Christianity, have also done untold harm. The Bible recognizes witchcraft in its infamous verse "Thou shalt not suffer a witch to live." (Eight words responsible for the deaths of hundreds of thousands of innocent people down through Christian history. John Wesley, founder of Methodism, wrote: "The giving up of witchcraft is in effect giving up the Bible."

Jesus Himself practiced exorcism when He cast devils from two possessed men into a herd of swine. The Bible recounts that "the swine ran violently down a cliff into the sea and were drowned."

Sporadic instances of belief in the devil still pop up in the news even in our enlightened times. A black pastor of a small Brooklyn faith-healing sect became greatly excited by his revival meetings. One day he threw a sofa and a chair out of his second-floor window under a delusion that the devil was after him. A few days later he jumped out of the window to escape the devil and ended up in the hospital.

A Houston woman began babbling scriptures after attending a prayer meeting and beat her two-year-old son to death claiming she saw the devil in his eyes. She beat him with a wine bottle and then sat on him.

A self-appointed exorcist was sent to prison for ten years for beating his handicapped roommate to death in exorcising the demons out of him. After seven hours of beating, the roommate died.

In the Middle Ages the blind and the insane were flogged to beat the devil out of them. The Catholic Church even today recognizes exorcism of the devil.

But the Middle Ages paid a heavy price for their religious superstitions. A belief arose that cats were possessed by demons, so a campaign was directed at killing all the cats in Europe. The campaign was successful enough to result in an explosion of the rat population, carriers of the bubonic plague. The ensuing Black Death bubonic plague wiped out one-third of the population of Europe.

We must not get the mistaken idea that massive harm was done by religion only in the distant past. Massive harm is still being done — the millions of victims of religion-based wars around the globe, the genocide attempt of the Syrian-backed Moslems of Beirut to destroy the Christian Phalangists, the fighting between the Jewish Israelis and the Moslem Arabs, the bloody ordeal between the Hindus and the Moslems in India, the fighting between the Catholics and Protestants in Northern Ireland, etc.

The superstition propensity of the right brain knows no bounds of absurdity, imagination and creativity. In Uganda in 1987 a priestess of the Holy Spirit cult attacked the government with thousands of troops she had convinced would be invulnerable to bullets because of the oil she rubbed on their chests. Seven thousand of her warriors marched into battle with sticks and stones they believed would explode like hand grenades. Government troops with modern weapons mowed them down.

History had repeated itself. A little over 300 years earlier an English cult calling themselves the Fifth Monarchy Men preached that Christ had come.

They believed that Christ was invisibly at their side and rendered them invulnerable and invincible as they attempted an insurrection. They refused to surrender, convinced that the Lord would protect them, as government forces shot them down.

In citing cases of harm done by religion, we must not overlook the People's Temple cult founded by the charismatic, mentally deranged Jim Jones. Jones brought about the deaths by suicide and murder of 913 men, women and children Temple members in their jungle retreat in Guyana in 1978.

In Mark 16:17-18 Jesus said: "In my name . . . They shall take up serpents; and if they drink any deadly thing, it shall not hurt them." So, many Holiness Church preachers and devout laymen took up handling poisonous snakes and swallowing poisons. Some of the preachers made great names for themselves handling rattlesnakes before their congregations. Skeptics suspected that the snakes were either defanged or milked of venom before the demonstrations.

But in 1945 two Church of God ministers devoutly believing in the protective anointment of the Holy Spirit, as proven by the other snake-handling preachers, were bitten and died. Skepticism would have served them better than faith did.

The cases of those two gained wide publicity and aroused some states to pass laws against snake handling, but the practice continued. Other snake handlers died. In 1974 in Ohio minister conducting a revival service in West Virginia was bitten by a diamondback rattlesnake. His arm swelled up to a grotesque size and he died the next morning. But the congregation was not dismayed nor disillusioned about anointment by the Holy Spirit. They saw his death as a godly sacrifice similar to that of Jesus on the cross. And they saw his death as disproving skeptics' accusations of fraud.

To demonstrate the anointing power of the Holy Spirit some ministers drank poisons, such as Drano, battery acid and strychnine. Two such ministers in Tennessee in 1973 drank strychnine and died.

In 1972 two members of the Church of Armageddon inhaled fumes from tuolene, lost consciousness and died. Their families were told that after three days they would rise again from the dead. When they failed to do so, their minister explained that the two were not strong enough in their faith.

Now let's look into some current worldwide bad effects of religion that even threaten our very civilization. We are slowly grasping the devastating magnitude of some of these indirect effects of religion beginning to appear on the horizons. These harmful threats are the result of our failure to restrain the population explosion, a failure for which religion is chiefly to blame.

Our society begins by denying that religion has any connection to overpopulation. Then we deny that overpopulation has any connection to our problems: pollution of our lakes, rivers, acquifiers and oceans; acid rain and smog, depletion of the ozone layer, the greenhouse effect, deforestation, overburdened sewage and waste-disposal systems, urban congestion and highway gridlock; overcrowded schools and jails, stress disease, increased violence and rising crime; growing hordes of homeless, starvation in Third World countries, and the increasing rate of depletion of Earth's unrenewable natural resources.

Fifty years ago we had few of these problems. Fifty years ago we had half the population we have today. But a cultural compulsive blinds us to the connection between the two. To blame our overwhelming problems on the population explosion seems to be tantamount to reviling motherhood.

Religion above all is to blame for abetting overpopulation with its disastrous consequences. As our population burgeons we do almost nothing to eliminate the cause of our troubles, but devote most of our attention to alleviating the effects of such population increases. We pass ever more stringent laws governing pollution, we design more efficient automobiles, we plan massive public transportation systems, we work at improving our waste disposal systems, we protect species endangered by the increasing population, we pass laws to decrease acid rain, we build more schools and jails, we try to feed the increasing hordes of starving Third World people, we pitch tents for our homeless. (And we cut off funds to support the United Nations population control efforts.)

But, so long as population continues on its explosive course we can never keep up with alleviating its disastrous effects. Our present approach is futile, stupid, foredoomed.

We are like the occupants of a sinking boat who bail faster and faster instead of plugging the hole in the boat, a hole that wears larger and larger from the rush of water through it.

Religionists find their rationale for opposing birth control and abortion in God's order to go forth and populate the Earth. But God didn't say to overpopulate it. When God ordered humankind to be plentiful and multiply, the population of Earth was two people, not five and one-half billion!

There are many enlightened people in the world aware of the increasing devastation being wrought by overpopulation. But their efforts to do something about it are regularly opposed by most churches. Pro-life religious fanatics attempt to shut down women's medical clinics by blockading them, by bombing them, and by calling abortion baby killing. The Catholic Church even opposes artificial birth control. Mother Teresa travels from one Third World country to another preaching against abortion and birth control—where overpopulation causes hundreds of thousands of deaths from starvation and malnutrition every year. For this she is awarded a Nobel Prize. In the name of religion, former President Reagan in 1985 canceled our country's contribution to a United Nations fund created to arrest the population explosion. President George Bush, yielding to right-to-life pressure, followed in Reagan's footsteps by denying U.S. funds to the United Nations family planning efforts.

A world facing devastation from overpopulation while fighting for laws to force women to have unwanted babies just doesn't make much sense.

If we go on doubling world population the Apocalyptic Horsemen of famine, pestilence, war, genocide, homicide and suicide will stabilize the population at a level bereft of cultural arts, science, education, democracy, decency and dignity.

The anti-abortionists, mostly religious-oriented, have a frenetic obsession with the sanctity of life and demand that every little scrap of embryonic tissue be preserved no matter how defective, how deformed, how demented or how unneeded.

They see the loss of such tissue as a loss to humanity. But how do they know that the embryonic tissue wouldn't turn out to be another Adolf like Hitler or Eichmann? Or a Josef Stalin or Idi Amin or a Pol Pot? Or a Ted Bundy who confessed murdering 29 women? Or a Lawrence Singleton who raped a young woman and then chopped off both of her arms and left her to die? Or a John Wayne Gacy Jr. who tortured to death 33 boys and young men and buried them under his house? Were these monsters' lives so very precious!

One may wonder why, if religion is so good for people, there have been so many religious leaders down through history who were ruthless tyrants, brutal sadists, evil monsters.

There was David (who achieved celebrity status by decking Goliath with a slingshot) who wanted to marry King Saul's daughter, Michal. The king's price for his daughter was a dowry of one hundred foreskins of his enemies, the Philistines. David, being no cheapskate, rounded up his soldiers and went out and slew two hundred Philistines and delivered their foreskins to his future father-in-law. (I Sam. 18:25-27)

There was Pope Benedict IX, whose life was so shameful, foul, adulterous and murderous that the people finally rose against him. Another Ninth was Pope Gregory, who published the imperial law to burn heretics.

Then there was Tomas de Torquemada, a pope-appointed inquisitor who is credited with ordering, during his five-year tenure, the burning to death of 8,800 heretics and blasphemers. Thousands of other victims of the Inquisition were tortured with molten lead, thumb screws, iron boots and racks.

The Reformation apparently didn't reform John Calvin. He ordered the anatomist Servitus burned at the stake with a small fire so Servitus would have more time to suffer and Calvin would have more time to enjoy it.

Jumping to modern times there was the recent Ayatollah Ruhollah Khomeini, a mean-spirited monster who incited young men and boys to high religious fervor and threw them against the better-armed Iraqis, who slaughtered them by the hundreds of thousands.

One might wonder whether ruthless, evil monsters gain religious leadership by means of such characteristics and then corrupt and debase their followers, or whether the populace is rotten itself and simply picks its own kind for leaders.

There does seem to be something about religion that encourages evil behavior. Voltaire said: "People will cease to commit atrocities when they cease to believe in absurdities."

Our country's most infamous racist and anti-Semitic organization, the Ku Klux Klan, has always been led by Christian fundamentalists.

The truth is that the horrible Christian leaders humankind has suffered from down through history found plenty of atrocious role models among the revered patriarchs of the Bible, as well as even God Himself.

Saul smote the Ameleks and utterly destroyed them, slaying both man and woman, infant and suckling, ox and sheep, camel and ass.

In another gruesome episode, King David commanded his soldiers to slay David's enemies, and cut off their hands and feet and hang them.

Joshua, warring against a consortium of kings, burned down their towns, smote all the souls therein, leaving not any to breathe, and burned their chariots and crippled all their horses.

According to the Bible, God shows little compassion or forgiveness, mouths morals to others and has none Himself, and frowns on crimes while committing them all. And, of course, God committed the greatest mass murder in history when He drowned everybody in the world but the nuclear family of Noah.

Sadistic Christian leaders can defend their infamies by arguing that if the Lord punishes his creatures with torture infinite in cruelty, why shouldn't His earthly ministers, so far as they can, imitate Him.

Three members of an Evangelistic Chapel near Seattle were charged with beating a small boy as punishment for spraying water on a rug in the church. For two hours three men beat him with sticks. The three were charged with second degree assault.

A couple living in a school bus in Virginia Beach with their own three children and 13 adopted children were charged with child abuse in the homicide death of one of their adopted sons aged 13. The father admitted that for a month he had been tying the boy to the floor of the bus and beating him with a switch.

The father told the media they were not ashamed of the way they treated their children, as God had guided their actions. The adoption agency had placed the children with the couple believing they were loving parents evident from their church-centered life. Sadistic parents especially like Proverbs 23:13-14: "Withhold not correction from the child. . . . Thou shalt beat him with the rod, and shalt deliver his soul from hell."

The self-righteous belief that God is on one's side leads to the easy justification of the most horrible criminal behavior. The victories of the Christian knights over the Saracens during the Crusades was an affirmation to the Christians that God was on their side (their victories were due to superior arms). One medieval story tells about a knight, Sir Torrent of Portugal, who killed a Saracen every Friday for seven years. (That's 364 Saracens.) One is reminded of the popular bumper sticker of the 1960s: KILL A HIPPY FOR CHRIST.

The right brain seems to be as gullible in swallowing lies as it is easily inclined to spread them. Garbage in, garbage out. The supernatural itself seems to appeal to dishonest people. Further, lying, cheating, tricking and deceiving are seen as virtues when done in the service of the Lord.

The body of a buried atheist hardly has time to adjust to ground temperatures before religionists begin inventing stories about how the atheist repented on his death bed.

Probably one of the reasons for the dishonesty of religionists stems from the impossibly high church standard of conduct that petitioners must agree to accept as the condition of membership. The new member soon learns to play the game of deception, dishonesty, coverup and hypocrisy.

For example, the Catholic Church's prohibition of divorce for members who had been married in the Church (those not married in the Church being considered not married) has been circumvented by annulment of their marriages (for a fee). Since the basis for annulment was liberalized to include incompatibility, the devious practice has skyrocketed. Annulment means that the couple are considered never to have been married in the first place—which seems pretty close to the border of dishonesty.

The Catholic Church's prohibition of artificial birth control is flagrantly disregarded. A 1987 *Los Angeles Times* poll of Catholics showed that only one out of four agree with the Pope that artificial birth control is a sin.

In 1989 CBS "48 Hours" revealed that Catholics are 30 percent more likely to get abortions than Jews or Protestants—explanation: Catholics' shame to let it be known that they got pregnant.

The over-stringent rules of churches force their members into disobedience of them, making it easier to also disobey the rules of their civil governments. Breaking inhuman religious laws in order to survive can unfortunately develop habitual patterns of law-breaking.

Nevertheless, the belief in the necessity and benefits of religion impels most people, including nonbelievers, to endorse religion. But one may wonder how the thousands of years of brutality, intolerance, torture, ignorance and murder fostered by religion can lead to such a belief!

If there were really anything to the moral uplifting claims of religion one would expect the prisons to be overflowing with atheists. Statistics show that there are actually more strongly devout people in prisons percentage-wise than atheists.

The theology of Martin Luther is anything but discouraging to criminality. In "Table Talk" Luther wrote: "He that says the gospel requires works for salvation, I say flat and plain he is a liar. . . . If men only believe enough in Christ they can commit adultery and murder a thousand times a day without periling their salvation."

Some modern spiritual innovators like to define God as love. Outside of the difficulty of defining love, Christianity hasn't exactly reeked with love over the centuries.

During the 1960s a young lady reacting to a hippy's badge "Make love, not war," remarked primly, "That's all right if it's Christian love."

One searches in vain for Christian love among the Crusaders who killed millions of Moslems and stole their land in the name of Jesus; or the love radiating from the Spanish Inquisition as it ordered the burning alive of heretics; or the love expressed by the Catholics in massacring thousands of Protestants on Saint Bartholomew's Day; or the love in the hearts of the Puritan Pilgrims of Massachusetts who burned to death most of the Pequot Indians by setting fire to their camp at night while they slept (the Pequots who escaped the holocaust were rounded up and sold into slavery in the Caribbean).

Christian love has too often been expressed by the rubric: If you don't accept our loving Prince of Peace we'll kill you. "He that believeth not shall be damned," is the Biblical verse that has too often bloodied the sword of the church.

But the Christian religion has no monopoly on cruelty. Even today some Moslem countries practice ghastly cruel punishments for those who break the laws of the Islamic religion, such as beheading for murder, rape, adultery and drug-trafficking. For theft merely the hand is cut off. Saudi Arabia's official executioner has cut off the heads of 600 condemned criminals (at $133 a head). He says he doesn't mind cutting off heads as much as he does cutting off hands. When a man's head is cut off, that's the end for him — forget him. But when a man's hand is cut off, he's still around, but with only one hand.

Another evil facet of religion is the emphasis on theology at the expense of virtue, compassion, kindness, love and charity. Charles Dickens wrote *The Life of Our Lord*, an honest attempt to tell the story of Jesus Christ in plain language, free from theological details. It was reverent and placed emphasis on good conduct and decent living. It was written for children and unconcerned with theological dogma. And churchmen attacked it viciously because Dickens failed to emphasize the Christian dogma that Christ died for the sins of man, and that Christians are saved by grace of God through the death of His son. (Perhaps Dickens hesitated to tell children how their God planned to have his only begotten, wholly innocent son murdered for the sins committed by long-dead ancestors to relieve current people from those sins, sins they never even committed.)

We must recall that tens of thousands of good people have been tortured, imprisoned, hanged or burned over petty differences in the interpretation of the ambiguous, murky Bible, such as the question of salvation by faith alone or by good works.

The worst kind of person is the erstwhile religionist who formerly behaved well because of his fear of Hell and his selfish desire to get his precious little soul into Heaven — one who has failed utterly to develop a conscience or humanistic feelings or secular ethics founded on the belief that good behavior leads to a good life on Earth, that virtue is good in itself. Upon losing his faith in religion, this rascal renegade is uninhibited from cutting people down right and left. One wonders how many of the "great" men and women of history fit such a profile.

Is belief in Heaven and Hell conducive to a better world? The atonement of Heaven and Hell in an afterworld would seem logically to encourage good behavior on Earth. That, no doubt, is the purpose of Heaven and Hell. But, it just doesn't seem to work out that neatly.

If fear of Hell prevented criminal behavior, atheists would not comprise less than one percent of the prison populations, as reported by L. E. Laws, a highly-respected warden of Sing Sing prison in earlier years. Psychiatrist and criminologist Havelock Ellis wrote in *The Criminal*: "In all countries, religion is closely related with crime. . . . Among 200 Italian murderers, Ferri did not find one who was irreligious. . . . Out of 28,351 Italian admissions to three large metropolitan prisons, remarks the Rev. J. W. Horsley, only 57 were atheists."

There are more important reasons for good behavior than fear of Hell. The greatest crime deterrent is not severity of punishment (everlasting Hell). More important are certainty and immediacy of punishment. What could be less certain and immediate than Hell!

Consciences, whether the result of religious or secular training, are effective deterrents. The religious conscience would seem to be the less effective because its guilt product is easily relieved by confession. It is significant that America's greatest criminal gang, the Mafioso, is made up of practically 100 percent Catholics.

But I believe that the two chief reasons for good behavior are fear of the consequences of bad behavior — fear of being caught with its attendant retaliation, embarrassment, court trauma, fines, imprisonment — and the general consensus that crime doesn't pay (for most people).

We should also note that secular ethics bind one to the spirit of rules, while religious ethics are based more on the letter of rules — easily dodged, twisted, convoluted. A good illustration of abiding by the letter is the practice of some Orthodox Jews in Eastern Europe in traveling on the Sabbath (which is prohibited except "over water") of putting a pan of water under their railway car seats.

In addition, the ethical focus of atheists and humanists is on their fellow humans, while the focus of religionists is primarily on God. While humanists and atheists are concerned with pleasing their neighbors, religionists are concerned with pleasing God.

Offhand, one would expect that in a society of 95 percent religionists, if religion were effective in insuring good behavior, we would need only enough prisons to incarcerate the five percent nonbelievers. But since prison statistics indicate the nonbelievers are among the least criminal, we would need scarcely any prisons at all.

There are verses in the Bible that might create considerable doubt among Judeo-Christians concerning an afterworld — doubts that might weaken the good effects of the religious system of reward and punishment. In Ecclesiastes, Solomon says: "The dead know not anything, neither have they any more a reward." Another time Solomon says: "For that which befalleth the sons of man befalleth the beasts, . . . All go unto one place." And in Job 7:9 we read: "As the cloud is consumed and vanisheth away: so he that goeth down to the grave shall come up no more."

Even the sincere and resolute belief in Heaven is not always conducive to what everybody would call good behavior. The Moslem suicide missions that blew up our peace-keeping headquarters in Beirut were carried out by religious zealots expecting instant passage into Heaven. The Japanese kamikaze pilots in World War II were likewise willing to make suicide crashes onto American ships, believing they would be rewarded by instant delivery to Heaven.

Of course, if atheists (and one-quarter of Judeo-Christians) are right in believing that Heaven and Hell are fictitious, those religionists who promote the lie are using the mails to perpetrate a fraud. In fact, atheists see religion as built on a foundation of lies and view the Bible as a great hoax whose revered patriarchs would today be thrown into prison or a psychopathic ward.

A noted opponent of Christianity, M. M. Mangasarian, concluded an address on Christianity: "Ladies and gentlemen, I have one objection against Christianity. It is not true. And not until this fantasy which has been imposed upon the world for two thousand years as fact has been overthrown, will the world swing in earnest toward truth, toward justice, toward love, toward liberty."

Needless to say, such a view is fervently opposed by the other 95 percent of the population, whose attitudes have been formed by the preponderant religious ethos — cultural compulsives, taboos, social pressures, desires to conform, economic forces, self-preservation and the will to believe.

Of course, there is no truth in fairy tales, Halloween witches, Santa Claus or the Easter rabbit. But these fantasies are not promoted as true, nor have hundreds of thousands of people been slain for not believing in them.

One is hard put to stack up enough virtues of religion — its beauty, moral uplift, spiritual solace, humanitarian and charitable achievements, acclamation of brotherhood, deification of love and, of course, much more — to counterbalance its persecutions, tortures, executions, massacres, religious wars, fight against science, subversion of education, acceptance of slavery, degradation of women, support of tyrants and its bitter fruits of hatred and cruelty.

The truth seems to be that the Prince of Peace brought more war to the world than peace, facilitated the destruction of Greece and Rome and ushered in a thousand years of tyranny, moral degradation, injustice, educational decline, brutality and religious warfare.

The shameful aspect to the Christian wars is that most of them are fought over inconsequential differences in interpretation of the Bible or over beliefs concerning the extent of the universe, the origin of humankind, life in the hereafter, the oneness or trinity of God, the substance of angels — questions still as unanswerable today as they were a thousand years ago. Men differ the most and fight the most brutally over their opinions about the things they know the least – the unknowable.

The theocratic system of the Dark Ages of Christianity combined church and state instead of separating them. An example of theocracy today is to be found in Iran, where their bible, the Koran, is both religious law and secular law, and where their supreme churchman, the ayatollah, is also head of the secular government. This is the formula for authoritarian tyranny. The people are totally subservient; there is no freedom of action or belief.

The Roman Catholic Church of the Middle Ages was abysmally corrupted by its absolute power. The Church was a well-organized parasitic theocracy of bigotry and brutality, fawned on by bureaucratic appointees, feared by scientists and intellectuals, and worshiped by the illiterate, benighted populace. Priests made every effort to frustrate reason and nourish in its place superstition, fear, faith and humility. The Christian religion had been created for the poor, but during the Middle Ages it was an instrument or power for the rich.

The Protestant revolt broke the absolute power of the Catholic Church. Unfortunately, the Protestant churchmen had all served their apprenticeships under the Catholics and carried on the brutalities they had learned from their mentors.

Despotism and brutality – torture, imprisonment, hangings, burnings at the stake – were continued under Protestant auspices.

The formula for autocratic rule is a universal one: the rulers maintain their power by bestowing favors upon their supporters – priests, preachers, civil servants, teachers, artists, policemen, judges, jailers – favors of good jobs, lives of ease, positions of prestige and power. In return the supporters narcotize the masses into subservience and docility and terrorize dissidents with a practice of torture, imprisonment and execution.

Ambitious ruthless men and women, aspiring to rule, use as tools in their drive to the top whatever religion or ideology is available – Catholicism, Muhammadanism, Marxism. The Ayatollah Ruhollah Khomeini used the Shiite sect of Islam to gain absolute power and to stir up religious fanaticism among the populace to support his regime until he finally died at age 89.

Selfish, dishonest, ruthless and destructive persons succeed, and having succeeded, come into control of religion as well as all the other instruments of information, propaganda and education. From such positions of power and influence they paint themselves in rosy hues. They transform themselves from unscrupulous, ruthless acquisitors into saintly, selfless paragons.

These rosy pictures are the material with which scholars construct history — a history studded with great men, legendary heroes. As Henry Ford is credited with saying, "History is bunk."

Churches have lost much of their power because their flocks have been seduced by the material goodies produced by science and industry. Politicians show little obeisance to enfeebled religion, but support the business and industrial interests that fund their elections, keep the enfranchised voters narcotized with consumer goods and hold in their hands the economic welfare of the masses. (People no longer put their trust in God, but in the employing corporations.)

No longer must the people be subdued by police terror, or threats of hellfire, or rendered humble by religion. The positive reinforcement of economic opportunities and copious consumer goods are more effective controls than the negative reinforcements of olden times (or of modern times in totalitarian societies).

The people no longer need to be steeped in ignorance, superstition and fear to reduce their threat to the establishments.

Even the churches have been seduced by the material goodies of our consumer society and become subservient to capitalism. As Heinrich Heine observed, "When religion can no longer burn us, it comes to us begging."

Chapter X

TEMPERAMENTAL SIMILARITIES BETWEEN FUNDAMENTALISTS AND ATHEISTS

Insightful, earnest atheists realize that temperamentally they are the brothers of the fundamentalists, not of the religious liberals. Eric Hoffer observed similarly that the bitter enemies — the Communists and Nazis — were temperamentally much more alike than either were like the liberal democrats.

Both militant atheists and fundamentalists are honest in their beliefs and courageous in expressing and promoting their beliefs (against the opposition of the great popular majority of establishment liberals, wimps and hypocrites); one has to admire them. A fanatic fundamentalist may be well defined as one who takes God seriously.

But, Christian liberals disdain fundamentalists. I think it is partly because fundamentalists are sincere and honest; they believe in the Bible, the foundation of Christianity. Standing beside them, Christian liberals professing to be Christians while doubting the Bible upon which Christianity is founded, appear as naked hypocrites. So they resent the fundamentalists.

Following the Book on which Christianity is based, fundamentalists condemn fornication, adultery and homosexuality; they believe in Heaven and Hell; they believe in the efficacy of prayer, faith healing and immunity of those anointed with the Holy Spirit to the bite of poisonous snakes; they believe in possession by the devil and exorcism therefrom; they believe that they should spread Christianity by whatever means necessary. Some of the

201

more fanatical fundamentalists even believe that atheists, blasphemers and sinners should be flogged, imprisoned, executed.

Based on the supposition that the Bible is true and inerrant, the fundamentalists are right and beyond criticism. But, of course, atheists see them as the hapless victims of a fraudulent book inherited from ignorant, dishonest ancients and promoted down through the ages by the successful (the establishments) to frighten the masses into subservience and docility.

Both atheists and fundamentalists are obsessed with the question of truth, and both believe they have it, while the vast majority of Christians, being pragmatic, are mealymouthed hypocrites with only perfunctory concern for truth.

If militant atheists believed that the Bible was the true word of God, they, being the earnest, sincere type, would surely act just as the sincere fundamentalists do. They would be in the fundamentalist camp. But being dominated by their rational left brain, atheists cannot accept the Bible as truth with no other proof than that some ancient story-telling ignoramuses said it was.

Fundamentalists, in believing that this short, insignificant life on Earth is like nothing compared with eternal life in a heavenly hereafter, follow a totally rational course in devoting their lives obsessively to religion in order to reap such a generous reward — pure left-brain logic. But where their left brain fails them is in their acceptance of the preposterous claims of a Bible that can't stand up under the loosest of tests as to its truth and authenticity.

There is nothing surprising about both the atheists and Christian fundamentalists thinking that what they believe is right. We all do; it is impossible to do otherwise. Try to come up with one opinion you hold that you think is wrong. Both atheists and fundamentalists are overwhelmed by their convictions that they are right.

One difference between atheists and fundamentalists compared with religious liberals is that the former take their beliefs more seriously and think about them more. Atheists and fundamentalists, being absolutely certain that all their opinions are right, often even display an elitist arrogance toward their neighbors.

Fundamentalists know they are right because they go by the inerrant Bible — so how could they be wrong! They communicate with God — how could they talk with God if there were no God! They see around them the marvelous world, the diversity of life, the incredible stellar space — could man have made it? Of course not! So there has to be a God to have made it.

Atheists look down cavalierly at such self-delusion, flawed logic and emotional excretions of the right brain. (But atheists may be a little miffed by the principle of American justice that grants more weight to positive evidence than to negative evidence. That is, a witness who claims there is a God because he has seen Him and talked with Him would carry more weight in court than a witness who says there is no God because he has never seen Him or talked with Him.)

The hostility atheists and fundamentalists hold toward each other is inevitable. In denying God, the atheists are saying that the fundamentalists are dupes wasting their lives on religious rubbish. And the fundamentalists in accepting the Bible are saying that the atheists are fools destined to burn eternally in Hell for rejecting God.

But neither side is content with leaving the other alone. The militant atheists and the zealous fundamentalists are intent on either converting one another or destroying one another. Why should either care what the other believes? But they do, deeply and viscerally. Intolerance is a common characteristic of both camps. Some fundamentalists demonstrate an urge to persecute or imprison those who don't believe as they do. (Now they want to imprison women for choosing abortion.) A few seethe in a democratic society that keeps them reined in.

While fundamentalists believe that Jesus was a perfect man, atheists have a few reservations. By modern standards Jesus fell short of being perfect. He showed little interest in liberty, freedom, democracy, equality. In fact, he condoned slavery. His concept of justice was flawed and inconsistent. He showed no mercy for those who disbelieved in Him but ordered them executed.

While people today see education as the savior of humankind, Jesus expressed no interest in it. He seemed unaware of the coming wonders of science that would change life on Earth. The only interest He showed in agriculture that was destined to feed the world was his cursing a fig tree for not bearing Him figs out of season.

Jesus didn't encourage music, architecture, painting, theater, literature and the other cultural arts that so enrich human life. He showed only a middling interest in encouraging better nutrition, exercise and health care.

His total accomplishment seems to have been to add another layer of ignorance and superstition onto a people already burdened with too much of it. Of course, the concept of a perfect man itself is an absurdity – perfect for what?

Avowed atheists and fundamentalist Christians, both being earnest and sincere in their beliefs, are deeply concerned with the question of good and evil. But there is a problem with good and evil. They are so subjective that they disintegrate under close inspections, leaving nothing but semantic illusion.

In nature there is no good and evil, no concept of right and wrong — no basis for morality and ethics. As Robert Ingersoll said: "Nature has no design, . . . produces without purpose, sustains without intention and destroys without thought."

A robin plucks a baby worm from the dew-drenched grass for her nestlings. Obviously, from the robin's viewpoint, this is good. But from the viewpoint of the mother worm — losing one of her babies to a predatory bird — this is evil.

Good and evil, like justice, are human concepts — man is the measure of all things.

William Jennings Bryan wrote: "The humblest citizen of all the land, when clad in the armor of a righteous cause is stronger than all the hosts of Error." But who judges whether it is a righteous cause? Obviously, W. J. Bryan (not Clarence Darrow).

Our winning World War II was a good thing for the Allies, but an evil thing for the Axis. But the opinions of victors prevail in history.

As mentioned earlier in this book the Moslem terrorists who bombed the U.S. Marines headquarters in Beirut didn't feel they were doing anything evil. They were killing Satanic U.S. Marines for Allah. The U.S. backing of Israel was what was evil.

Good and evil are the empty shibboleths of contending interests in human affairs.

One wonders why atheists and religionists argue over metaphysical questions. Neither religionists, atheists nor scientists can explain how the universe came about, when, if ever, it began, etc. Our minds can't conceive of a universe arising out of nothing, or having always existed. Nor can we conceive of a God creating Himself before He existed. So, why argue about the inconceivable, the inexplicable, the incomprehensible? We not only argue, but kill one another over such questions.

Religionists are probably more prone to intolerance, aggressive behavior and even violence than are atheists. Since atheists are more certain in their beliefs, they have little fear that they may be proven wrong and go to Hell when they die. But religionists, however intense their zeal and however loud the protestations of their faith, harbor a lingering doubt (in fact, faith implies doubt) about their beliefs. Some neuroscientists suspect that such subliminal doubts hover between the two cerebral hemispheres creating anxiety that sometimes expresses itself in hyperactivity and aggression.

THE GOOD SAMARITAN.

Charlatans, of course, are another story. There is no comparison of the temperaments of religious charlatans with atheists and fundamentalists. The biggest problem with charlatans is guessing how many preachers are charlatans and which ones. They don't wear CHARLATAN badges on their lapels. Most people would probably agree that religious charlatans are the sleaziest, greediest, and most dishonest reprobates on the religious scene. They exploit and make fools of their devout, sincere and vulnerable congregants. They even console them in their times of grief, shower them with concern and sympathy for their problems, commend them on their virtues, promise them divine rewards and, of course, overwhelm them with their charismatic, magnetic personalities — all for the singular purpose of stripping them of as much money as possible to enrich themselves.

Unfortunately, the greatest contumely is heaped on atheists, who are usually men and women of above average intelligence, honest, principled, humanitarian. But the popular concept of atheists as bad people persists even though crime statistics prove the very opposite. Society apparently sees something good and noble about ignorance and superstition, while seeing something bad and diabolic about knowledge and rationality.

Atheists are seen as degraded and malevolent, when their only major difference from their neighbors is that the rational minds of atheists cannot accept the superstitions of their neighbors.

Religion has made the left brain villainous, honest doubt a crime, freedom of belief a sin. Clarence Darrow complained: "Am I wicked because I know it cannot possibly be true? Have you got to get rid of all your knowledge and all your common sense to save your soul?"

Atheists are often isolated and alienated from society as a small, estranged, disapproved, widely-scattered minority. But atheists, although a minority, do not enjoy a sacrosanct status, are shown no respect, nor seen as a victimized minority to be protected—as blacks, Jews, women, homosexuals. (Atheists don't have enough economic and political power to demand respect.) Such a plight is not conducive to social integration, vocational success, contentment and happiness; it is more conducive to loneliness, mean-spirited ill will, bitterness and hostility.

Of course, there are exception; many outstandingly talented and brilliant atheists are protected by the buffer and buttress of their illustrious professional status—George Shaw, Clarence Darrow, Bertrand Russell, Robert Ingersoll, Mark Twain, Charles Darwin, Thomas Jefferson, James Madison, Voltaire, H. G. Wells, Herbert Spencer, Sigmund Freud, John Dewey, George Eliot, Margaret Sanger, Michelangelo, Beethoven, and William Shakespeare. It is the small-town atheist who gets pummeled, persecuted, prosecuted and becomes embittered.

Actually, we can divide atheists into several categories: the adaptive kind that accepts the inevitability of religion and avoids derision and abuse from the superstitious herd by either hiding in the closet or being as unobtrusive with his atheism as possible; the highly-principled militant atheist who is deeply absorbed in the fight against religion; the bohemian, dilettante nonconformist who espouses atheism as a standard form of opposition to the establishment.

Adaptive atheists are often found among businesspeople, professionals, scientists, politicians, teachers, and, I suspect, the clergy. Guided by an economic imperative, they are forced into a kind of hypocritical existence. Under ecclesiastical pressure many great scientists in the past have been forced to grovel before the Church. Bruno refused to grovel and was burned at the stake. Galileo was more pragmatic, and was allowed to live out his life under house arrest after confessing to the Inquisition that he was mistaken in stating that Earth orbits the sun. The Vatican even lifted the Church's condemnation of Galileo recently. In 1984 a commission appointed by Pope John Paul II decided after five years of investigation that Galileo was right the first time — Earth does orbit the sun. So, after 350 years the Church withdrew its censure of Galileo. (How progressive can the Holy See get!)

Today's scientists and college professors no longer risk their lives by offending religion — all they risk is an eminent position, fat salary, luxurious life style, secure tenure and comfortable retirement. Well, those are quite a bit too.

What to do about religion is a common quandary for atheists. To avoid the social, political and economic ramifications of religion, one would have to live in hermitage.

There is almost no end to what people do about religion. Some people take their religion seriously and some indifferently. Some people propagate their religion while others practice their religion with quiet humility, some harass and hate those who follow different beliefs, some lie about what they believe, some use religion to dupe fools out of their money, some adjust to the prevailing religion to gain social approval, some practice their religion piously in view of their faith in the promised heavenly reward, some create new religions (Joseph Smith, Mary Baker Eddy, William Miller, Sun Myung Moon, Shirley McLaine). Some people follow their religion down a road to insanity, and some people spend their lives trying to destroy religion.

And some people use religion for emotional release, spiritual joy, hedonistic pleasure. These are nominally fundamentalists of a different stripe than those discussed above. The fervor of a Holiness church meeting is described by psychiatrist Dr. Berthold E. Schwartz: "Now they are shouting, screaming, swaying, swooning, trembling, strutting, goosestepping, stamping; and incoherently they speak in new tongues."

Such emotional antics were imported from Europe and were characteristic of American religion from its earliest days. An 18th century meeting of New England Shakers was described by a disgusted former member: "Some will be singing, each one his own tune; some without words, in an Indian tune; some sing jig tunes of their own making in an unknown mutter, which they call new tongues; some will be dancing and others stand laughing heartily and loudly; others will be drumming on the floor with their feet as though a pair of drumsticks were beating a ruff on a drum-head; others will be agonizing as though they were in great pain; others jumping up and down; others fluttering over somebody and talking to them; others will be shooing and hissing evil spirits out of the house, till the different tunes groaning, jumping, dancing, drumming, laughing, talking and fluttering, shooing and hissing, make a perfect bedlam."

No rational explanation is necessary; if it feels good, do it. Atheists wonder how such people could possibly believe that God would be pleased by their shouting and screaming and jumping and jerking — maybe amused, but not pleased.

If this is what it takes to gain a following, I'm afraid atheists and humanists might as well fold their tents and go back up into their ivory towers.

The speaking in tongues may be the total surrender of Broca's area of the left brain, giving full sway of speech to the right brain — the hemisphere undeveloped and unskilled for speech; the result, nonsense gibberish.

Perhaps Freud had visited a Holiness camp meeting when he declared, "Religion is an obsessional neurosis of humanity."

Atheists and humanists wonder how religionists can act so irrationally and believe in the absurdities upon which religion is founded. The answer may be: Why shouldn't they if it satisfies their emotional needs, adds spiritual depth to their lives and delights them with its beauty and mysticism?

After all, there is nothing rational about art and music. Both are chiefly products of the right brain which fulfills human emotional needs. But, of course, atheists will point out the great differences between art and music compared with religion. Art and music don't depend on fraud, deception and lies nor cause the torturing of opponents, burning of witches, massacres, pogroms, bloody Crusades, terrorist bombing and wars. Religious superstition, not art and music, is responsible for the current atrocities and destruction going on in Ireland, Lebanon, Africa and Palestine.

Insightful atheists, nevertheless, do not see the right brain as intrinsically evil; it is responsible for most of our esthetic development — art, music, poetry, dance, theater, creativity, intuition. Atheists do not wish to destroy it but to curb some of the undesirable consequences of its religious superstitions.

Many religious practices are more injurious to the practitioners themselves than to society. One sometimes searches vainly the depth of the human psyche for an understanding of many religious practices. The German Baptist Church of Redding, Pennsylvania cuts a hole in a river's ice for the total immersion baptism of their converts.

Self-flagellation and excoriation are common religious practices around the world. Even self-castration is not unheard of. Jesus said: "There be eunuchs who have made themselves eunuchs for the kingdom of heaven's sake." (Mat. 19:12)

One wonders what kind of God would be joyed by the sight of His children beating themselves, excoriating themselves with broken glass, castrating themselves!

What possible good can such practices do for the victims, for society, for God? In what possible way can such practices prove the truth of religion!

Less sanguine and violent were the practices of ancient holy men enshrining personal filth in their worship of God. St. Hilarion lived his whole life in utter uncleanliness; St. Anthony was glorified because he never washed his feet; St. Abrahams never washed his hands and feet in 50 years. St. Sylvia never washed any part of her body but her fingers. One whole convent abstained from bathing. St. Simon Stylites lived in ordure and stench his visitors could not stand.

Had there been modern sanitary plumbing available, these holy men and women, of course, would have piously avoided it. They worshiped filth with their twisted minds.

Believing that disease was visited on people by the wrath of God, the saints saw no connection between the typhoid and bubonic plagues that regularly struck down the populace and the unsanitary living conditions they themselves advocated.

I am not cynical enough to suggest any Machiavellian motive, but the unsavory fact is that the Church inherited most estates and thereby became richer with each plague epidemic. One 14th century ecclesiastic remarked with considerable perspicacity that "pestilences are the harvest of the ministers of God."

Many fundamentalists are rational enough to see the course of action an inerrant Bible demands. But they aren't rational enough to perceive that the Bible is not only abounding with errors but totally lacking in authenticity.

Religion, being something about which sincere people are passionate, the behavior of both atheists and fundamentalists is often characterized by fanatical intensity. Fortunately, our society is protected by a great buffer between the two camps. This buffer — the religious middle of America — is made up of the multitude of less-than-earnest, weakly-principled, social church goers; of liberal wimps, backsliders, consumer addicts and hedonists; of New Agers, parapsychologists and closet atheists.

This inert mass interposes between the handful of sincere believers — the zealous fundamentalists, and the handful of sincere disbelievers — the militant atheists. The indisputable logic of each of these groups would, if their numbers ever became considerable, lead to social chaos, since each believes that the world would be better off with the liquidation of the other.

The center, by pure sluggish bulk, preserves domestic peace by keeping these extremists from each other's throats.

We can be thankful for this inert center including the bulk of nominal Christians — sensible, moderate, tolerant, even indifferent — who ensure a society's health, viability and stability. To be feared are cold, calculating atheists or morally-suffocating religious zealots.

THE FINDING OF MOSES.

Chapter XI
SPIRITUALITY OR POWER?

The question of how much of religion is motivated by the spiritual desire to serve God and how much by the lust for power is, I suppose, unanswerable as there is no way to quantify the two. Such a question, though unanswerable, is useful in opening another dimension to the religious conflict.

First, it should be pointed out that if hunters return from the forest with bears, it is most likely they went after bears, not butterflies. If clergymen achieve positions of power it is most likely they were more intent on seeking power than servitude to God or spiritual enlightenment.

Four chief characteristics of the successful are selfishness, dishonesty, ruthlessness and destructiveness. So, we should not be fooled by religious leaders' sanctimony and self-bestowed haloes of piety and righteousness.

No doubt many religious leaders grew up with a will to be recognized, to be listened to, to stand above the crowd, to be famous, to be powerful. With such compulsions, they surveyed the landscape and correctly concluded that religion was the field with the greatest opportunities; the field that demands the least talent, the least arduous application; the field with the fewest government restrictions and social restraints; the field with the quickest payoff and the richest rewards. So they chose religion.

The sinners who turn their lives around (find Jesus) and become zealous Christians are not such phenomena as they appear on the surface. They are often men and women who want to be outstanding—either outstandingly bad or outstandingly good. They want to be "somebodies," the most brutal and debased or the most saintly and righteous. They are people with big egos and strong dramatic impulses which they satisfy in the reformed role of born-again Christian hero as fully as in their role of gang leader or drug pusher. As preachers, they can fulfill their needs and enjoy adventurous, romantic, dramatic lives, rich with rewards and much safer and freer from hardships than lives of crime and sin.

Often the appearance of their conversion from non-believers to believers is illusionary. They always were believers. They have only changed from sinners to non-sinners because of their recognition of the greater opportunities for them lying in the path of religious leadership. (Sometimes even their change from sinners to non-sinners is phony: e.g., Jim Bakker, Jimmy Swaggart, Billy James Hargis.)

In addition, there are the out-and-out cynics, who believe nothing, but exploit religion by bamboozling the naive, vulnerable and superstitious.

Then, of course, there are the political leaders — politicians, bureaucrats, aristocrats, dictators. They use religion to gain popular support and to subjugate the people.

Sometimes the motives for the religious behavior of leaders are not very clear or certain. One African Ivory Coast president-dictator, Houphouet-Boigny, is building the largest Christian church in the world. An army of 1500 artisans has been working seven days a week on it. The basilica is to be bigger than St. Peter's Basilica. Stained glass windows will cover two acres, a 310-ton cupola with a gold-painted globe and cross will top the structure at a greater height than the cross on St. Peter's.

The drop in the price of cocoa, resulting in the Ivory Coast's suspension of payment on its $10 billion foreign debt, seems not to worry the president in the least. The project goes on.

Interestingly, only 15 percent of the Ivory Coast's 10 million people are Catholic, the rest being Protestant, Muslim and animist.

It seems that sometimes dictators, like religious institutions, get carried away by the material expression of power, glory and magnificence in the forms of great cathedrals, mosques, statuary, chapel ceilings.

Is this Ivory Coast leader expressing his love for God, demonstrating his faith in Christianity, embellishing his spirituality or indulging in self-flattery? One French press suggested that the president, who is 84, is building a backdrop for a spectacular funeral.

The simple mechanics of religion have always been a setup whereby the ruling element, whether theocratic, aristocratic or plutocratic, bestows favors upon priests and preachers in the form of lives of ease and positions of high status in return for which the latter buffer them from the truculent masses. It has worked for thousands of years. The interest of the rulers has never been saving the souls of their subjects but gaining power through enslaving them.

We should note that not only does government try to use religion, but religion tries to use government. When the Catholic Church was at its zenith of power in the Middle Ages it bent many a kingly knee before it.

The special nature of some religions, e.g., Christianity, Judaism and Islam, seems to be to drive toward theocracy. Many of our early American colonial settlements were theocratic, actually executing dissenters.

One of the chief themes the framers of our Constitution emphasized was separation of church and state. The fathers of our country had witnessed firsthand in their own time the evils of theocracy and were determined that religionists should never gain control of their new government.

A classical example of the attempts of religionists to use government to promote their religious doctrines was the law enacted by Tennessee legislators to forbid teaching the theory of evolution in the public schools of Tennessee — a theory in opposition to the biblical account of creation.

This law was the basis for the notorious Scopes Trial of 1925 in which Clarence Darrow, who represented Scopes, made a monkey of William Jennings Bryan on the witness stand. Although the Northern liberals lost the case, the trial so discredited the religious opponents of evolution that fundamentalism received an almost fatal blow.

But the evangelicals and fundamentalists did survive. They consoled one another over their moral defeat by the archeologists and evolutionists with the claim that "It is better to trust the Rock of Ages than the age of rocks."

They continued to work diligently and persistently in spreading their doctrines and proselytizing and multiplying their churches, all the while maintaining a low public profile.

Not until the 1970s did the fundamentalists become politically active again. This was due in a large degree to Jerry Falwell, pastor of the Thomas Road Church in Lynchburg, Virginia and head of Liberty Baptist College, giving up his belief that engaging in politics is forbidden by the Bible, and going all-out to politicize America's evangelicals and fundamentalists.

Falwell organized the Moral Majority and through it led the fundamentalists on a political rampage that scared the hell out of American politicians. By the late 70s fundamentalists had gotten sick of the liberal swing to homosexual acceptance, criminal coddling, sexual promiscuity and the crowning abomination — legalized abortion. Feeling left out and alienated from American culture, the religious right rallied behind the charismatic Falwell and his Moral Majority. The Moral Majority and other fundamentalist organizations raised untold millions of dollars to support right-wing political candidates, including Ronald Reagan. They blacklisted candidates who refused to subscribe to their agenda and brought defeat to many of them.

The Reagan administration maintained a favorable climate for the evangelicals, fundamentalists and charismatics. Even so, their decade of political explosion has subsided, the televangelist scandals have hurt and Jerry Falwell has closed the offices of the Moral Majority. Nevertheless, the political tide in America is still favorable to the religious right. They have a friend in President Bush and a Supreme Court now balanced in their favor.

They are still striving for political power on a state level to force their ideas onto the public through legislative action. They are bent on ousting evolution from public schools, introducing prayer into schools, subsidizing parochial schools, and stopping racially-determined school busing. They are working to obstruct the gay rights movement and most of all to abrogate women's right to abortion.

The degree of Rev. Falwell's threat to our democracy may be gleaned from his madcap vision of a fundamentalist takeover of American schools: "I hope I will live to see the day . . . we won't have any public schools. The churches will have taken them over again and Christians will be running them. What a happy day that will be!"

Lovers of freedom can be thankful that Falwell has given up winning elections and returned to winning souls.

But the cost of liberty is eternal vigilance and there are new threats to our liberty from the religious right. Author Hal Lindsey in his recent book *The Road to Holocaust* describes a new threat coming from Christian Reconstructionists whose belief, Dominion Theology, advocates that Christians should gain dominance over the whole Earth.

Lindsey says that the Reconstructionists want to set up theocracies around the world. It certainly appears even on the surface that power is the chief aim of these far-right Christians. Lindsey, a Christian himself, honors the constitutional doctrine of separation of church and state. "The problem is," says Lindsey, "once church and state merge it becomes very intolerant of other traditions. There has not been one case where the church merged with the state and the result was good."

The Iranian Shiites under the late Ayatollah Khomeini are a good modern example of the power developed by the merger of a political institution with a religious institution — Iran and Shiite Islam. It seems clear that Khomeini lusted for power, not spiritual power but political and military power. He instituted a brutal regime of oppression. He roused the youth of Iran to fanatical fervor and threw them against his religious and political Iraqi enemy whose more experienced and better-trained soldiers decimated them.

Khomeini was loyally backed by the vast majority of Iranians, who had or believed they had a stake in the preservation of the merged institutions of the Shiite religion and the Iranian state.

The problem with religious institutions is that their original vision or purpose gets lost in their competitive struggle to succeed, dominate and monopolize.

The Roman Catholic Church endured a fratricidal struggle with the Eastern Orthodox Church while fighting against the new Islamic religion bent on destroying both of them. These three religious institutions have kept the blood of zealots and innocent victims spurting all over the globe for almost 2000 years amidst their protestations of peace, love and brotherhood.

The Catholic Church was given a big boost by Constantine legalizing Christianity in 314. Near the end of that century Emperor Theodosius further boosted the power of the Church by making Christianity the *only* legal religion. The Church proceeded for a thousand years to grow and to increase its power by the most brutal means ever known to humankind. Millions of infidels, heretics, witches, and Christian rivals were tortured, imprisoned, hanged, beheaded, piked, burned. Christian grace, charity, piety, compassion, humility and love were lost in the bloody struggle of the Catholic Church to achieve and preserve its dominance.

Unfortunately, religions succeed only by violating the moral codes on which they were founded. A new convoluted, inverted, twisted and perverted theology is devised to serve the imperatives of the current religious institutions.

Aggressiveness, ruthlessness, chicanery, persecution, torture and murder have all played a part in the success of religious institutions — hardly Christian virtues. With institutions power always wins over principle.

Arthur Koestler maintains that people are driven more by self-transcending tendencies of love, devotion and ideology than by selfishness and aggressiveness. The problem here is the confusion between the people and the institutions, institutions which embody the selfish interests of the successful, the establishmentarians. The institutions possess no self-transcending tendencies, but exploit such tendencies of the people. Quite a different thing.

One of the virtues of democracy is the access the people have to their political institutions, access that keeps such institutions reminded of their true purposes.

One of the points made particularly clear by the framers of our Constitution was that our government was not to promote religion. Our country was founded by mostly deists and freethinkers who believed organized religion had no place in government. Every citizen was to be free to choose his own religion or to choose no religion.

This was a radical proposition for government, almost as radical as the idea of democracy itself. Quakers had been hanged in 17th century Boston for being Quakers. By the end of the American Revolution, nine of the 13 colonies had state religions.

Our Constitution does not mention God, divine law, the Bible, prayer, salvation; nor does it prescribe religious rituals. It is a secular document. Some religious zealots have never ceased their efforts to amend or do away with the Constitution that thwarts their dream of forcing their religion on the whole populace through theocratic power.

A recent rather ludicrous move by a few religious fundamentalists toward a theocratic state — a move the media treated as a Don Quixote battle against windmills — was their persuasion of the Arizona Republican Party to declare that the United States is "a Christian nation, a republic based upon the absolute laws of the Bible, not a democracy."

Although the United States government is nominally secular, religions do get much favorable government treatment in the forms of tax exemption and dozens of perks and special privileges.

Conversely, atheists are penalized. Some states still bar non-believers from holding elective office. Arkansas even bars court testimony of atheists — but not of blacks.

Atheists justifiably complain that because of the tax exemptions of churches, everyone (including atheists) has to pay higher taxes to make up for the church exemptions. In this indirect way atheists are forced to support the very religions that they see as social evils. Churches could never have accumulated the great wealth they possess in America had they not been tax-exempt.

Of course, churches supply many needed services — welfare, recreation, education, hospital care, child care, etc. — that the government would otherwise have to supply. So their tax exemptions, they contend, are well justified. But, atheists would argue that in a secular democracy the voters should decide how money (effectively partly out of atheist pockets) is to be spent — not the churches.

Former President U. S. Grant had a strong opinion on the taxing of churches: "Tax churches like any other business. Not one dollar of public money shall be appropriated for the support of any sectarian school. Keep the church and state forever separate. I most certainly recommend that a constitutional amendment be submitted prohibiting the granting of any school funds or school taxes for the benefit, or in aid, directly or indirectly, of any religious sect or denomination."

Being that the United States is a democracy, religionists have a perfect right to try to gain control of the government, propose laws favoring religion, seek government subsidies and financial support; they have a right to try to introduce prayers into public schools, to stop the teaching of evolution and to prohibit abortions. They even have a right to propose amendments to the Constitution the effect of which would turn our government into a theocracy. Of course, to succeed in a democracy they must first win the support of the majority of voters.

But the wisdom of the majority of American voters far exceeds that of the religious zealots. The effects of theocracies around the world and throughout history are too well known.

State-supported religions, even when the churches do not control the state, are detrimental to democracies. Clerics cease to be champions of the people against overbearing government bureaucracies; they are disinclined to bite the hand that feeds them.

A Roman Catholic archbishop complained: "The law of the land prohibits the teaching of any values in public education except secularist ones. . . . The child has a constitutional right to know about God. The child is not being taught about his Creator, his origin, his purpose in life or his destiny."

This sounds great at a superficial glance, but runs into difficulties with closer inspection. The right to know about God would be hard to find in the Constitution. And, of course, the archbishop has in mind the Catholic Church's God — not the Protestant's God, the Moslem's God, the Buddhist's God, the Jew's God, the Hindu's God or the God of native Americans — in a pluralistic religious society.

Andy Rooney wondered "whether the god Reagan wants in public schools here is the same god to which the Islamic Holy War members pray or not. We have never gone to arbitration to get a final decision on whose god, of all the gods of all the world's religions, we should recognize in our schools."

In the archbishop's mind the child's origin was from Adam and Eve, his purpose is to support the Catholic Church and his destiny is Catholic Heaven.

And besides, atheists strongly suspect that religionists getting a start in public schools is to be compared with the camel getting its nose under the tent. Atheists warn that our schools must never become conduits, paid for by the tax-paying public including the atheists themselves, for delivering religious doctrines, myths and superstitions to the minds of captive, innocent children.

One of the cornerstones of a democratic society is an educated electorate, and an educated electorate can't be produced by religious indoctrination. G. B. Shaw said, "There is no such thing as a Catholic university. If it's Catholic, it isn't a university; and if it's a university, it isn't Catholic."

But for the record, it is true that Britain, Denmark, Norway, Greece and Sweden all have established, state-funded churches. In addition, British and Norwegian children are required by law to pray in schools, though parents can have their children exempted. Voluntary school prayer, religious education and state-funded church schools are commonplace throughout Western Europe.

But the sophisticated Europeans do not have the aggressive, fanatic fundamentalists to deal with that we have in the United States. For example, the 1989 right-to-life demonstrations in Europe were planned, choreographed, financed and manned mostly by American pro-lifers. The latter do not only want to force their fundamentalist ideas on America but onto all of Europe as well. A democracy needs to guard itself against such zealotry.

But in Europe, even despite church opposition, abortion is no longer a major issue and is practiced in virtually every European country except Catholic-dominated Ireland. Both France and Italy have formally legalized abortion.

Today the fundamentalists are going all out to stop abortion, put prayer into classrooms, and teach biblical Creationism as science, although they have lost more court battles than they have won.

In 1948 the Supreme Court ended religious instruction in public schools; in 1962 it ended compulsory prayer in public schools; in 1973 it legalized abortion; in 1978 it banned Christmas caroling in public schools; in 1980 it prohibited posting the Ten Commandments in school classrooms; in 1981 the Supreme Court banned a cross erected in a public park; in 1987 the Court ruled that states may not require public schools that teach evolution to teach Creationism also.

Televangelist Jimmy Swaggart in 1986 said: "I don't have any good words about the public school system. If it weren't for the Christian school system, this country would have gone to hell in a hand basket." Of course, since the televangelist scandals, Jimmy Swaggart's good words have declined a tad in value.

Not only did President Reagan appoint two conservatives to the Supreme Court, but he established diplomatic relations with the Vatican, an act that must have caused many of our Founding Fathers to turn over in their graves.

Atheists, humanists, separationists and the American Civil Liberties Union, in exercising eternal vigilance, frequently bring law suits against local government authorities to enforce the constitutional mandate of separation of church and state — suits against religious training or prayers in public schools, crosses and creches on public property, teaching of biblical Creationism in science classes, etc. The public generally disfavors such suits, seeing them as petty interference in religious symbolism that harms nobody. But again, it may be a case of the camel getting its nose under the tent.

Religionists are not known for voluntarily stopping at a reasonable point in pressing their religion onto the public; so, for the sake of religious freedom they have to be stopped, even if stopping them brings opprobrium onto the upholders of the doctrine of separation of church and state.

The situation, however, may be that if ignorance and superstition predominate in our society, all the legal victories for separation will be reversed, one after another. On the other hand, if education and enlightenment prevail, there will cease to be any call to engage in petty litigation over separation. No one will want to construct creches, erect crosses, conduct school prayers or teach Creationism.

In a democracy the majority sooner or later gets what it wants. Gains based on the legal leverage of the Constitution, in defiance of the public's wishes, do not last long.

Certainly converts to atheism would be of greater value to atheism than unpopular, reversible court victories. One wonders how important such petty suits ultimately prove to be.

It is so easy to see how in the past scientists, psychologists, sociologists, philosophers and atheists adopted their beliefs, ascertained truth, formed perceptions and developed life styles according to their temperaments, cultural compulsives, economic interests and emotional needs. In addition we can see how greatly such persons were influenced by popular opinion, ego defense, national and ethnic bias and early indoctrination and conditioning. Yet they believed their conclusions and choices were products of pure reasoning.

Which leaves little doubt that we today are under similar illusions about being guided by pure reason. So, must we conclude that religionists, who claim to be informed by divine guidance, are as reliable a source of truth as rationalists because the thinking of rationalists is considerably tainted? Not at all.

At this point we must recognize the functions of the bicameral brain. The flawed reasoning of the rational left brain is still far superior to the so-called divine inspiration of the religious right brain. Consider the failure of right-brain reliability: there is no evidence that prayers are answered, that humans possess souls, that Heaven awaits the pious, that laying on of hands heals the sick, that the conformation of the stars controls human destiny, that demons possess the blind and mentally ill, that witches can cast spells, that a St. Christopher talisman protects motorists from accidents.

But there is ample evidence of the validity of the products of the reason and rationalism of the left brain. Airplanes fly, automobiles carry us about, cameras take pictures, radios send messages around the world, generators produce electricity that lights our homes, world news and entertainment do appear on our television screens, and wonder drugs cure us of diseases. The products of left-brain reasoning work.

Nevertheless, the reasoning capacity of the left brain is not perfect, and as extraneous influences change over a period of time, scientific attitudes and intellectual perceptions change. To some degree we replace one set of rationalized perceptions and beliefs with a new set to fit cultural requirements of a new age driven by new imperatives.

But we are not just riding a ferris wheel. The great advances in physical science indicate positive advancement in the improvement of our left cerebral hemisphere.

One may wonder why, if scientists and rationalists are intellectually superior to religionists, social and political life are dominated by right-brainers. A rationalist might say that it is because most people are right-brained religionists and power derives from numbers.

But, in many cases where left-brainers have gained power and attempted to rationalize society they have failed. Rationalists might attribute such failure to the impossible task of reining in the irrational behavior of right-brainers. But they have failed even in their attempts to set up small utopian communities of their own.

On what basis can we assume that rational behavior is more beneficial to society than irrational behavior outside the physical sciences? I suspect we assume it on the basis of faith only.

Then there are corrupting social mechanisms that enter the picture when rationalists achieve power, as will be discussed later.

More important than transcendent spirituality is the struggle for power.

The Catholic Church is a good case in point as it has been the world's most successful church in achieving power and retaining it.

Not everybody sees the Catholic Church as one of great spirituality and mysticism as most religionists, both Catholic and non-Catholic, see it. Some see the spirituality and mysticism primarily as tools in the hands of the church hierarchy to charm the lay Catholics into submission and obedience to the Church and see the Catholic hierarchy as a group of mostly hard-headed businessmen and practical politicians. (Who else could succeed in climbing to the top of such a monstrous organization but ambitious, ruthless practical men!)

Mussolini, although an atheist, enjoyed the wholehearted political support of the Catholic Church in Italy at the outbreak of World War II.

Throughout the history of Catholicism, wherever creed and dogma have threatened the Church's survival, creed and dogma have been changed. Such changes are proclaimed as liberalization, ecumenism, etc., as if the change represented a change of heart of the hierarchy. Instead such changes are cold, pragmatic, business decisions. (Today, communism is making radical changes in its dogma for similar practical reasons.)

Papal policy is directed more by practical considerations for the survival of the Church than by considerations for transcendent spirituality. The Church opposes inter-faith marriages because statistics show that the Church generally loses in such marriages, the children being more likely to be raised non-Catholic.

The Vatican's adamant stand against artificial birth control and abortion is seen by many as a practical policy, thinly veiled as morality, to increase the Catholic population. The war between Catholics and Protestants that used to take place on the battlefield now take place in the bedroom, and the Catholics are winning. Heavy-breeding Catholics are in the front line of the biological war.

In view of the biological war, one may wonder why the Church doesn't allow its priests and nuns to marry and produce more Catholics. One suspects that it is because the Church would lose its millions of priests and nuns who work for a pittance and without whom the Church could never have become the richest non-government institution in the world. The Vatican has no qualms about young men and women taking vows to work the rest of their lives wherever and at whatever the Church assigns them.

To succeed as well as it has, the Catholic Church has had to be successful in imbuing not only its lay people with love for and loyalty to the Church but its hierarchy as well. The success of an organization depends not only on the devotion, loyal support and selflessness of its members but also to a degree of its leaders. A hierarchy of leaders totally obsessed with their own selfish interests and without enough loyalty to the organization to induce them to transcend their own interests for the good of the whole would surely fail. So the success of the Catholic Church attests to sufficient loyalty, transcendence and brotherliness among its hierarchy to account for its survival.

In discussing power, we must understand the dynamics of success that leads to power. By the nature of social dynamics the selfish, dishonest, ruthless and destructive climb their way to the top. Utopian idealists, ignoring reality, visualize a society run by the virtuous — Plato's philosopher kings. But if by some rare happenstance virtuous, ethical people came into power, how long would they stay there with dishonest, ruthless, destructive competitors bent on deposing them? We see few good people at the top because it is contrary to nature. Even if good people did come to power, power corrupts, so they wouldn't remain good very long. Power wins over ethics as well as over spirituality.

The theory that not the best people but the worst people of society rise to the top is logically supportable. If the best people rise to the top and lead humankind, why would history be the story of one atrocity after another!

The selfish, dishonest, ruthless and destructive people become the leaders of the world, the helmsmen of society. As an inevitable result history is a wretched tale of massive mutilation and murder, or as historian Edward Gibbon expressed it more gently, "A register of crimes, sorrows, and misfortunes."

(A cynic might maintain that the best people really do get to the top.)

A sampling of the more notorious atrocities perpetrated by the successful (the *best* people) from ancient times to the present day would include Moses's army slaying all the Midianite soldiers, male children and adult women while keeping the young girls for themselves; the Byzantine emperor Basil the Bulgar Slayer blinding 15,000 captured Bulgarians in both eyes and 150 in only one eye to lead the rest back to their king; Genghis Khan massacring whole city populations to eliminate their threat to his power and to create terror in the next city to be attacked; the Spanish Conquistadors slaying 5,000 Incas and tricking them out of their wealth of gold and silver; the American slaughter of native Indians and driving them off their land; the sale and enslavement of millions of African Negroes, the working to early death hundreds of thousands of child laborers in the mills and mines of America and Europe in the early days of unrestrained capitalism.

And, of course, wars — generated by the world's best people, its successful, its leaders — are the greatest atrocities. In our Civil War 620,000 soldiers of both sides lost their lives; World War I resulted in 15 million deaths; following that war minor atrocities such as the Turkish genocidal attempt against the Armenians, Josef Stalin's starving to death seven million Russian kulaks, and the Japanese massacre of 300,000 Chinese in the Rape of Nanking.

Then a death toll of 40 million in World War II; separate atrocities during the war included Stalin's execution of 15,000 Polish officers in Katyn Forest; the U.S. bombing of Hiroshima and Nagasaki killing 240,000 civilians; and along with the war the Nazi Holocaust purportedly exterminating six million Jews, Poles and Gypsies.

Add 58,000 Americans and many times that number of Asians killed in the Vietnam War; a million Cambodians killed by the Khmer Rouge regime; Chinese Maoists slaying millions of their own people in a political purge; the Soviet-Afghan conflict in which an estimated million soldiers and civilians lost their lives; the Iran-Iraq war costing another million lives.

In Guatemala 60,000 citizens have disappeared since 1984, most of them presumed murdered by the successful regime in power; in Argentina the same kind of political murdering has been going on for many years; an estimated 500,000 people have been killed in Latin American civil wars since 1945; about 200,000 have been killed in civil wars in Greece, Hungary, Turkey and Ireland during the same period; the regimes of the three Ugandan leaders between 1970 and 1980 murdered an estimated 800,000 Ugandan citizens.

In total since the end of World War II, 16 million soldiers and civilians have been killed by war and political assassination around the world. And this during a period of relative peace.

What is important is that all these deaths were perpetrated by the leaders of society — the successful, the establishments. And according to popular belief the best people in society rise to the top and rule.

How is this obvious delusion achieved? Very simply. The successful, having risen to the top and come into control of the instruments of information, education, propaganda and indoctrination that mold public opinion — that is, the schools, libraries, churches, press, airwaves, politics and law — find creating the myth that invests them with virtue, nobility and honor an easy trick. They paint themselves as men and women whose superior virtues, nobility and diligence inevitably catapult them to the top.

The degree to which their hirelings — school teachers, writers, editors, preachers and politicians — uphold the myth determines *their* success.

This view, however radical, is difficult to escape once you see how consistent it is with the facts of history. It all fits together neatly into an extremely disturbing picture of reality. The truth shatters the Pollyanna world that the public has been taught to believe since childhood.

The view, however, is not new. The early Scottish economist Adam Smith in *Wealth of Nations* wrote: "The violence and injustice of the rulers of mankind is an ancient evil, for which, I am afraid, the nature of human affairs can scarce admit of a remedy." (But one doesn't apply such a view to his own society.)

Lord Acton's maxim that power corrupts doesn't explain where the powerful got their power in the first place. Obviously, they got their power by their corrupt character that they started out with. The rotten succeed and success rottens.

There surely are many good, honorable, talented people who are successful—but they, not the ruthless shysters, are the exceptions. Even the Communists are finally recognizing that their former honored leaders Josef Stalin, Mao Tse-tung and Ho Chi Minh were really murderous tyrants.

Ruthlessness under modern capitalism is more urbane. Today, success is attained by robbing small investors through stock market manipulation, by embezzling bank funds, by self-dealing savings and loan deposits at the expense of FDIC and U.S. taxpayers, by swindling Medicare and Medicaid through overcharge by doctors and hospitals, by adulterating food, by selling worthless nostrums, by hooking the public on the credit racket, by tax evasion, by corporate raiding, by corruption in granting government contracts, etc.

Competition produces ruthlessness under any kind of socioeconomic system. It is inevitable. All else being equal, the ruthless person enjoys the advantage of his ruthlessness.

Nineteenth century Social Darwinism was the enthusiastic response of the successful to Darwin's theory of evolution that described the survival of the fittest as a natural process that leads to the improvement of a species. Nothing could have pleased the successful more than to believe that in clawing their way to the top, they were following natural law and improving the human race.

Selfishness, dishonesty, ruthlessness and destructiveness are not always clothed in blood-drenched garments. The teachings of Dale Carnegie and Norman Vincent Peale that have had tremendous influence on American morality are soft-toned amorality presented as uplifting, self-improving, positive thinking.

Carnegie and Peale are modern Machiavellis instructing salesmen and businessmen how to succeed. Carnegie developed a strictly secular method for success; Peale preached a similar methodology, but threw God in to give the salesmen extra oomph. In either case honesty is replaced by deceit, principle by expediency and morality by success.

Carnegie, Peale and their horde of admirers and imitators have made positive thinking into a secular religion of America. They instruct people in dishonesty – always smile (conceal your true feelings), great people as if you are glad to see them (even when you're not), compliment people (even if they disgust you), make them feel important (deceive them even about themselves), etc. The chief thing is to always smile. Every entertainer, politician, celebrity and advertiser must cultivate a perpetual, phony Chessie Cat smile. Such teachings lead eventually to total amorality. Honesty becomes a vice that hinders one's popularity and progress. One's moral rule becomes: If it succeeds it is good.

There are still a few people around who have difficulty seeing anything *positive-minded about lying and deceiving.*

Although the successful are the chief architects of the world of make-believe, all people on the scale down to the smallest, have some interest in preserving the make-believe world, the world in which they have invested their careers that produce their livelihood, the world to which they are beholden for their destinies, the world in which their religions, sentiments and life styles have been inextricably woven. Most of us experience some success, and to that degree it is in our interest to support the make-believe.

There is little incentive to see the world as it actually is. One lives in a world of make-believe, accepts it, supports it, is largely unconscious of it. He succeeds in his subordinate role by conforming, not by questioning.

American liberals in their disillusionment with our own heroes, often search elsewhere for heroes. The dogged determination of Mao Tse-tung to bring freedom to the Chinese people and the noble effort of Ho Chi Minh to restore the freedom of Vietnam against American imperialism warmed the hearts of many liberals. But both of these Oriental revolutionaries turned out to be ruthless, power-obsessed butchers. Fidel Castro and Che Guevara were little better.

The myth of the best people rising to the top is supported by those at the top, by the hero- and royalty-worshiping people at the bottom and by the people in between whose welfare depends upon supporting the deceit.

The successful never lack toadies to paint them in rosy hues and to apologize for them. Exposés of unethical or immoral behavior by eminent people are passed off as exceptions. School teachers, writers and public spokesmen speak of the "bad" character traits of our great men and women as proof that they are only human, that even our best people have flaws, are not perfect. It is rarely suggested that those flaws or bad traits were what got them to the top.

In 1989 Al Neuharth, a highly successful business executive, came out with an autobiography, *Confessions of an S.O.B.* In his 16 years as head of Gannett Newspapers, he built the company from a regional chain with annual revenues of $390 million to a $3.3 billion giant. His best-known achievement was founding *USA Today*.

Neuharth got to the top through selfishness, chicanery, ruthlessness and destructiveness, but was honest enough to admit it. A rare bird indeed.

In his book he recounts a life of scheming and manipulating, how he swayed his college election with dirty tricks, acted as a newsroom spy to gain promotion to city editor and shoved aside his former boss and mentor at Gannett. Neuharth describes an S.O.B. as "someone who uses whatever tactics it takes to get the job done — and rise to the top."

Neuharth says, "I know a lot of CEOs in business who believe and practice some of my approaches but would rather not say so publicly." Among his favorite S.O.B.s are Malcolm Forbes, Lee Iacocca, Ted Turner, Rupert Murdoch, Tom Brokaw and Margaret Thatcher.

One of Neuharth's former wives doesn't dispute Neuharth's honest assessment of himself. "Al Neuharth is a snake. He's coldblooded. He's sneaky and slithers around and sheds his old skin as he grows and adapts to his newest surroundings." But how refreshing his honesty!

The successful love the bubble-brained, adulating, positive-minded sycophants of the press, air waves, churches and schools, who lick their boots and fight over scraps thrown down by their superiors. Certainly, rulers are pleased by subjects going around with positive thoughts in their heads and prescriptive, vapic smiles on their faces.

At this point, we might consider the functions of religion and morality in relation to power in a realistic Machiavellian world. Briefly, religion is an instrument in the hands of the successful to secure their status and to enrich themselves by narcotizing and duping the masses. (The ease with which rulers throughout history have convinced their subjects of the rulers' divine connections is as sad a commentary on the gullibility of the masses as it is on the chicanery of the rulers.)

A striking illustration of how the establishment determines morality is seen in the question of profiteering. Capitalist America, based on the profit system, holds its greatest profiteers in high esteem, while in Communist Russia (before perestroika) to profit from the labor of another person was a crime.

Naturally, there is a constant subtle effort by the ruling element to condition and indoctrinate citizens to act for the benefit of the ruling element. That is what religion, morality, ethics and education are mostly about.

Some children are born cynics. They are not hurt by moral training. C. Wright Mills said in *Power Elite*: "Blessed are the cynical, for only they have what it takes to succeed."

The successful behave in the manner they find most fruitful for themselves, while giving lip service to ideals of honesty, fairness and loyalty. They climb roughshod to the top, trampling all the rules along the way. Once at the top, not surprisingly, they support vigorously the rules they violated on their way up.

Humanists and religionists often face a thorny dilemma in rearing their children. They teach their children ethical behavior because they want nice children. They teach them moral discernment so that their children can select behavior for themselves that is right and good. But they also want their children to succeed, pouring thousands of dollars into their education. Unfortunately, the ethics they teach them so they will be nice children too often cripples them so they can't succeed.

The success of a society depends on the inoculation of its children with morality and ethics, i.e., a conscience, and on the few it fails to restrain with a conscience not destroying everybody in their greed and hunger for power.

Many successful people are troubled by doubts about their superiority. Daniel Goleman reported for New York Times Service: "Buried in the hearts of many high achievers is the secret sense of being a fraud, and the constant fear of being exposed. The conviction that one is an imposter may be prevalent in as many as two in every five successful people in all varieties of careers, in the estimate of one researcher who has studied the phenomenon."

Of course, the researchers, lacking the perspicacity to see that these successful people really are frauds, seek to find psychological explanations for such feelings, which the researchers call a phenomenon. There's nothing enigmatic about such feelings. They are just the conscious and unconscious realization by the successful that they are not successful because of the popular conception of their possession of superior talent and virtue, but because of their greater ruthlessness, self-promotion, dishonesty and chicanery — i.e., that they *are* frauds.

One might ask, so what if the world we live in is mostly make-believe? Well, granted we're not going to change it. But to deal with social problems as well as with our individual problems, it helps to understand the social dynamics that produce the problems.

We can't breed better cattle and develop higher-yielding grains without understanding genetics. We can't send vehicles to probe outer space without understanding astronomy.

We can't hope to achieve a peaceful and better world without understanding its structure and dynamics. More important to each of us personally is the grave trouble we run into when our actions designed for the make-believe world take place in the real world.

My theory of a make-believe world created by the successful—who upon achieving control infuse themselves with virtues—may be sound enough. But, unfortunately, because it places the successful in a dismal light it will never fly.

However power is achieved, it appears to be more important than salvation, spirituality or truth. In a glorifying sense, achieving power is emulating God, the all-powerful.

Chapter XII
THE SEARCH FOR THE HOLY GRAIL

The tenacity and persistence of religion have irritated, dismayed and frustrated atheists since time immemorial.

Religions are mortal but religion seems to be indestructible. A. S. Neill said in *Summerhill*: "No, religions are no more eternal than nations are eternal. A religion — any religion — has a birth, a youth, an old age, and a death. Hundreds of religions have come and gone. Of all the millions of Egyptians who believed in Amon Ra through the better part of 4,000 years, not a single adherent of that religion can be found today."

Arthur Brisbane confirmed that religions die, but asserted that religion can never die: "Religions die when their time has past, and a better one appears, but you can't kill them. That is proved by the failure of various religions to kill off their rivals. Religion itself can never die, since it is the expression of man's desire to know what he can never know."

Jesus had no doubt that his new cult would survive: "Behold, thou art Peter and upon this rock I shall build my church: and the gates of Hell shall not prevail against it." — Math. 11:18.

Religion was an attempt to discover the forces that control people's lives and to gain control of those forces. But religion has failed. It has failed to bring peace to the world — it has instead instigated wars — it has failed to eradicate evil, it has failed to obtain God's favor through prayer; religion has failed to cure the sick, to work miracles, to protect the faithful from disasters or to succor the starving poor.

While religion has flourished on unfulfilled promises, science has had to fight its way to produce undreamed-of goods and services for humankind's betterment — mass-produced luxuries for everybody, and a doubled life span through the advancement of medicine.

Science is affirmed by wondrous, palpable results; religion is affirmed by absurd visions and empty promises.

One might think that in view of its egregious failure, religion would be a pushover. Thomas Paine believed that religion was near the exit door. But Paine proved to be grievously mistaken. Paine hadn't realized that intelligence and rationality have little to do with belief. People believe in religion with their hearts, not with their heads — with their right brains, not with their left brains.

Highly educated people today, even scientists, make pilgrimages to Lourdes, or travel part way around the world to squat reverently at the Wailing Wall in Jerusalem. Or embrace astrology, parapsychology or pyramid power.

The promise of immortality may be the strongest allurement of religion. Even the comparatively Godless Eastern religions promise an afterlife. The forms of afterlife differ but they all cater to humankind's revulsion at self-extinction. Man, God's special creation, has to be exempt from the common death he readily grants to the trillions of other creatures on Earth. Man has a soul.

The notion I have previously cited that religion has been selected by evolution may be questioned. Religion may be just a fantastic excrescence that has developed in human society that neither helps nor hinders survival. The animal world is full of physical excrescences with no apparent utility — the fantastic plumage of the peacock, the breath-taking coloration of the scarlet flamingo, the useless stripes of the zebra. We have to assume that such excrescences can develop as long as they in no way interfere with the survival of the species. Every evolutionary development does not necessarily have to have utility.

So, religion may not be an evolutionary selection, but an excrescence that has not interfered with our survival.

As used in this chapter, the search for the Holy Grail symbolizes humankind's search for a better life, a better society — through religion, rationalism, education, science, humanism; through socioeconomic ideologies, political reform and revolution; through utopian ventures. The search goes on.

Science is our attempt to discover reality. Most people resist this attempt simply because they find the conforts of the old illusions of religion pleasanter than reality. Even many humanists follow science only as far as science does not offend some cherished irrational notion. Their difference from Catholics, Jews and Mormons is sometimes a matter of degree, not kind.

It seems that as long as we have voices we will talk and shout and sing; as long as we have right brains we will believe and worship and pray.

One may see science as chasing a will-o'-the-wisp. Who can seriously believe that science will ever learn the secrets of life and of the universe! One may rightly wonder how long humankind is likely to continue the frustrating probe of the unknown. Chasing a butterfly may be exciting to a boy for awhile, but when it becomes clear that he can never catch it, that the harder he tries the farther the butterfly gets away from him, he may quit in discouragement.

There is no basis for the assumption that humankind will everlastingly pursue an understanding of the world in which we live. After the Greeks' brilliant thrust toward knowledge, the world sank into a thousand-year period of ignorance and supernaturalism accompanied by the deliberate suppression of knowledge. Apparently, humankind had found ignorance and superstition more to its liking than knowledge and scientific enlightenment – and may do so again. If humankind finds greater emotional satisfaction in religion than in the painful, futile attempt to discover reality, higher natural wisdom may direct it to follow a pleasant rather than an unpleasant path to nowhere.

Historically, religion tends to ebb and flow and when religion ebbs, knowledge flows. Various societies have their own patterns of ebb and flow. Today Iran is flowing intensely in religion; Italy is ebbing. The United States seems to be flowing moderately.

America started out with the religious zeal of the Pilgrims. But along about the birth of our nation rationalists and deists had brought about an ebb in religious intensity. But the frontier life of the 19th century stirred up a strong interest in religion again. The 1920s saw an ebb in religion that continued to World War II. From then on, interest in religion in America, as based on mainline church membership, increased to a peak in 1952, then began a slow drop from 49 percent church membership to 40 percent in 1989.

Today (1990) regardless of the drop in church membership, we seem to be in a period of revived religious interest bolstered by cults, imported Eastern religions, the charismatic movement and the electronic pulpit, even though most of the older mainstream denominations are not keeping up in membership with population growth. (The percentage of churchgoers in America is actually the lowest since 1940.) But indicators other than church membership show a revival of religious interest.

George Gallup Jr., who oversees the Gallup polls, believes that "the final two decades of the 20th century could be a period of profound religious renewal." Gallup admits the recent drop in church membership in the United States, but maintains that it is more than made up for by an increase in religious belief. He calls it a widening gap between belonging and believing. In addition, it involves a current search for meaningful values replacing unquestioned obedience to authority.

Columnist Patrick Buchanan writes: "Looking about the nation and the world, it is the secular faiths from Marxism in the East, to humanism in the West, that appear to be desiccated and dying."

We have to call the status of religion in America ambiguous. The question persists whether the current surge is just a blip or a long-term trend.

The world's leading authority on religious statistics, Rev. David B. Barrett, says that the collapse of religion that was foreseen 20 years ago is just not taking place. Rather than humankind steadily "moving toward secularism and non-religion," he says, "there is a big swing away from all forms of anti-religion."

Barrett says that 79 percent of the world's people are religious, and only 4.4 percent are outright atheists, a sharp decline from the 13 percent outright atheists of about two decades ago. Barrett, however, foresees a proportional decline of Christianity in the world due to the high birthrates of the non-Christian Third World countries.

Previous to the 1978 China constitution, which granted citizens religious freedom, religion was banned and churches were closed. Since then over 4,000 Protestant churches and over 2,000 Catholic churches have opened, and over three million of the once-outlawed Bibles have been printed and distributed in China.

Even though the Catholic Church in China is under the control of the state, not the Vatican, and Protestant churches are also under strict government control, Christianity is exploding in communist China.

The story is similar in the Soviet Union. Despite over 60 years of intensive efforts to eradicate religion in the Soviet Union by closing churches and converting them to museums of atheism, imprisoning priests, granting job preference to atheists and teaching atheism in school, many citizens continued to baptize their babies, attend church services, observe religious holidays, and of course pray.

Belief has persisted in the Soviet Union despite government opposition and has been a continuous embarrassment to the communist leadership. Soviet satellite states have clung to their religions vigorously — Poland, Hungary, Czechoslovakia, East Germany, Bulgaria, Romania. In addition, the Soviet Union has 40 to 50 million Moslems to deal with.

As a result of the recent lifting of religious restrictions under perestroika, religion has been burgeoning in the Soviet Union. In July, 1989, the Hungarian Communist Party announced it would no longer require members to be atheists and that it would stop meddling in church affairs. At the time, evangelist Billy Graham was conducting one of his crusades in Hungary, where he overflowed a 70,000-seat Budapest stadium with the largest crowd ever gathered there.

In the same month the Vatican announced that it was restoring full diplomatic relations with Poland. The Polish parliament had just recently restored the Church to legal status in establishing religious freedom.

On Dec. 2, 1989 Soviet President Mikhail Gorbachev surprised the world by flying to Rome to meet with Pope John Paul II at the Vatican.

The religious changes going on in the Soviet Union are no less than startling: religious leaders are being elected to the new parliaments, thousands of new churches are being opened, seminaries are being started, churches are holding formerly forbidden catechism classes and Sunday schools.

On 1990 New Years Day 100,000 Muscovites gathered in Moscow's Red Square to hear the bells of St. Basil's Cathedral for the first time since the 1917 Bolshevik revolution. And for Christmas, celebrated in Russia in January, an hour-long religious service was broadcast by Moscow television.

Gorbachev, a pragmatist, may be saying and doing only what he believes is necessary to save the Soviet Union's shattered socioeconomic system. He told the Italians: "We have changed our attitude on some matters, such as religion. Now we not only proceed from the assumption that no one should interfere in matters of the individual's conscience, we also say that the moral values which religion generated and embodied for centuries can help in the work of renewal in our country too."

On the surface such a statement is purely pragmatic, but it is interesting to note that Gorbachev's mother is religious.

But one must not be too quick at drawing conclusions. Religion was supposed to vanish in the Soviet Union with the development of socialism. But socialism's development broke down. So atheism may not have been defeated so much by the will to believe as by the will to eat. The revival of religion may have been due more to the failure of the Soviet economic system than to the failure of the educational effort to eradicate religion. The success of Christianity in the West owes much to the success of Western capitalism.

The upsurge of religion in the Soviet Union, however, does seem to be consistent with a worldwide upsurge. Most of the European continent has given in to Vatican pressure to provide full government funding for parochial schools. Australia and Canada have followed suit.

Even the African Marxist state of Angola has been experiencing a surge in religion. Despite a decade of repression of religion, Protestant and Roman Catholic leaders say Angolan churches are packed on Sunday mornings. They claim that churches are growing by 8 to 10 percent a year despite Angola being one of Africa's most orthodox Marxist regimes.

In addition, the fanatic flareup of Islamic fundamentalism is one of the most fearful religious developments of our time.

Regardless of the decline in American mainstream church membership and regardless of the long-term trend away from religion, the recent renewal of religious interest is undeniable. Churchmen, sociologists, the press, television and the general public recognize it. Most atheists and humanists sadly admit it.

The worldwide Pentecostal-charismatic movement claims much of the credit for the current religious renaissance. One segment, the Assembly of God Church, has grown 66 percent in the last decade. Its U.S. membership is only two million, but through its missions its overseas branches have added an additional 16 million. It has 18 U.S. colleges and operates the Gospel Publishing House that turns out 24 tons of religious literature a day (that is probably more than American atheists turn out in ten years.)

Alexis de Tocqueville observed 150 years ago that despite America's separation of church and state, the American people were among the most religious on Earth. It seems to still be true.

Pollsters tell us that 95 percent of Americans believe in a God, 87 percent believe in prayer, 70 percent believe in life after death, and even 22 percent would like to see Christians in control — a theocratic government.

There is little question that in recent years the flawed characters of some televangelists have put a damper on the American religious revival. These persons came from humble backgrounds and struggled as tent evangelists preaching a sincere gospel. But when they got into the new highly-remunerative televangelism their careers skyrocketed. They became famous and they rolled in riches.

Their value systems became overloaded, their moral principles became blurred, their faith became contaminated. Money, fame, material luxury, power, vanity, arrogance and egotism took over in stark contrast to their Savior's selflessness, compassion, humility and love. So they fell.

Although televangelism is a flagrant, aggressive segment of the evangelical churches, it is a very small part. So the downfall of a few of its preachers may not be very damaging to the evangelical-charismatic movement.

Theologically, Christianity has been in a steady retreat for hundreds of years. God, as a symbolization of the unknown, retreats daily as the known encroaches upon the unknown.

According to former Southern Baptist President K. Owen Smith, the growth of liberalism weakens Christians. He defined liberalism as "an attitude which may cast doubt on the reliability, dependency and authority of God."

Liberals have softened Christian belief from a literal to an allegorical interpretation of the Bible, from belief that the Bible is the Word of God to belief that the Bible is the word of holy men divinely inspired, from belief in a jealous vengeful God to a God of love and mercy, from a male God to an androgynous God, from a palpable God to a spiritual essence, from a sectarian God to a universal ecumenical God.

Bible scholars arise from among religious liberals (Fundamentalists who believe the Bible to be inerrant, would see no purpose in a critical study of it.) New Testament scholars, for example, examine the sayings, parables and stories of Jesus to see which are most likely to have really been spoken by Him. They use the literary and historical methods of criticism generally used by scholars in checking the authenticity of any written material.

Their studies, as one would guess, do not confirm the inerrancy of the Bible, and they often come under heavy criticism by evangelical religionists who view the Bible as a book to believe, not criticize. Atheists see Bible scholarship as inevitably eroding Christian faith.

Under Christian liberalism we find ecumenism, greater tolerance of sexuality, feminist principles, acceptance of homosexuality, an allegorical interpretation of the Bible, and flexible demands on conduct.

A liberal spokesman of the U.S. Catholic Mission Association said: "I have prayed with Hindus in India. I prayed with the Buddhists. I prayed with the Shinto in Japan. It showed me how God is at work in the world. One can pray in the name of religious principles and peace."

But, objected a conservative member of Urban Outreach in Chicago, the church must guard against de-emphasizing the Biblical requirement to "teach all nations, baptising them in the name of the Father, Son and Holy Ghost." Don't pray with them, convert them.

Ecumenism seems to be growing more strongly among the mainstream churches, churches whose falling memberships frighten them into joining forces as a defense against the expansive cults and evangelical churches.

Ever since Martin Luther was excommunicated in 1521, the ecumenists have been struggling with the controversy between Catholics and Protestants over salvation by faith or by good works.

The Catholics had claimed that salvation could be earned by good works and by an array of ecclesiastical observances, including paying for Masses and indulgences to avert penalties in purgatory. Protestants generally held that salvation was by faith alone.

But now by means of semantic gymnastics they have reconciled their differences. The Christian doesn't do good works to be saved; he does good works because he has been saved. Good works are not the *cause* of his salvation, but the *result*.

Thus did a 20-member dialogue team of Catholics and Lutherans clarify the issue in a 21,000-word report after five years of work.

Salvation is a free gift of God's grace. If it had to be earned it wouldn't be a gift, it would be payment. This solution seems to satisfy everybody. People like something for nothing, and the solution retains that attraction. Offering something for nothing is a common gimmick in advertising — that suckers never seem to become disillusioned with. If it works for merchandisers, why not for religion? You don't have to tithe or do good works or live righteously; you merely have to believe in Jesus as your Savior and accept His gratuitous gift of eternal life. What a deal!

While the fundamentalists have generated the most heat with their literal Bible — a book of intolerance, authoritarianism and satanic terror — the liberals have been successful in swaying our nation in the opposite direction.

We have ceased burning witches, we freed the slaves and outlawed child labor. Women now enjoy equal political and economic rights, labor has gained the right to strike and blue laws have been abolished. Racial equality has been legislated, divorce laws eased, homosexuality legalized and abortion permitted. The accused have been protected by the Miranda ruling, the handicapped aided by access requirements, the aged succored by Social Security and the unfortunate provided with a welfare safety net.

Of course, many fundamentalists would say that most of this is what's wrong with our country. But other people would call such changes the signs of a maturing civilization.

Education certainly makes an important contribution to the quality of a society. But the word "education" needs some qualification. "Secular" does not in itself sufficiently qualify education. After all, Mao Tse Tung's cultural revolution was based on secular education. (While some people would call a Catholic education an oxymoron.)

Probably the best term we have for education that raises the level of civilization is liberal education. Fundamentalists, of course, dislike liberal education because it has a tendency to erode religion. Fundamentalists would like to get their hands on the schools and substitute religions indoctrination for free inquiry, accumulation of knowledge and scholarship—i.e., liberal education.

Even Biblical scholarship has helped to erode the foundation of Christianity. One wonders how much longer religion can last with scholars and scientists punching holes in its myths. Probably much longer. We must not forget that religion and superstition are emotional phenomena built deeply into our culture and possibly into our hereditary nerve patterns. They are punctured and pummeled by scientists, scholars, rationalists and positivists, but they obstinately persist to the consternation of atheists.

Nevertheless, salvation today is through knowledge and information. They are the driving force, the working religion of the modern world, despite the statistics of religious renewal.

The more fundamentalist religions and denominations emphasize strict creeds and authoritarianism. The Southern Baptists, for example, have a policy requiring their employees to profess that the Bible is true in all areas—historically, scientifically, and theologically. The editor of the United Methodist Reporter, writing on this Baptist policy, said "adopting a policy that attempts to dictate the beliefs of others is more likely to polarize and increase disunity among Southern Baptists than to produce the sought-after conformity."

Well, I wonder. Southern Baptists are the fastest growing major denomination in America while Methodists are in a sharp decline.

The saints and patriarchs of biblical days who talked with God were the source for the creation of our Judeo-Christian religion. Today such people are either laughed at or held for observation in mental institutions. Only a small percent of Oral Roberts' own followers believed that he had talked with a 900-foot Jesus, or was later threatened with death by God if he didn't come up with $4.5 million by the end of March.

Few people take the reports of current miracles seriously. Even the Catholic Church disavows the thousands of miracles claimed to take place around the world today. In biblical days miracles and prophetic revelations from God were common. Is it because God no longer suspends nature's laws to permit miracles to happen and no longer wishes to reveal Himself to his earthly children? Or is it because society has become too enlightened, too well-educated and too sophisticated to be easily duped? Or because we have too many investigative reporters around today?

Thomas Paine subjected miracles to an interesting logical question: "If we are to suppose a miracle to be something so entirely out of the course of what is called nature, that she must go out of that course to accomplish it, and we see an account given of such a miracle by a person who said he saw it, it raises a question in the mind very easily decided, which is, is it more probable that nature should go out of her course, or that the man should tell a lie?"

The Catholic Church was able to dominate Christendom for a thousand years because the few Bibles in existence were the property of the Church and the Church was the sole interpreter of the Bible. Lay people were even forbidden to read the Bible. But, thanks to Johann Gutenberg, Bibles became more widespread. In due time disputes over the interpretation of the Bible helped kindle the Reformation. But that was only the beginning of the fractionalizing of Christianity. The contradictory, ambiguous, disputatious Bible has spawned more sects in Christianity than are found in any other religion on Earth.

But the fractionalizing of Christianity over creed disputes has not been entirely detrimental to the religion. It has made Christianity more accessible to more people. It has given more followers an incentive for participation and leadership.

Besides arousing public interest in religion, fractionalizing also assures that no one religious group can become dominant enough to establish a theocracy in this country as in Iran. The fear that the fundamentalists, Pentecostals and charismatics will take over America may not be well-founded. First, these factious groups will have to take over one another. James Madison agreed that in a free government the multiplicity of sects would take care of each other.

Most of the traditional, mainstream Protestant churches are losing ground. Some of the reasons are the chipping away at their theology by liberals and scholars; the tendency of the free-choice spirit of younger generations to choose their own religion rather than follow that of their parents; the nature of aggressive, young people to rebel against authorities entrenched in an aged, fossilized bureaucracy; a lesser interest in a church's doctrine than in a church's location, parking facilities, recreational offerings, children's programs, friendly atmosphere, etc.

And of course there are demographic factors attributing to the decline of mainline Protestant churches: their members have fewer children, immigration greatly favors the Catholic Church, the population move from the Protestant strongholds of small towns and suburbs to large cities, etc.

To whatever one ascribes the causes of the decline of mainstream

Protestant churches, the decline is real: There are more Mormons and Muslims — than Episcopalians in the United States, as many Pentecostals as Presbyterians and nearly twice as many Roman Catholics as all the mainstreamers combined.

It is interesting to note that while the newer religions and cults in America often embrace strict discipline, Spartan living, self-denial, self-sacrifice, and authoritarian control, the oldline traditional Protestant religions have followed an opposite policy — one of increasing tolerance, permissiveness and democratic practice.

Some Protestants warn against too easy an accommodation to the demands of society. Ronald Knox expressed such an accommodation as the willingness to settle for whatever Jones will swallow.

Atheists believe that Jones has swallowed quite a lot and has been regurgitating for the past 50 years.

So what about many of the newer religions whose disciples eagerly swallow more than traditional religions ever did ask their followers to swallow? Man is a coprophagous animal.

To be as popular as it is, religion undoubtedly fulfills many human needs. Let me recapitulate some of them: the need of most of the people on Earth to believe in the mythical, the supernatural, the irrational, the mystical; the need of vain people to achieve sublimity through virtue and sacrifice. Religion satisfies the urge for immortality; it fulfills the need of the establishment for a means of keeping the masses subservient; the need of mountebanks for gullible sheep to be fleeced; the need of a respectable profession for those receiving the call. Religion furnishes a readily available structure for social and recreational needs; a heavy supply of the downtrodden and poor on which dogooders can indulge their compassion and a supply of sinners for reformers to straighten up; religion furnishes the means by which people with transcendental visions can work to create an ideal society — or at least a limited communal paradise; religion supplies the promises of heavenly rewards that make the injustice of life on Earth more easily suffered; it supplies the personal security of a divine guardian and a trustworthy friend in a lonely hostile world. Religion acts as a vehicle for artistic and musical expression; it furnishes an orgiastic circus for the venting of emotions, passions and physical energy. Religion furnishes the vehicle for scoundrels to make great pretensions of virtue and piety while lying, stealing, swindling and debauching.

Again I must ask the question: How many of these needs can atheists and humanists fulfill!

Humankind seems to be in the paradoxical situation where only irrational behavior can fulfill its needs, while such behavior is the cause of most of its problems.

Society valiantly struggles to build a solid foundation of religion to sustain itself. But it seems to forever fail, a failure atheists attribute to the illusory, fraudulent nature of the foundation. However much energy, zealotry, sincerity and dedication are devoted to building a foundation, if it is built out of mud instead of stone it will crumble under the weight of the house.

Pragmatists, however, say that it doesn't matter how true the metaphysical foundation of a society is. All that matters is how well a society can be convinced of its trueness. This is a valid observation, but atheists argue that it should be easier to convince people of truth than of falsehood. Well, not the right brain. In fact, truth seems to work against atheists. The English poet Dame Edith Sitwell wrote: "The public will believe anything so long as it is not founded on truth."

Truth is periodically discovered and then discarded by humankind, leaving a history of shattered hopes. History passes through cycles of great hope and enthusiasm, followed by disappointment, disillusionment and despair.

Christianity brought great hope of a world glowing in peace, love and brotherhood, but after a thousand years of bigotry, persecution, torture and religious wars, disillusionment swept over Christendom in the form of the Reformation.

The Reformation failed equally in bringing peace and love to the world. But the new despair was overshadowed by the enthusiasm of the Enlightenment, a growing belief that science would bring an end to human misery, poverty and disease. But the Enlightenment also ushered in sweat shops, child labor, industrial diseases, machine guns, poisonous gas and finally nuclear bombs.

However, the establishment of democracy in America aroused again the eternal hope of humankind for a better world. But the disappointment with capitalist democracy became the springboard for communism. Humankind became so enamored with the Marxist dream of a communist world utopia that idealists everywhere allowed their hopes to blind them to reality. Conditioned by religion to swallow almost anything fed them, many people were easy prey for the propaganda and lies of authoritarian communist governments. One should not be surprised that people taught to believe the monstrous lies propagated by religion would readily accept the much more believable lies propagated by communists. People falling for communism were often merely transferring their former gullibility at the hands of the authoritarian church to a new gullibility at the hands of the authoritarian communist party.

Marxism, the new truth that was to usher in a paradise of material comfort and equality, and to rescue humankind from the exploitation and poverty of capitalism, produced even greater exploitation and poverty of its own.

The most recent stirring of human hopes was spearheaded by the counterculture of the 1960s. Dreams of love, brotherhood, community and peace gripped the baby boom generation, energizing the protests against the war in Vietnam and embracing the movements for black liberation, women's liberation and sexual liberation, as well as environmentalism and Woodstock.

Of course, there were many minor disasters and disappointments along the course of history—the bubonic plague, two world wars, the Great Depression, Nazism, nuclear armaments and now AIDS. We are today in a period of disillusionment. During such periods, attention is turned to making money. This seems to indicate that young people prefer idealistic and spiritual experiences to the crass pursuit of money. They dedicate themselves to money-grubbing when there is nothing better going on.

But optimists find no difficulty in listing improvements such as those mentioned earlier in human society over the years. Such improvements come about naturally as a result of raised consciousness. Humankind is wont to go along blindly accepting and condoning gross injustices, appalling cruelty, callous insensitivity—until the wrongfulness of such practices is pointed out. Once such wrongfulness is realized, humans are quick to reject such behavior—and wonder how they could have been so blind for so many years.

Raised consciousness is just the recognition of how contradictory, hypocritical and irrational our behavior has been without our ever realizing it.

Even so, some reactionaries label such changes in behavior as effeminacy, enfeeblement, degeneracy. They fear that philosophical vegetarianism, advocacy of animal rights, opposition to capital punishment, denunciation of hunting, attacks against fur fashions and love affairs with whales and baby seals will result in a national wimpish character incapable of defending our nation against the real predatory world.

There is a close connection between conscious and conscience besides the spelling. Consciousness of wrong lays the foundation for conscience.

Conscience is not, as popularly supposed, some God-given guide telling people what is right and wrong. If it were that, the problem of morality

MARTYRDOM OF STEPHEN.

would be greatly simplified. But, as psychologists inform us, conscience is the internalization of the mores of a society. One might elaborate: as modified by an individual's rationalized desires and self-interests.

Morality is not a product of intelligence, but a product of conditioning—of inculcation of conscience. It has a societal purpose. Intelligence would not tell one to act according to moral principles but according to one's own best interest in terms of pleasure and pain.

The point is reached where the pain of guilt for violating moral principles, now internalized as conscience, outweighs the pleasure anticipated from wrongful acts. At that point society has its members efficiently shackled. Guilt becomes self-flagellation for violation of the internalized moral code of society.

However, people with consciences can murder, torture, steal, lie, cheat and rape without violating their consciences. Petty thieves easily justify their thefts by the magnitude of the billions of dollars stolen by crooked businessmen, politicians and bureaucrats. Income tax evaders justify their cheating by averring that everybody does it. Swindlers and con men feel little other than pride in their superior intelligence and cunning while feeling only contempt for the stupidity of their victims. Robin Hood's conscience did not bother him when he stole from the rich to give to the poor.

The Christians of the Inquisition did not violate their conscience when they tortured opponents of the church and burned heretics at the stake — they were doing it for Christ. The conscience of communists does not bother them when they kill capitalists and colonialists for the sake of Marxism. The disciples of Ayatollah Khomeini were not troubled by conscience when they murdered in the name of Allah. The PLO terrorists are no more inhibited by conscience from assassinating Jews, who drove them off their land, than Jews are inhibited by conscience from assassinating Palestinians, who vow to drive them into the sea. Hitler didn't suffer pangs of conscience in trying to exterminate the Jews, whom he saw as contaminators of the superior Aryan race, as world trouble-makers, as Antichrists.

No, we can't depend entirely on conscience for moral guidance. Consciences are flexible enough to be meaningless. All guilt is dissolved by the easy solvents of justification and rationalization. And although the development of conscience is necessary for a viable society, a Machiavellian would see conscience as a handicap for the individual — the greater his conscience, the worse for him and the better for the other fellow.

We might even speak of unusually sensitive consciences as pathological.

In view of the origin and nature of conscience, the religious notion that one's conscience should be regarded as inviolable becomes a bit ridiculous.

Guilt feelings are the emotion that put the teeth into conscience that make it more than an empty ethical exercise. The phenomenon of guilt is the carryover from childhood of the expectation of punishment for wrongdoing. The anxiety over expectation of punishment becomes permanently built into our emotional apparatus. Religion becomes involved with guilt mostly through its obsession with sexual sin.

The threat of Hell is just one of many anxiety factors in guilt and probably by itself is as little effective in curtailing bad behavior as the death sentence has proved to be in deterring murder.

People observant of the behavior of dogs are aware of guilt reactions of such animals. Guilt is a conditioned behavior and has no necessary connection with religion, even if religion is very effective in instilling it. The Marxists have attempted to imbue proletarian conscience with its attendant guilt into their countrymen, but with much less success than religionists have had.

Reforms, improvements and revolutionary changes of whatever nature are hard to come by. Religionists and idealists regularly fail to accomplish the changes in society they seek. The prototype humans necessary for the success of their idealistic dreams exist only in their imaginations. Besides this, for the dreamer to be successful in his endeavor requires the character traits upon which success depends—selfishness, dishonesty, ruthlessness and destructiveness. Traits few idealists possess; traits that would violate the principles most of them plan to espouse.

Reform and radical change involve the art of the possible. A good measure of realism and pragmatism is needed even for partial success. One must deal with a world that more nearly resembles a madhouse than a society susceptible to orderly improvement.

Reformers and revolutionaries must struggle with the human predicament. First, our reward and punishment system doesn't work. The mechanistic sociodynamics of society reward bad behavior more amply than good behavior. Man is not born evil, but evil behavior is encouraged by the mechanism that rewards such behavior by catapulting vicious people to the top. For this reason the world has a preponderance of aggressive, ruthless, dishonest and murderous people in most positions of leadership. By the mechanistic nature of society evil is rewarded and good punished.

This is the intrinsic nature of society that reformers must overcome. The reformer's success depends upon his ability to induce, coax, coerce or trick people, including ruthless leaders, to act against their own selfish interest for the good of the whole society. No small challenge.

It is notoriously true that the highest rewards of wealth and fame in our society go to entertainers, athletes, financial tycoons and criminals—not to scientists, educators and philosophers. Many of our wealthiest family dynasties were established with money from robber barons, bootleggers and Wall Street crooks. Today new dynasties are being established with drug money.

The challenge to improve society must face more than changing human behavior; the challenge must face altering the mechanisms that govern society.

To produce an ideal society, you must start with ideal people. Utopians have often attempted to create such societies by isolating themselves into select communities free from their evil fellow humans. But even they inevitably fail because, although they can escape the rest of society, they cannot escape the sociodynamic mechanisms that control societies, including theirs.

No matter what needs to be changed to improve a society, those in a position to effect a change have no desire to, and those who want the change aren't in a position to effect one. Certainly, the American legal system needs drastic reform. But neither the lawyers who grow rich from the legal system's flaws nor the influential clients they serve feel any pressing need for change.

If ideologists—religious or humanistic—ever come anywhere near creating a good society, that society would be foredoomed in this predatory world. That is part of the human predicament.

Finally, most revolutionaries aren't interested in improving society, but in controlling it.

Our present age is hailed as the age of information. Maybe we should do more bewailing than hailing. Even before the invention of the computer, Albert Schweitzer said, "Once every man of science was also a thinker who counted for something in the general spiritual life of his generation. Our age has discovered how to divorce knowledge from thought, with the result that we have, indeed, a science which is free, but hardly any science left that reflects."

We are becoming an ant-like society of specialists—each little ant doing his specific job with no concern or concept of overall results, with little thought about where the whole society is headed.

We may destroy ourselves despite our high efficiency, information resources and productivity. We need more philosophers and statesmen, more poets and artists; fewer specialists and information retrievers.

Before atheists, rationalists and humanists oppose religion they really should come to some general understanding of what it is they are to oppose. Is religion a mental disorder as Freud apparently thought; and if so is it curable? Is religion so deeply entrenched in the neural structure of the right brain as to be ineradicable? Or is religion just an excrescence that has developed in human society that has been neither selected nor rejected by evolution because of its inconsequence to human survival?

As mentioned earlier, the male peacock's fantastic tail feathers may not have been any more selected by evolution than the stripes of the zebra. In human history many behavioral excrescences have developed which seem to have been tolerated by the evolutionary process: in 14th century Europe, wearing stylish 30-inch-high platform shoes; in Zululand, embedding animal dung under the skin to create the body texture of a crocodile;

in Chad, stretching the lips with huge discs to the point where the individual can't talk intelligibly, can hardly eat, and must be accompanied when walking by maid servants to support their huge two-foot diameter lip discs; in China, binding the feet of girls that left them horribly crippled for life; in Australia, splitting boys' urethras the entire length of the penis (subincision); in Africa and the Middle East, excising the external genitals of girls (clitoridectomy) and sewing their vaginas shut (infibulation).

If religion is just another human behavioral excrescence tolerated by evolution, its eradication may be possible. Binding the feet of Chinese girls is now illegal, the practice of Zulus imbedding animal dung under their skins is diminishing as is the wearing of lip discs in Chad. Australian aborigines are no longer splitting the penises of pubescent boys. Organizations in Africa and Asia have been formed to stop the grisly practices of clitoridectomy and infibulation. There may come a day when Jews will quit mutilating the penises of baby boys, and Christians will quit drinking Christ's blood and eating His flesh.

The hourly recitation of catechisms required of Catholic school children and similar practices of other religions no doubt have a similar crippling effect on the brains of children that binding has on the feet of Chinese girls. (But one should not even suggest such a horrible thought.)

It would be hard to prove that belief in God and the practice of religious rites has anything much to do with the quality of life. It would be equally hard to prove that rejection of religious falsehood and the practice of free inquiry have anything much to do with the quality of life. Both are articles of faith. It is not surprising that religionists believe as they do because they posit a God to assure that their religious devotion will be rewarded. A just God would not reward dishonesty, punish kindness or exalt wrong!

But the faith of atheists is a little puzzling. They believe that truth will win, that right is rewarded, that honesty is not punished — all without positing a God to see to it. Perhaps such faith is a carryover from their early religious training. Or perhaps people just refuse to believe that there is no justice, no reward for honesty, no punishment for perfidy. Solomon didn't: "All things have I seen in the days of my vanity: there is a just man that perisheth in his righteousness and there is a wicked man that prolongeth his life in his wickedness."

The facts are that the human predicament is pretty lousy and the proposition life offers us should arouse our indignity and outrage. But in one sense, nothing could be fairer than life; we don't have to live it. What makes Hell so bad is the lack of any escape.

The grim inevitability of the end of our world really shouldn't be anything for anybody to get upset about. What difference should it make to us? We didn't expect to live on Earth forever anyhow. The world has ended with the personal doom of every man and woman who ever lived. So what's new?

The doomsday prophet must suffer taunts for his erroneous prediction up to the end. If his prediction did ever prove right, he'd no longer be here to say I-told-you-so, nor would there be anyone around to hear him say it. A no-win game.

We could theoretically start actions now that would diminish most of the threats to human survival. But we probably won't because our priorities are all screwed up by religion, nationalism, racism, ignorance, emotionalism, cultural compulsives, taboos, vested interests, greed and selfishness. I can't imagine what kind of horrendous peril humankind would have to face to come to its senses. The threat of nuclear annihilation hasn't been enough.

As pointed out in Chapter IX, most of our worst problems of today are caused by overpopulation. But mainly because of religion, we refuse to recognize it. In fact, our overall attitude is to encourage population growth rather than discourage it. How can humankind be so blind!

Global population should be compared with the multiplication of the bacteria that sour a crock of milk. They start as a small colony and multiply out of control until they have exhausted their food supply, polluted their environment with deadly toxicity and all die in their own excrement. This is the process of souring milk. A similar process turns fruit juice into wine, grain malt into beer, and milk curd into cheese.

If that small colony of bacteria in the milk had been able to control and stabilize its population it probably could have lived off the milk for billions of generations.

Humankind procreate with uncontrolled abandon not only for religious reasons, but also for political reasons. Competitive ethnic groups are in constant competition in biological warfare.

Perhaps the life cycle of creation, development, overpopulation and self-destruction that we are going through on our planet is an old, old story of the universe.

It is interesting to note that had the biblical commandment against killing (including abortions) been obeyed, humankind would have suffocated in its pollution from overpopulation centuries ago.

But still we pretend there is no problem. Or, even worse, we see our entry into space as the key to the solution of overpopulation. We will build colonies on other planets to ship our surplus population to. (At a cost of one million dollars per person for a world that cannot even afford prenatal care for half of its pregnant women!)

A strong cultural compulsive blinds us to the greatest threat to civilization. So we march on into the quagmire sinking deeper with each step while denouncing those who plead for a change of direction, proclaiming our right to have all the babies we desire, singing the praises of motherhood, honoring heavy begetters and feeling self-righteous all the way.

Prolife people in their ignorance work to assure a supply of millions of unwanted children destined to die of starvation in countries too poor to feed their present population, and bring closer the day in our own country when children will starve to death as we reach a similar condition.

The abortion issue is a classical case of the right-brained prolife response of blind compassion and the left-brained pro-choice response of reason. Ultimately, a society's need to survive will dictate its moral choices. RU486, not Jesus Christ, may be the savior of humankind.

From this chapter it is fairly clear that the search for the Holy Grail is not the purpose of life; it is the substance of life.

Our individual holy grails are the ends we pursue. Some call it happiness; the more crass call it money. As the comedian said, "Money can't buy happiness, but it isn't happiness I want — it's money."

Most of us say we are pursuing happiness. But this happiness seems to be an illusion that is always over the horizon. Nevertheless, we pursue happiness through achievement, hard work, perseverance, financial prudence and reaching out for recognition and fame.

The happiness we attain is in the pursuit, but it often takes a lifetime to realize it. The happiness is in the quest. Like a dog chasing a car — what's he going to do with it if he catches it? The fun is in the chase.

Chapter XIII
THROUGH A GLASS DARKLY

Besides ideologues, both religious and secular, the makeup of humankind also includes an assortment of pragmatists, realists, skeptics and cynics. These down-to-earth people recognize the limitations of human improvement, the absurdity of utopian dreams, the historical evidence of humankind's inveterate malevolence and the shades of grey that distinguish one society from another.

They also recognize the contradistinction between good and evil. Without evil, good would have no meaning. Heaven without a Hell would have no value. But human society hardly needs to worry about virtue becoming meaningless.

The above assortment of people are not necessarily good or evil. That depends upon how they react to their realistic conceptions of society. A cynic, for example, is never turned bitter and vengeful by the pervasive injustice, hypocrisy and inhumanity that surround him. He doesn't expect anything better. While optimism is imbecilic and pessimism is sick, cynicism is robust and healthy. But there is always the danger of cynicism becoming the foundation for evil. But fortunately, one's philosophic outlook seems to be of less importance to good behavior than one's genetic temperament and early moral conditioning.

Pragmatists see societies in shades of grey, and they judge puddings by the eating. They rate America as one of the light grey societies, based on the judgment of the emigrants of the world, who choose America overwhelmingly. Pragmatists, not being governed by ideological delusions of black and white, work persistently to improve human life on every little front and in every little way they can and are thereby probably the real salt of the earth.

Nevertheless, pragmatists are sometimes viewed as men without principles — other than pragmatist principles. Pragmatists might support superstition and religion, on the basis that if that sort of stuff is what people want, then they should have it — even if it is founded on falsehood, lies and nonsense. Delusion, they might argue, may still be a better foundation for society than reality.

Pragmatists might suggest, in view of our modern materialistic civilization in which consumption is our greatest value, that we should emphasize physical science and technology because they are the source of our consumer goodies. We should downplay social sciences and the humanities because they are sources of controversy, disruption and doubts. Technology is what produces high incomes and the mountains of consumer goods that people want. People's sensual and spiritual needs can be fulfilled by wallowing in religion, superstitions, supernaturalism, parapsychology, mysticism, eroticism and gormandism. (Atheists wonder if pragmatists haven't already imposed their agenda.)

Humanism, a secular philosophy-ideology with bonds to the Ethical Culturists, Unitarian-Universalists, agnostics and atheists, has received considerable publicity in America in the past decade, not because of the PR skills of its leaders, but because the politicized, right-wing fundamentalists (mostly Jerry Falwell and his Moral Majority) have singled out secular humanism as a convenient satan-figure to scare the American public.

One is rightly dismayed at the shamelessness of these Christian fundamentalists depicting humanists as the devils of society. The Christians with their history of burning heretics at the stake, hanging witches, torturing unbelievers with racks and thumbscrews, murdering tens of thousands of Saracens and stealing their lands, massacring whole city populations over doctrinal differences — these Christians depicting humanists as the devils of society, humanists whose ethical philosophy dedicates them to the betterment of humankind through the acceptance of science and learning and the repudiation of superstition and ignorance!

The Christian fundamentalists speak of secular humanism as a religion taught in our public schools. Of course humanism being primarily atheistic, is not a religion in the usual sense. In addition, the organized humanists of America have negligible influence on the public schools.

But the fundamentalists do have a point. If because of separation of church and state, religion is kept out of public schools — that is, the religious basis for moral training is excluded — about all that is left in the way of moral training is secular.

Religious moral training is based on divine edicts; secular moral training is based on what experience has shown to be the best behavior for producing a happy, harmonious society.

Humanists, rationalists and other left-brained realists generally avoid the error of viewing the world as black and white. They see in the improvable nature of society an opportunity that warrants optimistic enthusiasm. They work toward small realizable increments of improvement in the quality of life, foregoing the grand dreams of ideologues — both religious and secular — that stir great hopes but end in disappointment and despair.

The humanist foundation for ethics and morality is intellectually so far superior to the religious foundation — a foundation based on the hearsay edicts and commandments of a supposititious god — that only the theory of the right brain can explain the incredible choice by 95 percent of humans for the latter.

But to be realistic, humanist and religious ethics may not have as much to do with behavior as generally thought. Behavior is molded mostly by early conditioning and role models as well as by the fear of embarrassment from being caught, of retaliation, of fines and imprisonment. It is molded by the desire to be liked, loved and respected, and by the lure of the economic rewards for good behavior.

Humanist ethics do not differ greatly from religious ethics except in their foundation. For religion, the threat of divine punishment is the last desperate effort to deter evil-doers. But the bicameral brain, which believes and disbelieves at the same time, undermines the threat.

There is no question about religion's success in (as atheists see it) bamboozling the human race. But religion's success in improving moral behavior and in enhancing human existence is not so certain. Has religion made men nobler, more merciful, more honest, more just? During the Middle Ages when religion dominated, were people better behaved and happier?

Robert Ingersoll in a burst of rhetoric questioned the claimed benefits of Christianity: "For thousands of years men and women have been trying to reform the world. They have created gods and devils, heavens and hells; they have written sacred books, performed miracles, built cathedrals and dungeons; they have crowned and uncrowned kings and queens; they have tortured and imprisoned, flayed alive and burned; they have preached and prayed; they have tried promises and threats; they have coaxed and persuaded; they have preached and taught, and in countless ways have endeavored to make people honest, temperate, industrious and virtuous; they have built hospitals and asylums, universities and schools, and seem to have done their very best to make mankind better and happier, and yet they have not succeeded."

In contrast to the fabulous growth of organized religion, humanists and other nonbelievers have to admit, however sadly, that their association and their influence in America are very close to nothing. Religion is a hundred times — a thousand times — more successful in organizing, proselytizing and winning the public to its views and beliefs than humanism. With the total backing of science, history and common sense, humanists still gain only a trivial number of advocates.

There is little competition between humanism and religion. The real competition is between different religions vying for the souls of believers. Humanists and atheists occasionally pick up a stray apostate.

The failure of humanism vis-a-vis religion is attributable to many factors humanists can do little or nothing about:

(1) The human will to believe.
(2) The absence in humanism of the promise of a reward of eternal life to followers.
(3) Humanism's appeal to the head rather than the heart.
(4) The irrelevance of truth in gaining popular support.
(5) The difficulty of organizing nonbelievers, who feel little need to reinforce their nonbelief by joining an organization.
(6) Humanism's innate inability to fulfill emotional needs.
(7) The humanist disfavor of herd-like subordination and devotion to strong leaders.
(8) The stigma attached to nonbelief in religion.
(9) The handicapping effect of humanist ethics.

But there are things that humanism could do something about to increase its popularity. One of them, as mentioned earlier, is to get rid of the ivory-tower mentalities dominating humanism, and then bring humanism down to the grass-roots level. As one letter-writer expressed it: "Reflecting on my thirty-odd-year association with Humanism, what concerns me is that most of my fellow Humanists are white, relatively well off, and well educated. Humanism in its present form is incapable of reaching the blue-collar class (from which I came), the minorities, and the impoverished. I'm sorry to say that at this stage we are nothing but a tiny group of bourgeois Humanists who have little, if any, influence in making this a better world in which to live."

The elitists, whose erudite analyses of religion seldom reach beyond those people already committed to humanism and atheism, are possibly as much of a problem as a solution. Humanist Lawrence Hyman made some interesting points along this line: "I would like Humanism . . . to be less a philosophy for superior intellects and more a 'common faith' (to use John Dewey's term) that can gain universal acceptance."

To achieve public acceptance, humanism must offer more than skepticism, insults and ivory-tower snobbery.

After all, in view of the nature of Christianity, built as it is on a foundation of sand, it is no great feather for anybody's hat to thoroughly discredit it with rational arguments, historical data and scientific evidence. Any 12-year-old child of normal intelligence can debunk the Bible.

Paine proved that the Bible is a fraud 200 years ago and gained only public abuse for his effort. Humanists and atheists who get hung up on the Bible waste their time exposing its errors to people who believe with their hearts, not with their heads. Once skeptics conclude that the Bible is false, their interest in it should end. It might even be a good idea after humanists once conclude that religion is a fraud to dismiss religion and devote their time and energy to promoting the positive philosophy of humanism instead of wasting their lives fighting religion.

From the standpoint of reason and logic Christianity is a pushover. One wonders how such an easy pushover could stand even if there were no opposition.

Obviously, reason and logic have nothing to do with the tenacity of this monument to the right brain. The ivory-tower intellectuals aren't even needed.

What are needed are people of understanding, people with the ability and talent to organize, publicize and proselytize; people to develop a saleable humanist lifestyle. And it wouldn't hurt to have a few charismatic orators like Robert Ingersoll.

Religion does offer much more to people here on Earth besides commandments and superstitions. Humanism must learn to compete. Humanists are egregious failures in human relations partly because of their self-centered absorption with their ratiocination and partly because of their elitist hubris. One cannot easily persuade people one hates or holds in contempt.

Humanists would do well to adopt the successful ways that have made religion so popular. They must learn the skills of public relations, offer social and recreational opportunities that appeal to the public and develop an attractive humanist life style. They need to discover ways of competing with the passionate appeal, mystique and pizzazz of religion.

Human relations should start with a shift from the negative approach of Bible-bashing, deriding priests and preachers and debunking religious myths to the positive approach of enhancing the appeal of humanism to make it competitive with religion. People aren't ingratiated by having their emotional props kicked out from under them, nor are they endeared by being called fools. Attacking the Bible turns off even people who no longer believe in it but still retain a warm feeling in their hearts for the Bible from childhood.

Friendliness, openness, warmth, kindness, love, sympathy, charm and flattery are some of the ammunition used successfully by churches. Religionists have perfected ingratiating tactics for welcoming lonely, alienated people to their churches. The church members fall all over the newcomers to make them feel wanted and loved. The love is mostly feigned, but it works. Humanists must learn the tricks of the trade. They must concentrate on filling the needs and wants of the public, not their own needs and wants. The public does not want intellectual arguments deploring religion.

Churches make the same kind of positive approach as do successful advertisers and salesmen. The prospective buyer of a new washing machine or television set is seduced by the description of the new product, not by the advertiser's attempt to run down the old, obsolete product the prospect presently owns.

New Age religions have made spectacular gains by promoting their highly appealing new nonsense. They devote no effort toward decrying the established religions. (They leave that unproductive work to humanists and atheists.)

Once new people have been lured into the humanist fold and have developed a positive attitude toward the group, the new people will pick up the humanist viewpoint more or less osmotically. (The deliberate attempt to change people's minds by rational arguments usually turns them away.)

So, the smart tactic is to lure prospects, win their friendship, and then convert them. Once their affections have been won, their minds will open up to the logic and reason humanists present.

At present humanists have little to offer to fulfill people's needs for social and recreational activities that is comparable to that offered by the churches. Humanists must offer an attractive life style that yields happiness and emotional fulfillment. Rational competency is not enough.

And it is important that humanists direct greater attention toward reaching the young. As Isaac Asimov said: "There is always a new generation coming up. Every child, every new brain, is a possible field in which rationality can be made to grow."

Some humanists have suggested that humanism should be called a religion in order to make it more palatable to the public. Promoting humanism as a religion might result in millions of people swarming into humanism, people who can't stomach the theology of churches but feel that to be a good person they have to have a religion. But then, the humanistic Universalist-Unitarians call themselves a religion, and their success has been less than spectacular. It won't happen, anyhow, because too many ardent supporters of humanism oppose the idea.

One letter-writer ensconced the humanist predicament in a bit of humor: "Sure, I've looked at the philosophy of the regular secular humanists, and it's boring, believe me. There's no room for prejudice, mythology, self-righteousness, hatred, inquisitions, or even cable TV shows. Most importantly, the profit motive is missing. I now offer you the earthly immediacy of secular humanism combined with the good, old-fashioned, buns-kicking, arbitrary mindlessness of southern fundamentalism. You don't have to use your brain, as orthodox secular humanists advise, or wear a diaper on your head, as is the custom of Islamic fundamentalists."

Humanists would do better by dropping their misplaced faith in the old Socratic notion that truth, goodness and beauty will always win by their sheer superiority. There is no natural law or divine authority behind such a notion.

Success has to do with popularity, not truth. Humanists have to learn that whether they are right or wrong is irrelevant. They will succeed when they master the skills of proselytizing, promotion, propaganda and public relations.

Of course, there may be a few humanists who prefer to remain a small elite group uncontaminated by the stupid, superstitious multitude. They believe that what is wrong is the coprophagous, gullible, superstitious, irrational, 12-year-old mentality of the human herd. (I have the arrogance to agree.)

The philosophy of humanism is rationally unassailable. Humankind is abandoned on Earth to its own devices to either create a useful civilized society or to destroy itself. Humankind's hope lies in accepting the responsibility for its own welfare rather than in trying to shift the responsibility onto some mythical God. The good life the gods failed to deliver, humankind must find the courage and intelligence to build itself. This is essentially the existential view of the human situation.

Humankind must place its faith in the scientific methods that have yielded fabulous tangible results rather than in religion, which has an uninterrupted record of failure since the first ape-man prayed for rain 500,000 years ago.

Although humanists are few in number in America, many have worked diligently to promote humanism. In some foreign countries humanism has made a greater impact than it has in America.

But American humanists are active in organizations to abolish corporal punishment in schools, to stop genital mutilation of children, to aid runaway teenagers, to promote population growth control. They are active supporters of free choice for women, of a substance abuse alternative to the religion-oriented Alcoholics Anonymous, of the fight for civil liberties, of the struggle to maintain the separation of church and state.

Friedrich Nietzsche saw Christianity's view of life as extremely negative. The world was a vale of tears, an ugly sinkhole of sin, an abomination. Christians posited a heaven to better slander this life. Such a view produced lugubrious, downcast Christians.

What more could humanists want? Such a theology begs for a competing ideology with a really positive view, an ideology to hearten and gladden with a promise of a bright and happy life here and now.

Of course, with the failure of socialism and communism has come an increasing skepticism of earthly solutions to human discontent. Nevertheless, the current worldwide breakdown of communism inspires a renewed interest in humanism and democracy. I speak of humanism and democracy because the founders of our country were humanistic deists along with a handful of Christians. Our Constitution leaves little doubt about who dominated the framing of it, in view of its rigorous safeguards against its ever being perverted into a theocracy. The United States was founded de facto as a secular humanist nation.

Albert Schweitzer asked if there was a harder task than to make what is used up usable. "Never hitherto have worn-out ideas risen to power among the people who have worn them out. Their disappearance has always been a final one," said Schweitzer.

Communism seems to be worn out, and Christianity has been around thirty-times longer. Humanism has not been worn out because it has never been tried as an explicit ideology. Should religion decline, there is no other moral-ethical guide on our horizon but humanism, and humanism and democracy fit together like a handshake.

Instead of wasting its energy fighting religion and defending itself against the Christian fundamentalists' charge that humanism has been imposed on the public schools and permeates our government, humanists should take a positive attitude and go on the offensive: Yes, humanism dominates our public schools and is well represented in our government, and as a result America is the greatest nation on Earth, the choice for emigration by all the peoples of the world.

If the fundamentalists insist on giving humanism the credit for America's superlative civilization, why should humanists decline it!

Humanist Lawrence W. Hyman suggests: "Although I have no formula to reconcile the difference between religion and humanism, I am convinced that some kind of convergence is taking place between the major religions and humanism and that the rise in the religious right is the result of a fear that this convergence would result in an end to the non-humanistic elements in Christianity (and in Judaism)."

Humanism as a reform movement (aside from its radical atheist ideology) can address itself to many societal problems of mutual concern to religionists. The duty of people of good will is to help make life better for everyone within their sphere of influence. This can be done by direct humanitarian aid and by the manipulation of the mechanisms that govern human behavior, such as the reward and punishment system. Such manipulation can be effected by political means and by the practices in the realm of the private sector.

Of all the mechanisms determining the quality of a society, the reward and punishment system is by far the most important. When virtue is not rewarded, it declines; when vice is not punished, it flourishes.

People of good will must strive to improve the reward and punishment system (justice). Indifference and neglect lead to a society governed by the amoral laws of the jungle.

Speaking of people of good will working to improve the world sounds a bit naive, almost Pollyannish. Much of the contention and turmoil of the world *is* the result of people of good will trying to improve the world. Conflicts arise over how to improve it, by what means, in what ways, for whom, by whom, etc., etc.

About all we can say is that if citizens of good will make a sincere effort to establish a just reward and punishment system, are not too violently divided ideologically and practice tolerance, their efforts should enhance tranquility, harmony and happiness.

One thing we can all agree on is that there are great differences in the quality of life between various countries, e.g., between Sweden and Lebanon. Since some societies are unarguably much better than others, it is logical to conclude that all societies are improvable. This is an apt optimistic basis for humanism.

It was communism's poor reward and punishment system in the

economic sphere that finally brought it to its knees. Citizens received too little reward for production effort.

But America has little to brag about re reward and punishment. In fact, no society has. They all reward bad behavior more amply than good behavior because of the mechanistic nature of human society rather than because of any intrinsic malevolence in man's character. People of good will must work at mitigating the effects of this natural social dynamic.

Most people are practical, pragmatic. If lying is rewarded, they lie; if cheating is rewarded, they cheat; if stealing is rewarded, they steal. Play the game. Forget about morality, ethics, justice. Follow the amoral, positive-minded Norman Vincent Peales and Dale Carnegies of the world.

The attitude of college students toward repaying student loans is an example of the direction America is moving. According to one justice department official, the losses from default of such loans amounted in one year to more than American banks had lost in robberies during this entire century. And this from the cream of American youth!

Since cheating and stealing are so persistent and ubiquitous, they must be highly rewarded. The council for the regional administrator of national banks in Atlanta, commenting on the light sentences bankers receive when convicted of embezzling millions of dollars, said that bankers do it because they think they can get away with it and that even if they don't, the penalty is trivial. He called such people a danger to society because they show that it pays to steal.

Fame and fortune are two of the primary rewards that propel a society. The more widely they are dispersed, the healthier the society. But in America, fame and fortune tend to become heavily concentrated; our system encourages it. For example Michael Jackson, the entertainer musician, makes as much as $140 million a year. In this case the public, not Jackson, is responsible for such an unhealthful distribution of entertainment money.

Besides our society's preposterous range in rewards, we fail miserably in the allocation of rewards according to the value to society of the services performed. Patti Davis, ex-President Reagan's actress daughter, was deluged with movie, TV and night club offers after her father won the election. Two Las Vegas hotels each offered her a reported $150,000 a week for a six-week stint as a singer and entertainer. That adds up to $900,000 for just six weeks — $700,000 more than her dad was getting for a whole year as President of the country!

When the 52 hostages were returned from Iran in 1979 after 444 days of captivity, they were greeted as heroes. The frenzied celebration of their homecoming made thoughtful people wonder what the hostages had done to deserve it. Actually, the whole Iranian episode, including the disastrous attempt to rescue the hostages, was shameful and dishonorable. But the American public inverted the humiliating return into a glorious victory, and celebrated with unsurpassed extravaganza. All of this, of course, was bitterly resented by the Vietnam veterans, who had only recently struggled through years of dismal and dehumanizing fighting in Southeast Asia. When they returned home they had been given not a hero's welcome, but had been received with shabby neglect, even contempt.

Reward and punishment are often transposed. Some of the Watergate criminals were enriched by writing and lecturing about their perfidy, and received millions of dollars for movie rights chronicling their crimes.

The quality of a society is largely determined by who is rewarded and who is punished. Those most responsible for productivity—the workers, engineers, inventors and scientists—receive far less than those who expend their time and brains manipulating for control of the profits. Created by science, operated by labor, industry pays its greatest rewards to those who gain financial control of it.

Probably the biggest reason for skewed reward and punishment systems is that most of those at the top—those in a position of power to improve the system—got to the top by virtue of the skewed system. They got up there by ruthlessness and dishonesty; they like the system. Justice would probably require hanging some of them and throwing the rest into jail.

Notwithstanding, our reward and punishment system is still better than one in the hands of religionists who have convinced themselves that they are acting under the guidance of God.

The ultimate in reward and punishment, of course, are Heaven and Hell. The carrot and stick combination does tend to inhibit and cripple naturally good people, but has little effect on naturally evil people. The canonical threats down through the centuries of punishment after death have failed to prevent wars, pogroms, genocide, torture, enslavement, murders and massacres.

Not to be overlooked are compassion, mercy and charity that some-times sabotage and cancel our sanctions of punishment. Because of our forgiving natures, we often sin against victims. "Who spares vice wrongs virtue." Criminals and crooks are all aware of the compassion of their fellow men and take full advantage of it.

Probably next in importance to reward and punishment is the training and education of children. Here we find considerable disagreement about what children should be taught. Religionists, of course, are less interested in cultivating reason in new brains than in planting predigested dogma. One wonders how filling a child's head with superstition, myths and lies can be called education.

In discussing the status of American education, we should start with a realistic view of the nature of society. Briefly, the successful climb to the top by whatever means necessary, including ruthless, dishonest, unethical, immoral and illegal means. Once up there, they proceed to describe the qualities leading to success as honesty, decency, fairness, law obedience and talent. This self-flattery implies a perfect world.

The job of school teacher then is to teach the imperfect child to adjust to this perfect world. In accord with this flattery is the picture of the newborn baby as a ruthless, selfish beast. By educating him in the virtues and values acclaimed by the successful, parents and teachers transform the beast into a civilized human being.

Of course there is a contrary view of the newborn child that sees him as untainted and uncorrupted and with an unlimited capacity for reason and understanding, a child more prone to virtue than to vice. But the processes of acculturation and education pervert his natural goodness, stunt his moral growth and poison his brain with propaganda, bigotry and superstition.

Further, according to this contrary view, the shape of the person is not inherent in the malleable child, but inherent in the die in which the person is cast. And this die is designed by the successful to shape a child to become a conforming, obedient, technologically-trained employee of the establishment, and to love his servitude. Schoolteachers and preachers, smugly entrenched, are the hirelings who operate the forge. The reader will have to weigh these two views for himself.

Too often the universities play the role of preservers of the status quo through propagating prevailing beliefs and values. Professors learn quickly that the path to the head of the department is paved with the solid marble of conformity. And the mind, if induced to teach what it doesn't believe, sooner or later adapts to a more comfortable situation by coming around to believe what it teaches.

But the decline of intellectual vigor in universities is merely a part of the general decline throughout society brought about in good measure by the growing emphasis on economic security. Few persons in a society dedicated to security and enslaved by mortgages have the courage to stick out their necks for righteous causes. G. A. Borgese said of Italian Fascism: "We imagined that the universities would be the last to surrender. They were the first."

Particularly in democracies, there is an ongoing controversy over whether education should be aimed at developing excellence in a relatively few elitists or at raising the general level of literacy of the populace. However offensive to the opponents of royalty, racism, slavery and the rule of wealth, the truth is that without the inequality and slavery of the past, science, learning and the cultural arts could never have been developed. They are the product of privilege.

There is also a continuous controversy over teaching children morality or adaptivity—should the child be taught to do the right thing or the successful thing?

Children taught adaptivity do what is required to succeed, and adjust their tactics accordingly—whether the requirement is corrupt politics, crooked finance, or ruthless business practices. The successful, of course, have always practiced amoral adaptation. But now it is beginning to be taught in the schoolhouse. The Watergate people were the product of such an education trend. Teaching adaptivity is the antithesis of character building.

Parents are subject to an uneasiness about education, a fear that their children will not be indoctrinated to believe as their parents do, that they may be exposed to ideas in conflict with their childhood nurturing. Other people, however, are more troubled by the spectacle of hundreds of thousands of young people being exposed to four years, six years, eight years of college and coming out having lost not one ounce of the bigotry with which they entered, having shed not one feather of childhood superstitions, having changed not one significant view of the world since walking through the institution's portal on their freshman day!

Possibly most to be feared from American education stems from the excessive emphasis put on success. Our schools arouse aspirations for success, but because success is relative, only a few students can reach the top; the rest are dumped into the dustbin of frustrated failures. The successful, too, are often frustrated because the drive that got them to the top is insatiable. So, it is not surprising that our country is full of people twisted by frustration, and given to venting their feelings through sadistic behavior, crime and violence.

Rationalists hope that religion, based on superstition and supernaturalism, will eventually falter in the face of the increasing historical research proving the man-made basis of religions, along with the increasing advances of science disproving the purported evidence of a supernatural world.

Should religion come to a timely end, it will leave the world to secular

ELIJAH FED BY RAVENS.

humanism, and when the successful secularists get the idea that they, not God, are in control, will they not be tempted to play God? Since they believe that man is improvable — man is what man makes of himself — will they not proceed to fashion man according to the way they think he should be? Then will not democracy be crushed in the process? When successful rulers assume the authority of God, tyranny follows.

This was well illustrated by what the Catholics did when they attained dominant power in the Middle Ages, by what the Protestant Puritans did when they ascended to power in early America, by what the communists and fascists have done whenever they have attained power, by what the Iranian Islamic Fundamentalists are doing today now that they have attained dominance. There is understandable fear that religious doctrine may be replaced by political doctrine pursued with religious fervor.

Is there any sound reason to believe that secular humanists are different — that humanists aren't human! Should they come into power will they not do the same thing? Well, not necessarily. Our own political leaders have never succumbed to the temptation in over 200 years of our democracy to turn it into a dictatorship — although some Republicans became a bit apprehensive of Franklin Roosevelt's New Deal administration. Leastwise, I doubt that anyone needs to fear that humanists will ever attempt to impose a dictatorship on the American people. Humanists are too conscientious, too restrained by ethics and moral principles to rob the people of their liberty. The ethics that humanists teach their children produce nice people, but not winners. So it is unlikely that humanism will ever establish itself as America's predominant ethos. (Of course, by the time humanists achieved very much status and power, the ruthless successful would wrench control from them.)

So where is America headed? In the present confused situation it is difficult to tell whether liberalism, or specifically humanism, as a scientific outlook, is progressing, regressing or just holding its own. Humanists and atheists can take satisfaction in the knowledge that regardless of continuous changes, truth remains exactly where it has always been. (Precisely the satisfaction religionists take!)

Rationalists have always had an uphill battle against the benighted supporters of superstition and supernaturalism. So what's new?

The emotional reactions to religious words and symbols built up in the past when people believed more earnestly in religion may be much of the sustaining force behind modern religion. Without the foundation of deep belief to reinvigorate the momentum, modern religion may be coasting to its end on the diminishing heritage of semantic residue from past ages of belief.

In Christ's day the discussion of religion was not taboo. Judging from the religious obsession of the Middle Ages discussion must have been a daily commonplace. And certainly such discussions were not taboo during the turbulent Reformation.

But modern, business-oriented middle-class societies have hung a taboo on the discussion of religion. Religion evokes heated arguments that a staid, business-oriented society can do better without. Religion is not discussed in polite society. Sex was also a tabooed subject for discussion in polite society for most of American history. Victorianism denied there was such a thing as sex. If it doesn't exist, of course, you don't talk about it. But the discussion of sex has been considerably liberated in recent years and is now widely accepted. The once-tabooed subject has entered the newspapers, magazines, airwaves, schoolrooms and churches. Preachers no longer camouflage sex with the generic euphemism sin, but speak explicitly of sexual intercourse, oral sex, sodomy, homosexuality, rape and child molestation.

Atheists and humanists wonder if the taboo will be lifted from the discussion of religion as it has been from the discussion of sex. Is discussion of religion the last no-no? Atheists foresee that when people "look into" their religion, discuss it, study it, reason about it, they will begin to doubt it and leave it. As Socrates said, when you expose the roots you kill the tree.

The radio and television talk shows have pretty well shredded the taboo against discussion of sex and here and there show signs of a similar pattern of de-tabooing the discussion of religion. For example, a Phil Donahue talk show of October 24, 1988 on the question of life after death dealt openly and spiritedly with every facet of religion. On the panel were a rebel Catholic priest, a fundamentalist Christian, a representative from the International Council of Community Churches, a reincarnationist and an atheist. A year later Sally Jessy Raphael aired a talk show titled "Lost and Found Religion" in which three religionists turned atheists, a born-again Christian and two atheists turned religionists discussed religion in an open way that would have shocked an audience a decade ago.

The growth of religion in America may be reversed as better-educated, more sophisticated Americans begin to realize what an anachronism Christianity is.

Polls of religion in America indicate around 95 percent believers in the supernatural against 5 percent nonbelievers. One would expect such polls to be greatly skewed in favor of believers. A believer is very unlikely to report that he is an atheist, while an atheist could have many reasons to report that he is a believer.

One can only guess at how many closet atheists there are in this country, non-believers who discreetly keep their mouths shut to protect their reputations, their professional jobs, their businesses, their marriages, etc.; college professors who teach evolution through the week and attend church on Sunday to hear a preacher talk about the biblical story of creation; timid atheists who feel isolated, insecure, alone.

If the taboo against open, candid discussion of religion is lifted and religion is released from most of the cultural compulsives now sustaining it, and the momentum of semantic reactions to religious words and symbols spends itself, could atheism and humanism burst into bloom in the new intellectually liberated environment!

Could there be an atheist coming-out day as doubters and atheists throughout society realize that they are not alone, when each doubter realizes that his neighbor is also a doubter, when each realizes that his own adherence to religion is a defensive pretense against a society hostile to atheism—when all realize that the emperor wears no clothes! When they realize that *they* are the moral majority—not the deluded, superstitious fundamentalists!

Americans are herd-minded followers of trends, vogues and styles. The whole country can shift to new popular trends with amazing speed and alacrity. If the herd ever turns to secular humanism, religion is finished.

Julian Huxley said that once there are enough people who believe in transhumanism, "the human species will be on the threshold of a new kind of existence, as different from ours as ours is from that of the Peking man."

Once the humanists and atheists sense that the tide is turning, that they are no longer fighting a lonely, outmoded and hopeless battle against the forces of mass credulity, they will be inspired to intensify their efforts to reach the millions of potential converts who need only to learn that there are organizations with whom they are already substantially in agreement.

But there are profound impediments to this vision. The first great impediment to the progress of atheism and humanism is right-brain preference—the human will to believe superstitious nonsense over rational explanations. H. L. Mencken expressed it simply: "The men the American people admire most extravagantly are the most daring liars; the men they detest most violently are those who try to tell them the truth."

The second great impediment is the cultural compulsive blinding humankind to the population explosion—a catastrophe slowly sinking humankind deeper and deeper into a quagmire that may eventually destroy science and learning and loose religious zealots to swarm over humanity like maggots over a putrescent carcass.

But let us leave speculation and get down to what's really happening in the world. We are witnessing one of the most historic watersheds of history—the breakdown of the atheistic Union of Soviet Socialist Republics.

Not surprising, many religionists see the breakdown as a great victory for religion. To them it proves that God exists, and that God has finally triumphed over the communist atheists. One wonders, though, why it took this omnipotent God of the universe 70 years to do in the evil empire.

To rational minds the breakdown of the Soviet Union seems more likely to be due to the failure of socialism—a system dependent on ideal citizens sacrificing their selfish interests for the good of all—to compete with realistic capitalism whose success depends on individuals working for their own selfish interests under a better reward and punishment system (justice) than any socialists ever dreamed up.

In addition, because of the failure of socialism to achieve its unrealistic, idealistic aims, totalitarian slavery became necessary to hold it together.

Under Marxism, the Russians not only attempted to radically change one-sixth of the world from capitalism to communism, but tried to convert their God-fearing population into a God-sneering population.

These two radical transformations of human nature would have ranked second only to the transformation of apes into Homo sapiens. No wonder the Marxists failed.

Even with the clandestine backing by enchanted liberals, romantics, ideologues and dupes around the world who believed that atheistic communism was destined to supplant Christian capitalism, the Russian experiment still fell flat on its face.

The failure of communism to replace religion in fulfilling the spiritual need for a transcendent ideology, to replace religious conscience with proletarian conscience as a moral guide for social behavior, and to supply the physical needs of its citizens with a new kind of economic system has created the crisis of today's world. The secret hope of rationalists for the success of Marxist attempts to eradicate religion has been shattered.

Some religionists are acclaiming the breakdown of the Soviet Union as heralding a great and glorious return of God's viceroyalty to again dominate human society as it did in the centuries of the Dark Ages.

Yes, it is possible. After what has happened in Eastern Europe anything must be considered possible. We shall see.

The religionists have good reasons to believe that a great tide of superstition and supernaturalism is coming in. Freedom and democracy are unfortunately being associated with religion. There is, of course, a connection: Give human beings freedom and their coprophagous nature and need to believe will sink them in the slough of religion every time. The pleasure principle of the dominating right brain finds more joy and fulfillment in ignorance and superstition than in education and rationality. Nor is humankind elevated much by its vaunted education establishments, dominated as they are by fear and greed. Nor can any auspice be found in the aphorism that ignorance and folly are more powerful than science and reason.

It is high time for a viable substitute for the failed Christian and Marxist dreams. The breakdown of Soviet communism has left a void in Eastern Europe begging to be filled. Organized humanists, unfortunately, are too inconsequential to do much about it. About all they can do is disconsolately observe the religious vultures of the world flocking in vast well-heeled numbers to the Soviet Union to pick over the moribund body of the failed communist experiment. Adding to their despair is religion's record of being as much of an enslaver of the human mind and spirit as communism has been.

History shows religion to be quite durable. We must not sell it short from wishful thinking. The routing of communism from the Soviet Union and its satellites is more likely to be followed by a burst of repressed religion than by humanism.

But humanists do see some hope. Eighty percent of all the scientists and engineers who have ever lived are alive today. In addition, every generation produces a minority of concerned citizens with skeptical predispositions and noncoprophagous temperaments to fight ignorance and superstition. Humanist Isaac Asinov said: "There is always a new generation coming up. Every child, every new brain, is a possible field in which rationality can be made to grow. We must therefore present the view of reason, not out of a hope of reconstructing the deserts of ruined minds that have rusted shut, which is all but impossible — but to educate and train new and fertile minds."

Moreover, the record of religion rescuing failed societies is not very impressive. More often societies have been saved from religions that had gone quite berserk as religions tend to when not restrained and modified by saner elements.

In time humanism might take hold in Eastern Europe after everything else fails. In America? Well, humanism has a lot going for it. A Constitution written by humanists, a discredited worn-out religion, a youth starved for an ideology, grossly underestimated humanist closetarians and an educational system with physical infrastructure that has the greatest potentiality in the world.

The future of humankind may be determined by the conflict between the right and left cerebral hemispheres for domination of the human brain.

The right hemisphere has a lot going for it, including Freud's pleasure principle. As long as religion, supernaturalism, superstition, mysticism and magic bring more pleasure to most human beings than does rationalism, religion will continue to dominate human behavior. After all, who is to say what rational behavior is? If religion brings people the greatest pleasure, isn't their pursuit of their greatest pleasure entirely rational?

While religionists find happiness, joy and self-fulfillment in religion, others may not be able to stomach the lies, deceptions, humbug and mummery that underlie religion. Such people could be compared with those who might enjoy ocean fishing if they weren't subject to seasickness.

The world has never lacked religious shysters and charlatans as well as sincere psychotics suffering from delusions of grandeur to keep religion at an ardent pitch. Their frequent appearances are no great wonder because genetic mutations can produce anything. The phenomenon isn't the popping up of megalomaniacs with their weird and bizarre theologies; the phenomenon is the eagerness with which the public follows them, worships them, deifies them — these zanies, holy men, prophets and saviors, as well as the greedy charlatans exploiting the public's imbecility.

But it is difficult to sort the conscious frauds from the self-deluded kooks. There have been such charismatic leaders as Zoroaster, Moses, Krishna, Christ, Buddha, Mohammed, Joseph Smith, Mary Baker Eddy, Sun Myung Moon, Maharishi Mahesh Yoga, Jim Jones, Bhagwan Shree Rajneesh and more to come. The only difference between the ancient ones and the modern ones is that the ancient ones have accumulated more patina.

Of course, science is producing increasing mountains of material pleasures — automobiles, airplanes, televisions, computers, microwave ovens, video games and what have you. But all these goodies seem to fail to fully satisfy the spiritual and emotional needs of the people. So far the public has been able to enjoy the pleasures of both religion and science, and the conflict between them has been successfully ameliorated by the separation of the two cerebral hemispheres.

But one wonders how long this can continue with dynamic science leaping forward while religion remains bogged down in the ignorance and folly of the past. There are no great new developments in static religion while science is exploding. Science has made more progress in the past half century than it had in the previous entire history of the world, ever widening the gap between progressive science and static religion. One might reasonably expect dynamic science to overtake, overrun and overwhelm moribund religion.

But to look upon scientific progress as good is an act of faith. Exploding science may be accelerating us rapidly toward extinction. On the other hand, religion, in its blindness to the population explosion, may be bringing civilization to an end — even if not the human species.

I will close my book with a quotation from the great horticulturist Luther Burbank:

> I prefer and claim the right to worship the infinite, everlasting almighty God of this vast universe as revealed to us gradually, step by step, by the demonstrable truths of our savior, science.

ORDER FORM

YOU'RE OK
THE WORLD'S ALL WRONG

by
C. W. Dalton!

ISBN 0-916969-00-2   LC 8470707

    This well-written book faces the most controversial issues of the day headon--drugs, crime, poverty, religion, war, sexual freedom, women's liberation, Wall Street chicanery, the fragility of democracy, doomsday.

    Sheer, stark and Machiavellian, the book penetrates and shatters the veneer of the world of make-believe.

    Taking a critical, skeptical, iconoclastic view, the author recognizes that doubt, as Socrates said, is the origin of truth, and that criticism, as Philip Wylie said, is the ultimate positive contributor to progress of any kind. 542 page hardcover including illustrations and extensive index.

$17.95. No postage or handling charges.
California residents add $1.30 sales tax for a total of $19.25

Book title _____ Enclosed $ _____

Name _____

Address _____

_____ Zip _____

BIG BLUE BOOKS
P. O. Box 1627
Lakeside, CA 92040

How to
Raise a
Winner

C. W. Dalton !

The price is $7.95 postpaid.
California residents add sales
tax for a total of $8.53.
ISBN 0-916969-01-0

Not the usual Pollyannish treatise on success, but a practical Machiavellian guide on how to raise a winner. If you are wondering why your children aren't succeeding, it may be because you are throwing roadblocks in their paths or are loading them down with balls and chains.

The book is packed with new ideas and insights that may seem at first glance outrageous, but are soundly based on experience, observation and common sense.

The book is predicated on the the assumption that winning is good, but you are warned as you read the book that you may develop second thoughts about success.

Forty-two cartoons keep the book light, even though the concise style itself makes for easy reading.

Book title _____ Enclosed $ _____

Name _____

Address _____

_____ Zip _____

BIG BLUE BOOKS
P. O. Box 1627
Lakeside, CA 92040

ORDER FORM

THE
RIGHT BRAIN
AND
RELIGION

A DISCUSSION OF
RELIGION IN THE CONTEXT
OF THE RIGHT- AND LEFT-
BRAIN THEORY

C. W. Dalton!

A GREAT GIFT FOR YOUR RIGHT- OR LEFT-BRAINED FRIENDS, RELATIVES, INLAWS OR CELL MATES.

A NEW CONCEPT OF RELIGION THAT COULD TAKE HOLD AND ALTER THE COURSE OF HISTORY.

ISBN 0-916969-02-9
LC 90-81587

The price is $11.95 postpaid. California residents add sales tax for a total of $12.82

Book title _____ Enclosed $ _____

Name _____

Address _____

_____ Zip _____

BIG BLUE BOOKS
P. O. Box 1627
Lakeside, CA 92040